TRADITION AND COMPOSITION
IN THE PARABLES OF ENOCH

SOCIETY
OF BIBLICAL
LITERATURE

DISSERTATION SERIES

edited by
Howard C. Kee
and
Douglas A. Knight

Number 47
TRADITION AND COMPOSITION IN THE PARABLES
OF ENOCH
by
David Winston Suter

David Winston Suter

TRADITION AND COMPOSITION IN THE PARABLES OF ENOCH

Scholars Press

TRADITION AND COMPOSITION IN THE PARABLES OF ENOCH

David Winston Suter
Department of Religion
Wichita State University
Wichita, Kansas 67208

Ph.D., 1977
The University of Chicago

Adviser:
Norman Perrin

Copyright © 1979
Society of Biblical Literature

Library of Congress Cataloging in Publication Data

Suter, David Winston.
 Tradition and composition in the parables of Enoch.

 (Dissertation series ; no. 47 ISSN 0145-2770)
 Originally presented as the author's thesis, University of Chicago, 1976.
 Bibliography: p.
 1. Bible. O.T. Apocryphal books. 1 Enoch—Parables. I. Title. II. Series: Society of Biblical Literature.Dissertation series ; no. 47.
BS1830.E7S95 1979 229'.913 79-17441
ISBN 0-89130-335-9
ISBN 0-89130-336-7 pbk.

Printed in the United States of America

TO NORMAN PERRIN

PREFACE

My interest in the Ethiopic Book of Enoch (1 Enoch) began with a paper that I wrote some years ago for a course on the Son of Man taught by Norman Perrin. I argued that, while the Synoptic tradition as a whole does not reflect the treatment of "Son of Man" in the Parables of Enoch (1 En. 37-71), the special Matthean Son of Man material does. Some parts of that paper have found their way into chapter II below.

The dissertation itself began as a redaction-critical study of the myth of the fallen angels in 1 En. 6-11. In the course of research, however, I concluded that the versions of the myth in the Parables of Enoch were not simply dependent on chapters 6-11 but provided evidence for the state of the tradition, evidence that, in spite of the later date of the Parables (first century A.D. by my estimation), had a bearing on the tradition-history behind chapters 6-11. The dissertation thus came to deal with the structure of the Parables itself, the role of the fallen-angel and Noachic material in it, and the relation of the Parables to tradition.

Some three years have elapsed between the completion of the dissertation and its publication in the Society of Biblical Literature Dissertation Series, and a number of articles and books related to 1 Enoch have appeared during that time. Given the nature of the series, it is impossible to revise the dissertation to take account of these publications. I have, however, included a supplementary bibliography to give the reader access to them. James H. Charlesworth of Duke University, director of the Pseudepigrapha Institute, has kindly made available to me his bibliographical resources, which will appear in an update to his <u>The Pseudepigrapha and Modern Research</u>, and is therefore responsible for the thoroughness of this bibliography.

Unless otherwise specified, the quotations of the works of Josephus,[1] Philo,[2] Hesiod,[3] and Lucian[4] have been derived from the translations of the Loeb Classical Library. In addition, quotations from the Apocrypha of the Old Testament have been taken from the RSV.[5]

vii

PREFACE

For chapters of 1 Enoch where more than one version exists, translations in the dissertation have followed the Gizeh papyrus Greek text unless otherwise specified. For chapters 37-71, I have, of course, followed the Ethiopic version. Publication of the Aramaic Enoch manuscripts from Qumran[6] came subsequent to the completion of this work. It was, therefore, impossible to utilize the Aramaic version here. J. T. Milik, in publishing the Aramaic fragments, amplified his position on the dating of the Parables,[7] a position with which I deal below in chapter II. I remain unconvinced, however, by his efforts to treat the Parables of Enoch as a Christian writing of the third century.

The transliteration of Ge'ez consonants follows the system found in Carlo Conti Rossini's grammar.[8] The vowels are indicated as follows:

1. first order a
2. second order u
3. third order i
4. fourth order $\bar{a}$
5. fifth order $\bar{e}$
6. sixth order e (or unvoiced)
7. seventh order o

Gemination has been indicated only in the cases of B (intensive) stems, imperfects, and final t's of verbal prefixes that have been assimilated to following dentals. I am grateful to Gene Gragg of the University of Chicago, my Ge'ez teacher, for suggestions concerning the treatment of Ge'ez in the dissertation.

I would like to express appreciation to a number of persons who have assisted with the writing or publication of this volume: to Jay A. Wilcoxen, who has taught me much of what I know about apocalyptic literature; to Newland F. Smith, librarian at Seabury-Western Theological Seminary, who gave me access to the Hibbard Library during the early seventies; to Lloyd M. Benningfield, Dean for Graduate Studies and Research at Wichita State University, for support for the cost of typing the manuscript; to Karla K. Kraft for the care with which she has typed the camera-ready copy; to Dale C. Allison, my former student, who survived a severe automobile accident to complete the proof-reading; and to numerous fellow students

PREFACE

at the University of Chicago and colleagues at Wichita State University, and elsewhere, whose conversations have taught me much. I am also grateful to the Society of Biblical Literature, its editor, Howard Clark Kee, and the anonymous readers, for the selection of this dissertation for publication in the SBL Dissertation Series.

Finally, I would like to express appreciation to--or, more accurately, for--my teacher, Norman Perrin, who died Thanksgiving morning of 1976, three weeks after accepting this dissertation. It is to him that this volume is dedicated. Norman should be remembered not only for the number of important books he produced during the last years of his life but also for the excellence with which he wedded publication and teaching. He thrived on the interchange available in an American university, and by doing so, he helped to give American Biblical scholarship its own distinctive flavor.

D.W.S.

Wichita State University
August, 1979

TABLE OF CONTENTS

PREFACE vii

TABLE OF ABBREVIATIONS xiii

Chapter
I. INTRODUCTION 1

    PART I. LITERARY CRITICISM AND THE
              PARABLES OF ENOCH

II. THE PROVENANCE OF THE PARABLES OF ENOCH 11

    Recent Discussion of the Problem of Provenance
    The Parables and the Hekhaloth Tradition
    The Date of the Parables of Enoch
    The Provenance of the Parables and the Enochic
      Literature

    PART II. A FORM-CRITICAL EXAMINATION OF
              1 EN. 54:1-56:4 AND 64:1-69:12

III. THE IS. 24:17-23 MIDRASH 39

    Excursus 1: Midrash as a Method and a Genre
    Excursus 2: The Date of the Isaiah Apocalypse
    1 En. 54:1-56:4 and 64:1-68:1 as Midrashim of
      Is. 24:17-23
    The Structure of the Midrashic Unit
    Parallels in Content between Is. 24:17-23 and
      the Midrashic Tradition in the Parables
    Utilization of Other Passages of Scripture in
      the Is. 24:17-23 Midrash
    Mythological Patterns in the Is. 24:17-23
      Midrash
    The *Sitz im Leben* of the Is. 24:17-23 Midrash

IV. THE LISTS OF FALLEN ANGELS 73

    The *Sitz im Leben* of Angel Lists
    Exegesis of Scripture and the Angel Lists
    Mythological Patterns and the Angel Lists

V. THE ESSENTIAL ELEMENTS OF THE IS. 24:17-23
MIDRASH AND THE LISTS OF FALLEN ANGELS 91

    The Is. 24:17-23 Midrash
    The Lists of Fallen Angels
    The Tradition History of the Two Units
    Conclusions

PART III. THE ROLE OF THE IS. 24:17-23 MIDRASH
AND THE LISTS OF FALLEN ANGELS
IN THE COMPOSITION OF THE
PARABLES OF ENOCH

VI. THE IS. 24:17-23 MIDRASH IN THE THOUGHT AND
STRUCTURE OF THE PARABLES OF ENOCH   107

    The Second Parable: 1 En. 45-57
    The Third Parable: 1 En. 58-69
    The Role of the Is. 24:17-23 Midrash in the
      Parables of Enoch

VII. THE PARABLES OF ENOCH AS AN ORAL COMPOSITION AND
AS A PSEUDEPIGRAPHON   125

    Tradition and Literature in Ancient Judaism
    The Editorial Framework of the Parables
    The Three Parables as an Oral Composition:
      Formulas and Formulaic Language
    Structure and Oral Composition
    Ornamentation: Lists and Similar Themes from
      Other Patterns
    The Genre of the Parables of Enoch
    Oral Poet and Scribe: Types of Authorship
    The *Sitz im Leben* of *Mašal* and Pseudepigraphon
    Conclusions

VIII. THE PARABLES OF ENOCH AND THE STUDY OF
APOCALYPTIC   157

    Continuity, Hellenization, and the Parables
      of Enoch
    The Kings and Mighty and the Understanding of
      History in Apocalyptic

NOTES   169

SELECTED BIBLIOGRAPHY   203

INDEXES   213

TABLE OF ABBREVIATIONS

ABBREVIATIONS OF THE NAMES OF BIBLICAL BOOKS (WITH THE APOCRYPHA)

Gen.	Ko.	Zech.	Rom.
Ex.	Song of Sol.	Mal.	1-2 Cor.
Lev.	Is.	1 Bar.	Gal.
Num.	Jer.	4 Ezra	Eph.
Deut.	Lam.	Jdt.	Phil.
Josh.	Ezek.	Let. Jer.	Col.
Judg.	Dan.	1-2 Macc.	1-2 Thess.
Ruth	Hos.	Pr. Man.	1-2 Tim.
1-2 Sam.	Joel	Sir.	Tit.
1-2 Kings	Amos	Song of 3 Y.	Philem.
1-2 Chron.	Obad.	Tob.	Heb.
Ezra	Jon.	Wsd. Sol.	Jas.
Neh.	Mic.	Mt.	1-2 Pet.
Esther	Nahum	Mk.	1-2-3 Jn.
Job	Hab.	Lk.	Jude
Ps.	Zeph.	Jn.	Rev.
Prov.	Hag.	Acts	

GENERAL ABBREVIATIONS

Abr.	Philo, *De Abrahamo*
ANET	J. B. Pritchard (ed.), *Ancient Near Eastern Texts*
Ant.	Josephus, *Jewish Antiquities*
ARW	*Archiv für Religionswissenschaft*
ATR	*Anglican Theological Review*
Barn.	Barnabas
BH	R. Kittel, *Biblia hebraica*
Bib	*Biblica*
BibOr	Biblica et orientalia
B. Meṣ.	*Baba Meṣi'a*
BSOAS	*Bulletin of the School of Oriental and African Studies*
ConB	Coniectanea biblica
1-2-3 En.	1-2-3 Enoch
Flacc.	Philo, *In Flaccum*

xiii

ABBREVIATIONS

Gen. Rab.	*Genesis Rabbah*
Gig.	Philo, *De Gigantibus*
GKC	*Gesenius' Hebrew Grammar*, ed. E. Kautzsch, tr. A. E. Cowley
Ḥag.	*Ḥagiga*
HTR	*Harvard Theological Review*
HTS	Harvard Theological Studies
Ign. Eph.	Ignatius, *Letter to the Ephesians*
JA	*Journal asiatique*
JBL	*Journal of Biblical Literature*
JJS	*Journal of Jewish Studies*
JRAS	*Journal of the Royal Asiatic Society*
JTC	*Journal for Theology and the Church*
JTS	*Journal of Theological Studies*
Jub.	Jubilees
J.W.	Josephus, *The Jewish War*
KB	L. Koehler and W. Baumgartner, *Lexicon in Veteris Testamenti libros*
Kil.	*Kil'ayim*
LCL	*Loeb Classical Library*
Leg.	Philo, *De Legatione ad Gaium*
LXX	Septuagint
Mid. Ps.	*Midrash on Psalms*
MPAIBL	*Mémoires présentés à l'Académie des inscriptions et belles-lettres*
MT	Masoretic Text
nif.	*nif'al*
NTS	*New Testament Studies*
Praem.	Philo, *De Praemiis et Poenis*
PVTG	Pseudepigrapha Veteris Testamenti graece
1QH	*Hôdāyôt (Thanksgiving Hymns)* from Qumran Cave 1
1QM	*Milḥāmāh (War Scroll)* from Qumran Cave 1
4QpIs^a	*Pesher on Isaiah* from Qumran Cave 4
4QSl	Strugnell Texts (*Angelic Liturgy*) from Qumran Cave 4
Quod Omn. Prob.	Philo, *Quod Omnis Probus Liber*

ABBREVIATIONS

RB	*Revue biblique*
RE	*Realencyklopädie für protestantische Theologie und Kirche*
RechBib	Recherches bibliques
RevQ	*Revue de Qumran*
RHR	*Revue de l'histoire des religions*
RSR	*Recherches de science religieuse*
RSV	*Revised Standard Version*
Sanh.	*Sanhedrin*
Šabb.	*Šabbat*
SBT	Studies in Biblical Theology
SD	Studies and Documents
SPB	Studia postbiblica
SVTP	Studia in Veteris Testamenti pseudepigrapha
TDNT	G. Kittel and G. Friedrich (eds.), *Theological Dictionary of the New Testament*
Vit. Cont.	Philo, *De Vita Contemplativa*
VTSup	Vetus Testamentum, Supplements

ABBREVIATIONS IN SUPPLEMENTARY BIBLIOGRAPHY

AnBib	Analecta biblica
BETL	Bibliotheca ephemeridum theologicarum lovaniensium
BWANT	Beiträge zur Wissenschaft vom Alten und Neuen Testament
CBQ	*Catholic Biblical Quarterly*
ETL	*Ephemerides theologicae lovanienses*
Exp Tim	*Expository Times*
IDBSup	Supplementary volume to *Interpreter's Dictionary of the Bible*
JSJ	*Journal for the Study of Judaism in the Persian, Hellenistic and Roman Period*
JSS	*Journal of Semitic Studies*
NovTSup	Novum Testamentum, Supplements
SBLSCS	Society of Biblical Literature Septuagint and Cognate Studies
SEA	*Svensk exegetisk årsbok*
Sem	*Semitica*

ABBREVIATIONS

TS	*Theological Studies*
VT	*Vetus Testamentum*
ZTK	*Zeitschrift für Theologie und Kirche*

CHAPTER I

INTRODUCTION

This dissertation has three parts, which are distinguished, more or less, by the methods involved in each. Part I uses literary-critical methods to deal with the question of the provenance of the Parables of Enoch, an unresolved problem in the current discussion. In addition, the problem of provenance raises questions concerning the relation of the work to the rest of the Enochic literature. Given the absence of the Parables from Qumran and the lack of any Greek manuscripts of the work, the possibility must be considered that the work was produced in a tradition isolated in some unknown degree from the one that produced and preserved the rest of 1 Enoch. While a possibility may not automatically be transformed into a probability, it does set the stage for an examination of the fallen-angel material in the Parables, an examination that concludes that this material is based on traditions that are independent of the form of the myth of the fallen angels found in 1 En. 6-11. Independence here could imply lack of knowledge of the rest of 1 Enoch, or it could merely imply that the circle that produced the Parables found tradition more relevant to its needs than 1 En. 6-11.

Part II of the dissertation is a form-critical examination of the fallen-angel material in the Parables. This material is to be found in 1 En. 54:1-56:4 and 64:1-69:12. In these two passages it is possible to isolate two distinct traditional units, which appear side by side and which have not been intertwined. The situation may be contrasted to 1 En. 6-11, where the same two traditional units have been utilized, but in a manner that leaves them thoroughly interwoven. These two units are an Is. 24:17-23 midrash, found in 1 En. 54:1-56:4 and 64:1-68:1, and two lists of fallen angels, found in 1 En. 69:2-12. They are based on two distinct genres, the former being an excerpt from a midrashic tradition and the latter a list or catalog of angels.

If these two traditional units are examined separately, instead of being taken uncritically as a single myth of the fallen angels or an interpolation from a Book of Noah, they are seen to have two distinct sets of basic elements. The Is. 24:17-23 midrash is the result of the traditional interpretation of a passage from the Isaiah Apocalypse (Is. 24-27), a passage that sandwiches an allusion to a cosmic catastrophe between passages dealing with the judgment and punishment of the inhabitants of the earth or the host of the heights and the kings of the earth. The two passages in the Parables, 1 En. 54:1-56:4 and 64:1-68:1, follow this pattern. They also reproduce the parallelism of Is. 24:17-23 by juxtaposing the judgment of the host of Asael[1] with that of the kings and mighty of the earth. Where they mention any angel name at all, it is that of Asael. They seem to characterize the sins introduced by the angels as sorcery or idolatry, including, apparently, emperor worship, and are not concerned with the chastity of the angels. Furthermore, they have a distinct eschatology, based on Is. 24:17-23, that relates the flood to the eschaton. Ultimately, the Is. 24:17-23 midrash is ideally suited to deal with the limits of royal power, a theme that fits well into the concerns of the Parables of Enoch.

In contrast, to the extent that the lists of fallen angels are associated with Biblical passages, they are related to Gen. 6:1-4, the passage dealing with the sons of Elohim and the daughters of men. The first list, in 1 En. 69:2-3, treats Shemiḥazah[2] as the leader and Asael as the tenth angel. The second list, in 1 En. 69:4-12, is concerned with the chastity of the angels as well as the introduction of violence, sorcery, and false wisdom to man. If the connection to Gen. 6:1-4 is seen as the most important element of meaning in the lists, then the major concern of this traditional unit is with the problem of purity, which it has projected upon the cosmic level. When this traditional unit was used in 1 En. 6-11, the problem of purity raised by the use of Gen. 6:1-4 was the most important element.

Once these two traditional units and their basic elements have been distinguished, writing tradition histories for them is not difficult, since there is one major passage

INTRODUCTION

with which to deal, 1 En. 6-11. Most of the other fallen-angel passages from the period are dependent to some degree on chapters 6-11 and provide no further evidence relevant to the independence of the two units. With these units in mind, the reason for the careful distinctions, maintained in chapters 6-11, in the responsibilities of Asael and Shemiḥazah for the introduction of evil becomes obvious--these responsibilities correspond more or less to the roles that the two angels play in the two traditional units. In addition, the punishment of Asael in 1 En. 10:4-6 corresponds more closely to that of the host of Asael in 1 En. 54:4-6, one of the passages using the Is. 24:17-23 midrash, than the punishment of Shemiḥazah in 1 En. 10:11-13 does. 1 En. 6-11 seems to be more interested in the Is. 24:17-23 midrash for its description of the punishment of the angels, a feature that may be missing from the interpretation of Gen. 6:1-4 associated with the angel-list tradition, and for its eschatology, which treats the flood as a prototype for the eschaton, than for its attack on kings who exceed their power; however, in spite of the degree to which these two traditional units have been intertwined in chapters 6-11, some vestiges of their individuality have remained. The literary critics were correct in their recognition of the importance of these traces; however, the resulting doublets are best treated as indications of distinct traditions rather than of two literary sources.

It is fairly clear that the Is. 24:17-23 midrash is used in the Parables of Enoch independently of 1 En. 6-11. While the midrash is found in the latter passage, the essential element of importance for its use in the Parables, the parallel punishment of the host of the heights and the kings of the earth from Is. 24:17-23, does not appear there. Even if the poet responsible for the Parables were aware of the earlier writing, it would have been necessary for him to turn to tradition for the form in which he used the midrash. In chapter VI below, it will become apparent that the Parables utilized several different midrashic excerpts that deal with the limits of royal power in order to elaborate its central concern. The Is. 24:17-23 midrash was one of these, and its most likely source would have been the traditional interpretation of Isaiah familiar to the poet.

The case for the angel lists is not as clear, since the concern of this unit with purity seems more at home in 1 En. 6-11 than in the Parables. There is, however, some reason to believe that, of the parallel versions of the second list in 1 En. 8:1-3 and 69:4-12, it is the former that has undergone redaction to fit it into its context and the latter that presents a more or less unredacted version of the tradition. In addition, examination of the Parables as an oral composition in chapter VII below will suggest that the lists of fallen angels function as traditional lists or catalogs used to ornament a narrative: a stylistic feature of oral composition.

Part III of the dissertation is a redaction-critical examination of the utilization of the fallen-angel material in the Parables. It has two parts. First, there is a study of the relation of the Is. 24:17-23 midrash to other traditional materials in the Parables, a study that serves not only to support the argument that this midrash is an integral part of the traditional material used in the Parables but also to uncover the central theological concern of the work: theodicy as it relates to the problem of a king who claims to be a god. Second, an examination of the structural and stylistic evidence suggests that the three parable collection that is the basis of the Parables was originally composed through the use of the techniques of oral composition. An examination of the recurrence of midrashic traditions and patterns of thought from parable to parable in the Parables of Enoch supports this conclusion and provides a basis for an examination of the relation between traditional material and an apocalyptic pattern in the work. The determination of the genre of the Parables is also an important part of the discussion. The three sections of the work represent a variety of *māšāl*, a traditional form concerned with the vision of the reward of the righteous and the punishment of the wicked. The genre is one that is spoken, and a comparison with the interpretation of Is. 24:17-23 in the Targum indicates that the midrash on

INTRODUCTION

that passage is related to the concern of the Parables of Enoch with the punishment of the wicked.

The concern of this study with oral modes of expression will require a discussion of the role of oral tradition in Judaism of the Hellenistic period. While there may be societies that preserve their traditions through memorization of a fixed text--the Vedic tradition for example--the model that best describes the Parables of Enoch is that of oral composition as developed by Milman Parry and Albert B. Lord[3] in their study of Yugoslavian heroic songs and the Homeric epics. The contrast between Jewish apocalyptic literature and that studied by Parry and Lord is that the society that produced the former was probably more literate than those that produced the latter. This difference will require a discussion of the interplay of oral and written modes of expression using Philo's descriptions of the literature and assemblies of the Essenes and Therapeutae as a typical *Sitz im Leben* for such interchange. It should be noted that, since modern English is inadequate for a discussion of oral "literature," the terms "literary" and "literature" will be used for written expressions and "tradition" or "traditional" for oral expressions.

Part III of the dissertation will also examine the role of the editorial material in the Parables. This material serves to transform the work from a set of three *mešalim*, which seem to be independent of the name of Enoch, to a pseudepigraphon attributed to the antediluvian sage. While the editorial work may have been closely associated with the composition of the three parables according to the techniques of oral composition, a pseudepigraphon is a literary type, and the techniques of composition necessary for the creation of such a work must be distinct from those used in the composition of the three parables. The former are the skills of a scribe, the latter, of an oral poet. It is therefore possible to examine the relation between oral and written forms of communication in Judaism of the Hellenistic period. The three parables reflect a traditional, or oral, performance, and they derive their authority from the status of the poet, one of those responsible for the interpretation of scripture in the public assemblies of the sect. The editorial work is designed to transfer this authority from the traditional to the literary *Sitz im Leben*, where a writing, in order to command respect, must claim to have been written by one of the ancients.

A final chapter will deal with the significance of the fallen-angel material and the Parables of Enoch for the study of apocalyptic. The work uses these traditions as part of a polemic against the kings and mighty of the earth, who are probably to be identified with the Emperor and powerful men of the Roman empire sometime during the first century A.D. The polemic represents a profound alienation from history as a sphere in which a people can control its own destiny, an attitude that leads toward a visionary experience of a coming re-creation of the cosmos in which God destroys the forces of chaos and reestablishes the society of the righteous in the midst of an orderly cosmos. In this eschatological scheme, the eschaton does not merely reflect creation, but history itself takes on the role of the time of the creation myth, in which the forces of chaos rebel and must be defeated. The important version of the myth of the fallen angels in the Parables, which parallels the imprisonment and punishment of angels with that of the kings and mighty of the earth, provides an important part of the cosmic dimension in this eschatology.

Another problem raised by the study of apocalyptic is the role of continuity in a religious tradition. Jewish apocalyptic was not an isolated phenomenon in the Hellenistic world. Even though it represents a religious reaction to the incursion of Greek and Roman civilization and power, it has been profoundly affected by Hellenistic religious traditions, and it has parallels within other national cultures of the period that have been placed in a similar situation. It is the task of the historian of religion not only to determine the points at which discontinuity is to be found as a result of either inner development of a tradition or syncretism but also to define the element of continuity that makes Jewish apocalyptic *Jewish*. The problem could be more sharply defined in an examination of 1 En. 6-11; however, such a study of that passage is beyond the scope of this dissertation. The material in the Parables of Enoch is, however, relevant to the problem,

INTRODUCTION

and the solution that it suggests is that midrash, as a type of hermeneutic, is characteristic of a particular stage of cultural development in which a society turns to its ancient traditions to reinterpret them in order to discover meaning in the present. The element of continuity in Jewish apocalyptic, as well as in Jewish religion as a whole in the Hellenistic age, is to be found in the *perception* of the source of meaning in the national "epic" tradition, the scriptures, although hermeneutic methods and traditions seen as relevant to the interpretation of particular passages of scripture may be brought forward from various sources in order to apply the ancient words to the present situation.

PART I

LITERARY CRITICISM

AND THE PARABLES OF ENOCH

CHAPTER II

THE PROVENANCE OF THE PARABLES OF ENOCH

An important concern of literary criticism is the determination of the provenance of a writing. To be properly interpreted, a work must be placed in its historical context. While form criticism works backward from the composition of a writing in a particular time and place and is concerned with a more general *Sitz im Leben* in the life of a community, the historical context of a writing is of importance for both literary criticism and redaction criticism. In the case of the Parables of Enoch, it is important to coordinate the discussion of the provenance of the work with the discussion of its thematic interests. The historical context, however, is also of importance for form criticism, since its determination provides a starting point for the examination of the relationship between different versions of the same or similar traditions appearing in different works or in distinct sections of a composite book.[1] It is important, in a discussion of the fallen-angel traditions in 1 En. 6-11 and the Parables of Enoch, to know that the latter has a distinct origin from the former. 1 En. 6-11 is pre-Maccabean,[2] while the Parables seem to belong to the first century A.D. The following discussion will also suggest that the latter work is from a fairly distinct strand of tradition and is therefore likely to preserve traditions that are in some degree independent of similar ones found elsewhere in 1 Enoch.

*Recent Discussion of the
Problem of Provenance*

Soon after the publication of the Ethiopic Book of Enoch in the nineteenth century, the Parables of Enoch was recognized as a distinct literary unit and attempts were made to determine its provenance. The initial stage of this discussion by the literary critics has been summarized by Charles,[3] and there is no need to repeat his discussion here. However, the Qumran discoveries have reopened the discussion, and it will be necessary to examine the several options available at the present.

J. C. Hindley[4] relates the account of the attack on Palestine by the Parthians and the Medes in 1 En. 56:5-8 to a historical invasion by the Parthians in A.D. 115-17. He believes that the Parables of Enoch was produced by a Jew living in Antioch at that time who wished to refute the Christian use of "Son of Man" by identifying the Jewish sage Enoch with that title. Some of the parallels that Hindley draws to historical and natural events are interesting; however, they are limited to 1 En. 56:5-8, a passage that has definite roots in apocalyptic mythological traditions, roots that make any historical interpretation problematic.[5]

Subsequent discussion in this dissertation will conclude that the Parables are primarily concerned with an anti-royal, and probably an anti-Roman, polemic, and this conclusion has two implications for Hindley's argument. First, since the Parthians had been the major enemy of the Romans to the east from the beginnings of Roman power in Palestine, it is not surprising to find the Parthians substituted for their predecessors, the Persians, in a version of the apocalyptic motif dealing with the movement of alien armies.[6] This substitution could have taken place at any time during the Roman period. Second, while it is entirely possible that "Son of Man" in the Parables could have been influenced in some way by Christian usage,[7] the polemics of the book are directed against men of power, the kings and mighty of the earth, rather than against the powerless Christian heretics. Hindley's position rests on only a portion of the Parables and does not take into account the work as a whole.

A second approach to the dating of the Parables of Enoch is the position of J. T. Milik.[8] He has argued from the absence of the Parables in the Qumran fragments and from the presence of what he claims are Christian elements in the work that it is third century Christian in origin and is to be attributed to the circles that produced the Christian portions of the Sibylline Oracles.

PROVENANCE OF THE PARABLES

> Il me semble tout à fait certain qu'il [the Parables of Enoch] n'existait pas à l'époque préchrétienne, dans un texte araméen, hébreu, ou grec, puisqu'aucun fragment sémitique ou grec n'en a été repéré dans les très riches lots manuscrits des grottes de Qumrân. C'est donc une composition grecque chrétienne. . . .qui s'inspire visiblement des livres du Nouveau Testament, en particulier des Evangiles, en commençant par les titres du Messie préexistant: "Fils de l'homme" (Mat 9,6; 10,23; *etc.*) et "Elu" (Luc 23,35).[9]

Milik makes the assumption that the library at Qumran, rich as it may have been, contained every pre-Christian Jewish work composed. In fact, the Enochic literature found at Qumran predates the development of that sect's distinct literary style, and, as Milik notes, the period of interest in Enoch at Qumran is prior to the Herodian period.[10] Continued interest in Enoch indicated by the Slavonic Enoch (2 Enoch) and the *Sefer ha-Hekhaloth* (3 Enoch)[11] must be assigned to other circles.

While Milik attempts to derive the title "Son of Man" in the Parables from the Christian gospels, it may more properly be explained as part of a Dan. 7:9-14 midrash that has been used at several points in the composition of this work.[12] The first reference to this figure is in 1 En. 46:1: *wa-mesleḥu kāleʾ za-gaṣu kama reʾyata sabeʾ*, "And with him [the Head of Days, *reʾsa mawāʿel*, who is clearly the Ancient of Days of Dan. 7:9] there was another whose face was like the appearance of a man." The reference is clearly to the "one like a son of man" of Dan. 7:13 rather than to the Son of Man of the gospels, where the Ancient of Days plays no role. It is also interesting to note that the Ethiopic phrase resembles the description of the likeness of God in Ezek. 1:26: דמות כמראה אדם, and it is likely that the midrash reflects both passages.

The distinctive developments that accompany the title "Son of Man" in the gospels are absent from the Parables, and, as Norman Perrin notes,[13] the title in the gospels is likewise the result of exegetical traditions based on Dan. 7:13, combined in this case with Ps. 110:1. The messianic title "the Elect one" is predominant in the Parables[14] and can probably be traced to Is. 42:1 rather than to Lk. 23:35. "Son of Man" and "Head of Days" are seldom used outside of the context of an apparent midrash in the Parables of Enoch; however, the divine title "Lord of Spirits," which seems to be associated with "the Elect one," is freely redacted into the passages dealing with the Son of Man and the Head of Days.[15] The former two titles represent, at least initially, the preferred usage of the Parables, while the latter two are introduced in the course of its development. By 1 En. 62:5 and 69:26-29, "the Elect one," the major messianic designation of the work, has been reinterpreted in light of the exegetical tradition on Dan. 7:9-14 so that "Son of Man" seems to displace "the Elect one." While it is possible that Christian usage of a similar exegetical tradition or of "Son of Man" as a title could have prompted the use in the Parables of a Dan. 7:9-14 midrash, it would not be correct to conclude that the Parables were produced by a Christian working with the gospels as a model.

The Parables and the Hekhaloth Tradition

A third position in the current discussion effectively resolves the problem raised by the absence of the Parables of Enoch from the library at Qumran by relating it to another tradition that seems to have some degree of independence from the Dead Sea Scrolls. That tradition is Merkabah mysticism, which produced the Hekhaloth writings, Jewish mystical books, including 3 Enoch, that deal with the palaces (*hekhaloth*) of the seventh heaven and the vision of the divine throne-chariot (*merkabah*), which was the ultimate goal of the mystic's ascent.

Gershom G. Scholem argues that the Hekhaloth tradition has Palestinian origins and that the Enochic literature contains its seeds.[16] Although he does not concern himself with defining precisely the relationship between apocalyptic writings and the Merkabah mystical tradition, he does, in a later book, trace some of the earliest features of the mystical ascent of this tradition to pre-Christian Judaism.[17] He maintains that the Christian mystical traditions were derived from Judaism, since the Jewish traditions seem more closely related to Hellenistic elements than to Christian ones and since it is unlikely that, in the polemic atmosphere existing between Christianity and Judaism, the Jews would have knowingly adopted Christian mystical traditions, while the numbers of Jewish converts to Christianity could have easily taken Jewish traditions with them. It is interesting to note that Scholem is cautious about relating the Merkabah tradition too closely to the Dead Sea Scrolls.[18]

John Strugnell, in an important article in which he publishes two unique texts from Qumran and makes a contribution to the discussion of the typology of the angelology and ouranology of ancient Judaism, treats the Parables of Enoch, as well as the rest of 1 Enoch, as part of the Hekhaloth tradition.[19] 4QS[trugnel]1 40:24.2-9, one of the texts published by Strugnell, contains a description, based on Ezek. 1-3, of the heavenly throne-chariot.[20] He assigns this work to the middle of the first century B.C.[21] and argues that, in respect to its angelology, 4QS1 40 is somewhat more primitive than the Parables of Enoch. In 4QS1 40, the אופנים are the wheels of the divine throne-chariot of Ezek. 1:15-21, while in 1 En. 61:10 and 71:7 they appear as a band of angels, the *Ophannin*.[22] This band belongs to Jewish rather than Christian angelology, and its existence depends upon the mystical use of Ezek. 1-3 in the Merkabah tradition.

Jonas C. Greenfield also presents an important discussion of the relationship between the Parables of Enoch and the Hekhaloth writings.[23] He notes several correspondences between the language of the Parables and that of Qumran. The title "Lord of Spirits" is more or less peculiar to the former while רוחות play an important role in the angelology of the latter, and בחירים is apparently used in both places to refer to the righteous.[24] However, important differences exist between the Parables of Enoch and the Qumran texts, an insight that Greenfield attributes to David Flusser. 1 En. 41 assigns a role to the moon equal to that of the sun, a detail that would have been unthinkable at Qumran, where the liturgical calender was based on a solar year.[25] Greenfield suggests that "It may then be best to see the Similitudes as part of a different Enoch cycle that was at a later date made part of the *Vorlage* of the Ethiopic Enoch."[26]

Greenfield sees a connection between the developing role of Enoch in the earlier Enochic literature and the identification of Metatron as Enoch in 3 Enoch.[27] Elsewhere in Merkabah mysticism, Metatron is a primordial being unrelated to Enoch. The closest tie between Enoch/Metatron in 3 Enoch and the role of Enoch in the earlier literature is the identification of Enoch as the "Son of Man" in 1 En. 71:14 at the conclusion of the Parables of Enoch. It should also be noted that 3 En. 6:3 identifies Enoch as "an elect one" (בחיר), the only antediluvian to achieve perfection and to be taken up into heaven with the Shekinah before the flood. While בחיר does not have the messianic sense that it does in the Parables of Enoch, there is a remote possibility of a connection between its use in the Parables as the major messianic title and in 3 En. 6:3. Greenfield does not specifically relate the identification of Enoch as the Son of Man in the Parables to Enoch/Metatron in 3 Enoch, but he may have had it in mind. He also follows Gershom Scholem in relating the angelic songs of 1 En. 47:2 and 61:9-12, which are offered "with one voice," to the angelic hymns of the Hekhaloth tradition; however, he seems to have overlooked the song in 1 En. 39:9-14, which Hugo Odeberg identified as an early version of the *Qeduššah*, similar to one of the versions of this song found in 3 Enoch.[28]

The heavenly ascent. There are several other points at which relationships might be established between the Parables of Enoch and the Hekhaloth tradition. First, the heavenly ascent of the sage needs further attention. Scholem has identified 1 En. 14-16 as the earliest Jewish account of a heavenly ascent extant.[29] It dates, most likely, from the late third century B.C. Both this passage and 1 En. 71, the conclusion to the Parables, share a proskynesis and a call to a task with Ezek. 1:28-2:7; however, these are part of the formal elements of a prophetic call tradition[30] and cannot be used to establish a positive relationship between the Enochic ascents and the call vision in Ezekiel, which is the major source of material dealing with the ascent in Merkabah mysticism. To establish a relationship between these two passages and Ezekiel, it is necessary to turn to the description of the throne in 1 En. 14:18, which seems to grow out of Ezek. 1:15-21. In 1 En. 14:18, the wheel(s) (τροχός) of the throne should be noted. They are a major feature of the vision in

Ezekiel, and in 1 En. 71:7 they have become the *Ophannin* mentioned above. The *Cherubim* appear in connection with the wheels of 1 En. 14:18 and the *Ophannin* of 1 En. 71:7 and could possibly be related to the vision in Ezek. 10, which is similar to the one in chapters 1-3. The *Cherubim* and the wheels are associated in Ezek. 10:9, and Strugnell notes that the two are also paralleled several times in 4QSl 40.[31]

The throne of his glory. In Merkabah mysticism, the goal of the mystical ascent is the "throne of his glory," כסא כבודו, and this phrase occurs frequently in this body of literature.[32] It originally meant "his glorious throne," and the two nouns are related through the construct state so that the second noun indicates an attribute of the first. While the pronominal suffix belongs with the first noun, כסא, it must be attached to the second, since the construct state does not permit it to fall between the two.[33] The construction is necessary because Hebrew has no adjective for "glorious." The phrase appears in Jer. 14:21 with a second person singular pronominal suffix, where it should be translated "your glorious throne"; however, as כבוד becomes identified with the Shekinah,[34] it becomes a technical term and the translation, "Throne of his Glory," seems correct. In 3 Enoch, the identification with the Shekinah is so complete that the pronominal suffix falls away to permit כסא כבוד, "Throne of Glory."[35]

While thrones are frequent in apocalyptic texts, this particular phrase is not. A Greek version of it, θρόνος δόξης σου, an obvious Semitism,[36] is found in Wsd. Sol. 9:10, and a similar phrase occurs in T. Levi 5:1; however, in the latter case the suffix is missing. Although the situation may change with the publication of texts dealing with the angelic liturgy, the phrase is rare in the Qumran texts. 4QpIs^a D,3 has כס[א] כבוד, which is in a quotation from Is. 22:23 and is not a reference to the divine throne. However, in 4QSl 40:24, a passage that deals with the throne-chariot, ממחת מושב כבודו appears, and, in this context, it can only refer to "his glorious throne," although מושב generally means "dwelling." The phrase θρόνος δόξης αὐτοῦ appears in Mt. 19:28 and 25:31. It is found nowhere else in the New Testament. It appears in 1 En. 9:4, and the Ethiopic equivalent, *manbara sebḥātihu*, occurs six times in the Parables of Enoch at 1 En. 45:3; 55:4; 61:8; and 62:2,3 and 5, where it refers to the throne of judgment that the Lord of Spirits turns over to the Elect one/Son of Man. While the throne does not function in quite the same way in the Parables as it does in the later Hekhaloth tradition--it is the throne of judgment rather than the object of the mystical ascent--the phrase does seem to be on the way to becoming a technical term, and its frequency in the Parables points toward the later mystical writings.

The Qeduššah. The role of the angelic songs, including the *Qeduššah*, in the Parables and the Hekhaloth tradition has been mentioned above. The *Qeduššah* is important for the Parables of Enoch because it identifies that work as Jewish and because there are accounts of heavenly ascents in the Parables and in 3 Enoch in which that song plays an identical role. The following passage is the climax of Enoch's ascent at the beginning of the Parables:

> (1 En. 39:10) And for a time my eyes looked upon that place, and I blessed and glorified him, saying, "He is blessed, and may he be blessed from the first and forever. (11) And before him there is no limit: he knows before the world was created what is forever, and for generation after generation what will be. (12) They continually bless you, those who never sleep [the Watchers]37 and who are standing before your glory and are blessing and glorifying and magnifying, saying, '*Holy, holy, holy is the Lord of Spirits; he is filling the earth with spirits.*'" (13) And there my eyes saw all of those who never sleep; they were standing before him and blessing and saying, "*You are blessed, and blessed is the name of the Lord for ever and ever.*" (14) And my face was changed, for I was unable to observe.

R. H. Charles related the chant in verse 12 to the Christian Sanctus;38 however, Odeberg is correct in coordinating it with the chant in verse 13 and identifying them as an early version of the Jewish *Qeduššah*.39 The latter has two parts derived from Is. 6:3 and Ezek. 3:12:

קדוש קדוש קדוש יי צבאות מלא כל־הארץ כבודו:
והאופנים וחיות הקדש ברעש גדול מתנשאים לעמת שרפים לעמתם
משבחים ואומרים׃
ברוך כבוד־יי ממקומו:

> *Holy, holy, holy is the Lord of hosts: the whole earth is full of his glory.*
> And the Ophanim and the holy Chayoth with a noise of great rushing, upraising themselves towards the

Seraphim, thus over against them offer praise and say:
Blessed be the glory of the Lord from his place.[40]
Odeberg observes that the antiphonal response of 1 En. 39:13 is actually closer to a second version of the *Qeduššah* peculiar to the Hekhaloth tradition: ברוך שם כבוד מלכותו לעולם ועד, "Blessed be the name of his glorious kingdom for ever and ever."[41]

The account of the climax of Enoch's ascent in 1 En. 39:10-14 should be compared to that of R. Ishmael in 3 En. 1:10-12:

> (10) After that (moment) there was not in me strength enough to say a song before the Throne of Glory of the glorious King, the mightiest of all kings, the most excellent of all princes, until after the hour had passed. (11) After one hour (had passed) the Holy One, blessed be He, opened to me the gates of *Shekina*, the gates of Peace, the gates of Wisdom, the gates of Strength, the gates of Power, the gates of Speech (*Dibbur*), the gates of Song, the gates of *Qĕdushsha*, the gates of Chant. (12) And he enlightened my eyes and my heart by words of psalm, song, praise, exaltation, thanksgiving, extolment, glorification, hymn and eulogy. And as I opened my mouth, uttering a song before the Holy One, blessed be He, the Holy *Chayyoth* beneath and above the Throne of Glory answered and said: "HOLY" and "BLESSED BE THE GLORY OF YHWH FROM HIS PLACE!" (i.e. chanted the *Qĕdushsha*).[42]

This account obviously represents a more highly developed conceptualization of the mystical experience; however, it has four elements in common with 1 En. 39:10-14: (1) the pause in 1 En. 39:10a and 3 En. 1:10-11a, (2) the praise of the might of God in 1 En. 39:11 and 3 En. 1:10, (3) the seer breaks into song, and (4) the angelic beings respond with the *Qeduššah*. It seems probable that both works belong to the same mystical tradition, although the account of the heavenly ascent in the Parables of Enoch should be placed at the early levels of that tradition.

The cosmological oath. Another point of contact between the Parables of Enoch and the Hekhaloth tradition is the oath mentioned in 1 En. 69:13-25. Although the oath itself is never given, the writer goes to great length to list its powers: it maintains the order of the entire cosmos. The material is based on older traditions regarding the creation of the world, traditions that are found in several psalms of thanksgiving (Ps. 104; 136:4-9; 148; see also 135:6-7;

19:1-5; 24:2), in some of the older prophetic books (Is. 40:21-26; Jer. 5:22), in wisdom literature (Prov. 8:22-31; Job 38-41; see also Job 26:5-14; Gen. 1:1-25; Wsd. Sol. 7:17-22; 1 Bar. 3:29-37; Jub. 2:1-16; Song of 3 Y. 35-68), and in the Qumran literature (1QH 1:8-15; 13:7-9). At the basis of this entire tradition there seems to be a traditional onomasticon listing in a particular order the phenomena of the universe.[43] 1 En. 33:4 seems to imply that Enoch received such a list in a written form from Uriel, although it is likely that the general pattern that all of the above material follows is traditional rather than literary in character. In the case of the oath in 1 En. 69:13-25, the list of its powers seems to have been composed with some of the passages of scripture listed above in mind, since there are points of contact in phraseology.

> (1 En. 69:13) This is the number of Kasebel, the chief of the oath, which he revealed to the holy ones when he was dwelling on high in glory, and its name is Biqa. (14) This one asked Michael to show him the secret name that they might recite it in the oath, that those who had revealed all that was hidden to the sons of man might tremble on account of that name and oath. (15) And this is the power of this oath, for it is powerful and strong, and he placed this oath Aka in the hand of Michael. (16) And these are the secrets of this oath, and [it is] strong, and through the oath heaven was suspended before the world was created and until eternity. (17) And through it the earth was established on the water, and from secret places of the mountains beautiful waters issue forth, from the creation of the world and until eternity. (18) And through this oath the sea was created, and as its foundation for the time of wrath he established for it the sand, and it shall not pass from the creation of the world and until eternity. (19) And through this oath the abyss was made firm, and it stood [fast] and was not moved from its place from eternity and until eternity. (20) And through this oath the sun and moon complete their circuit, and they do not transgress their law from eternity [until eternity]. (21) And through this oath the stars complete their courses, and he calls their names and they answer him, from eternity and until eternity. (22) And likewise the spirits of the water, and all the spirits of the winds, and their various paths from the districts of the winds. (23) And in that place the voice of the thunder and the light of the lightning are stored, and there are kept the storehouses of the hail and the storehouses of the snow and the storehouses of the mist and the storehouses of the rain and dew. (24) All these are faithful and offer praise before the Lord of Spirits, and they glorify with all their power, and their sustenance is in

every praise, and they praise and glorify and exalt the
name of the Lord of Spirits for ever and ever. (25) And
this oath is powerful over them, and through it they
are preserved and their paths are preserved, and their
circuits are not destroyed.

As it stands, this passage is attached to a list of fallen angels in 1 En. 69:2-12, although the way in which it is attached has raised questions in the past. Charles reads "task" for "number" in verse 13.[44] The transitional material in verses 13-14 makes it appear that Kasebel is one of the fallen angels who wants to obtain the secret name for those angels to use in the oath, which they already know. It is understandable that the fallen angels would want to obtain the powers of such an oath; however, this interpretation of verses 13-14 does not explain why Kasebel turns the oath over to *Michael* in verse 15. In addition, it appears in verse 14 that it is Kasebel and Michael who are to recite the oath and cause the fallen angels to tremble. *Kāseb'ēl*, "Ram of God," does not seem to be thought of elsewhere as a fallen angel. The name כשבאל is probably equivalent to כבשיאל, which, besides the names of the four archangels, was the most frequent name on amulettes designed to obtain good will or favors.[45] Therefore, there is reason to question the assumption that Kasebel is a fallen angel, and the last angel of the list beginning in 1 En. 69:4, who wants to obtain the power of the oath for use by the fallen angels.

The correct interpretation seems to be that Kasebel and Michael are joining forces to use the oath to restore the cosmic order disturbed by the fall of the angels. If *yaḥădder*, "he was dwelling," were changed to *yaḥădderu*, "they were dwelling," this interpretation is restored. 1 En. 69:13 should thus be seen as the beginning of a new unit rather than as a continuation of the list of fallen angels in 1 En. 69:4-12.

That the tradition concerning this oath was once independent of the fallen-angel material is demonstrated by its clear presence behind 1 En. 41:3-44:1, where it is again associated with an angel list: in this case, a list of the four archangels in 1 En. 40:9-10. 1 En. 41:3-7 and 43:1-2 contain language that is close to 69:13-25, and in 41:5 an oath that serves as the *natural law* of the cosmos (cf. 69:20) is mentioned. A similar block of material is to be found at 1 En. 60:11-23, although an oath is not mentioned there.

Moses Gaster[46] has called attention to a magical text, the *Logos Ebraikos*, which at first glance seems to be based on 1 En. 69:13-25; however, although some of the language is quite similar to 1 En. 69:18 and 22, the reference to the giants in lines 44-45 (Gaster's enumeration) of the *Logos Ebraikos* is dependent on Greek rather than Jewish tradition. Although the *Logos Ebraikos* may in fact depend in part on 1 En. 69:13-25, it seems more likely that it merely depends on the same or a similar exegetical tradition. Note that, like the *Logos Ebraikos*, Ps. 135 and 136 include, in addition to the creation tradition, the Exodus motif, although the latter is not found in 1 En. 69:13-25.

Closer parallels to the oath are to be found in the Hekhaloth tradition:

> Because of the great love and mercy with which the Holy One, blessed be He, loved and cherished me [Metatron] more than all the children of heaven, He wrote with his finger with a flaming style upon the crown on my head the letters by which were created heaven and earth, the seas and rivers, the mountains and hills, the planets and constellations, the lightnings, winds, earthquakes and voices (thunders), the snow and hail, the storm-wind and the tempest; the letters by which were created all the needs of the world and all the orders of Creation.[47]

Scholem quotes a similar passage from 3 En. 41:1-4 in his discussion of theurgic elements of the Hekhaloth tradition and later adds another passage from the Lesser Hekhaloth:

> This is the spell and the seal
> By which the Earth is bound
> And by which the Heavens are bound
> And the Earth flees before it
> And the Universe trembles before it
> . . . .
> It opens the mouth of the sea
> And closes the waters. . .of the firmament.
> It opens the Heavens and waters of the Universe
> It uproots the Earth and confuses the Universe.[48]

The latter passage explains the reason for the trembling of the fallen angels in 1 En. 69:14: it is in response to the divine power of the oath, which is intended to preserve, or restore, the order of the universe.[49] As in the case of 1 En.

PROVENANCE OF THE PARABLES   23

69:13-25, the spell itself is not given. What these two
passages have in common with the oath tradition in the Parables
of Enoch is the memory of the onomasticon of natural phenomena,
which has come to be a means of listing the powers of the oath,
and the idea that a word, spell, or oath is involved in the
creation or maintenance of the universe. The cosmic dimensions
of the tradition have been greatly obscured by the *Logos
Ebraikos*, which, like the Akkadian cosmological incantation
against a toothache,[50] should be classified in the terms of
Mircea Eliade[51] as an *infantilization* of the creation myth.
However, in both the Parables of Enoch and the Hekhaloth
tradition, the oath has not undergone infantilization, although
it does have an obvious theurgic aspect. It is, of course,
impossible to determine to what private uses the Jewish
apocalypticists and mystics may have put the oath, but in the
literature it functions at the cosmic level.

Examination of the heavenly ascent and the oath
traditions in the Parables of Enoch leads to the conclusion
that the work is Jewish rather than Christian in origin and
that it belongs to an early stage of the Merkabah tradition.
It might be better, perhaps, to classify the Parables as
proto-Merkabah, since the throne plays more of a central role
in the later mystical tradition than it does in the Parables.
The apocalypticist responsible for the latter work is concerned
more with a vision of order beyond the chaos of the present
than in a vision of the throne itself. At the same time, the
role of the "throne of his glory" is in the process of
development: its *wheels* have become a band of angels, the
Ophannin.

The Date of the Parables of Enoch

The date of the Parables of Enoch still remains a
problem. Charles dates the work by identifying "the kings and
mighty of the earth" with the last of the Maccabean princes
and the Sadducees.[52] He assumes that the author was a Pharisee
and that the work was composed after the beginning of conflict
between the Pharisees and Alexander Jannaeus, which he dates in
95 B.C., and before the coming of the Romans in 64 B.C.
However, his argument that "the kings and mighty" must be Jews

and that Rome was unknown to the author is not convincing. It is also not obvious that the author was a Pharisee, although the Hekhaloth tradition and the Pharisaic movement are not mutually exclusive.

Recent attempts to date the Parables have centered on 1 En. 56:5-7, which is said to be related to a Parthian invasion of either 40 B.C.[53] or A.D. 115-17,[54] or on 1 En. 67:7-9, which is said to be a reference to Herod the Great's final illness and his journey to the thermal springs at Callirhoe to seek a cure.[55] The former passage, as has been noted, should be understood as an apocalyptic motif rather than a historical reference. In addition, it is not by any means certain that the latter passage is an allusion to Herod. Josephus reports that Herod was dipped into the bath once at Callirhoe and did not respond very well; however, 1 En. 67:8 implies that the kings and mighty are using the warm springs daily and yet fail to understand that they will become the instrument of their punishment at the eschaton.[56] The identification of the springs with Callirhoe likewise ignores 1 En. 67:4, which locates the place of the punishment of the kings and angels in the west.[57]

Typological approaches. Since the material in the Parables of Enoch does not seem to provide any firm historical allusions, it is necessary to turn to other methods in order to date the work. Strugnell's argument, that the description of the divine throne-chariot in 4QSl 40 is more primitive than the Parables,[58] has already been noted. He assigns the Qumran manuscript to the middle of the first century B.C. Another feature that suggests a typological approach to dating is the twofold ouranology of the Parables. In 1 En. 71:5-7 there is a distinction between heaven and the heaven of heavens where the divine throne is located. In 1 En. 14:10-17 the same idea is represented by two houses, one of crystal and the other beyond it of fire and containing the throne. Such an ouranology seems to be more primitive than the sevenfold one that dates from the first century A.D. Strugnell has noted the lack of the concept of seven heavens in 1 Enoch; however, he also notes that Revelation also lacks such a concept, making it dangerous to use this criterion alone in dating a work.⁵⁹ The various manuscripts of the Greek version of T. Levi 2:7-3:9 seem to show a development from a twofold to a sevenfold ouranology; however, as Strugnell notes, it is necessary to await the publication of the Qumran fragments of the Testament of Levi to pursue further a discussion of the typology of the Hellenistic Jewish concept of the heavens.⁶⁰ It would seem, however, that the lack of seven heavens would make a date too far into the second century A.D. unlikely.

The Son of Man in Matthew and the Parables. Another approach to the dating of the Parables suggests that Matthew is dependent upon the work for special Son of Man material. This suggestion is not new, and in the past it would not have been necessary to argue for a relationship between Matthew and the Parables.⁶¹ However, Vermes⁶² and Perrin⁶³ have demonstrated that the use of Son of Man as a *title* in Christianity is dependent upon exegesis of Dan. 7:9-14 rather than upon a pre-Christian use of Son of Man as a messianic title. In fact, the two Jewish uses of Son of Man, the Parables of Enoch and the sixth vision of 4 Ezra, are likewise examples of the exegetical use of Dan. 7, where the phrase is a simile intended to distinguish an anthropomorphic figure from the four beasts of the first part of the vision.⁶⁴ The variations in the functions of the figure described in the Parables of Enoch, 4 Ezra, and early Christianity suggest that what the passages have in common is a traditional interpretation of Dan. 7:9-14 as messianic.⁶⁵ While there is no reason to suggest that the Son of Man material in Mark and Luke is dependent upon the Parables of Enoch,⁶⁶ the special Matthean use of the title portrays the Son of Man as eschatological judge in a way suggestive of the Elect one/Son of Man in the Parables. In addition, in two of these passages, Matthew associates the Son of Man with the θρόνος δόξης αὐτοῦ, echoing the phraseology of the Parables, where the Elect one/Son of Man is associated with the *manbara sebḥātihu*, or "throne of his glory."

In Daniel as well as in Mark and Luke, the Son of Man functions eschatologically as a sign of the eschaton and as the ruler of the righteous in the new age; however, his role as an eschatological judge is limited to the eschatological judgment sayings, Mk. 8:38 and Lk. 12:8-9, where, in fact, the title may be a later addition to the earliest form of the saying.[67] In Dan. 7, judgment takes place before the appearance of "one like a son of man," and the figure therefore does not occupy a throne as a seat of judgment.

In the Parables of Enoch, "that Son of Man" appears largely in the context of an exgetical tradition based on Dan. 7:9-14 and derives his judicial function from "the Elect one" as this tradition is used to amplify the latter title. In 1 En. 46:4, which is in the context of the midrash on Dan. 7 found in 1 En. 46-47, the kings and mighty of the earth, who are the objects of the eschatological judgment, are the usual opponents of the Parables and are therefore to be understood as redactional in this context (cf. 1 En. 38:5; 53:5; 54:2; 62:1,6,9; 63:1,12; 67:8). Their crime is also redactional: they have denied the name of the Lord of Spirits (cf. 1 En. 38:2; 45:2; 46:7; 63:7; 67:10). While Dan. 7:11-12 and 7:26 suggest the removal of kings from their thrones, the Parables goes a step further and makes the Son of Man responsible for this action in 1 En. 46:4-8, after the Elect one has already been introduced in 1 En. 45:2-3 as the judge of those who deny the name of the Lord of Spirits. It is also important to note the shift from the Elect one to the Son of Man in 1 En. 62. That chapter begins with the Elect one being seated on the throne of his glory by the Lord of Spirits to judge the kings and mighty of the earth; however, in the midst of the passage, at 1 En. 62:5, the poet changes from "the Elect one" to "that Son of Man." The change establishes the Son of Man as a judicial figure who sits upon the throne of judgment. The interplay of exegetical traditions in the Parables will be examined again in chapter VII below. That analysis will demonstrate that various traditions that have appeared independently in the first two parables (1 En. 38-44 and 45-57) are brought together and intertwined in the third parable (1 En. 58-69). Chapters 62-63 seem to be the focal point of this compositional technique.

The Elect one seems to have been associated with the function of judgment prior to its use in the Parables as a messianic title. In Is. 42:1-4, where the origins of the title are probably to be found, the primary task of Yahweh's chosen one is to bring forth justice to the nations, משפט לגוים יוציא, or to establish justice in the earth, עד־ישים בארץ משפט. In 1 En. 55:4 and 61:8, the Elect one seems to have been associated with traditions concerning the judgment of heavenly beings.

Carsten Colpe notes that statements concerning the Elect one are made in the Parables prior to the appearance of the Son of Man; however, he refuses to differentiate between the two terms, treating them as part of a single messianic conception.[68] His position seems to assume that a Son of Man tradition[69] has some type of an independent existence in pre-Christian Judaism, although he admits that the term is not used as a title in the Parables.[70] He attempts to validate this position by turning to the Christian tradition as evidence for the existence of the Son of Man in Judaism.[71] If "that Son of Man" in the Parables is not a title, the Jewish evidence for Son of Man as a title evaporates, leaving solid evidence only for a messianic interpretation of Dan. 7:13-14. This tradition is represented in the Parables by a Dan. 7:9-14 midrash, which has been interwoven into the fabric of the work in such a way that it could easily have acquired in the process some of the features of the broader messianic conceptions represented by the Elect one. Since Dan. 7 does not assign the function of eschatological judge to its messianic figure, and since this function is not an important element of the early Christian use of Son of Man as a title, the position that "that Son of Man" in the Parables derives its judgmental role from "the Elect one" is a viable one.

Matthew introduces new Son of Man sayings that picture the figure as an eschatological judge. In Mt. 16:27 the evangelist displaces the eschatological judgment saying of Mk. 8:38 with a more explicit saying: at his coming the Son of Man will repay each man for his deeds.[72] This change seems to be part of a redactional process that is intended to strengthen the role of the title, Son of Man, in Mt. 16:13-17:13. The title is moved to the beginning of the Confession narrative at Mt. 16:13. Mt. 17:9-13 is rewritten to emphasize the authority of Jesus as the Son of Man.[73] The reference to the suffering of the Son of Man in Mt. 17:12 now appears after the two references to Elijah (cf. Mk. 9:12-13),[74] and the phrase "it is written" from Mk. 9:13 is not used by Matthew, so that the teaching concerning the suffering of Elijah is given on the authority of Jesus rather than on the authority of scripture. The latter change is remarkable given Matthew's concern with the fulfillment of scripture; however, it is possible that it merely indicates that Matthew knew no exegetical tradition that would support the teaching that Elijah must suffer. In any case, he seems to be treating the Confession of Peter and the Transfiguration narrative as a unit by moving the title Son of Man to the beginning of the Confession and closer to the end of Mt. 17:9-13,[75] the section that concludes the Transfiguration narrative. Between the Confession and Transfiguration he has accentuated the role of the Son of Man by heightening his function as the eschatological judge in Mt. 16:27 and replacing "kingdom of God" in Mk. 9:1 with "Son of Man" in Mt. 16:28.

Mt. 19:28 introduces the Son of Man into the saying regarding the twelve apostles sitting on thrones judging the twelve tribes (cf. Lk. 22:30) and has the figure seated ἐπὶ θρόνου δόξης αὐτοῦ.[76] Mt. 13:41-43 introduces a new Son of Man saying regarding the last judgment as an interpretation of the parable of the weeds of the field in Mt. 13:24-30. Finally, Matthew introduces the parable of the last judgment in Mt. 25:31-46,[77] which is obviously dependent on the judgment scene in the Apocalypse of the Animals, see 1 En. 90:20-27. In Matthew, the sheep are to be separated from the goats, while, in the Apocalypse of the Animals, Israel and the nations are represented by sheep and wild animals respectively, and in 1 En. 90:26 the blind sheep, sinful Israelites, are cast into the burning abyss. In Mt. 25:31, it is the Son of Man who sits ἐπὶ θρόνου δόξης αὐτοῦ, while the "Lord of the Sheep" sits on the throne of judgment in 1 En. 90:20. Tödt notes that, while Matthew places "Son of Man" at the beginning of the parable, throughout it the judge is termed βασιλεύς and addressed as κύριος.[78] The introduction of the Son of Man as judge in a judgment scene based on 1 En. 90:20-27 suggests that Matthew knew both the Apocalypse of the Animals and the Parables of Enoch; however, it is not possible to determine if he possessed an edition of Enochic writings more or less identical to the Ethiopic version now extant. If the Parables of Enoch have influenced the Matthean treatment of Son of Man, the work must be dated earlier than the last decade or two of the first century A.D.

Apocalyptic and the fall of Jerusalem. It is possible to argue that the Parables was composed prior to the fall of Jerusalem in A.D. 70. One would not expect to find 1 En. 56:7 if the work was written after that date: *wa-hagara ṣādqāna zi'aya yekawwen māʿqafa la-'afrāsihomu*, "But the city of my righteous ones will be an obstacle for their [the Parthians' and Medes'] horses." The "city of my righteous ones" should most certainly be taken as Jerusalem, since the reference is to an apocalyptic motif based on the ancient Zion tradition that God would defend his city,[79] and it does not seem likely that the motif would be used after the fall of Jerusalem. Jewish apocalyptic writings composed after A.D. 70--namely, 4 Ezra and 2 Baruch--are obsessed with the destruction of the holy city, but there is no evidence of a similar concern in the Parables of Enoch.

The lack of concern with the destruction of Jerusalem, coupled with the apparent influence of the Parables on the Matthean Son of Man and the lack of a concept of the heavens as sevenfold, indicates that the work was composed prior to the last third of the first century A.D. On the other hand, Strugnell's position,[80] that 4QSl 40 is more primitive than the Parables in the description of the divine throne-chariot, suggests that the composition of the Parables should not be placed too far back into the first century B.C. It is not possible to be more precise in dating the work. It is possible, however, on the basis of its major concerns, to suggest some circumstances under which it might have been composed.

Anti-royal polemic and the divinity of the Roman emperor. Chapter VI below will examine several midrashic traditions that are intended to develop a polemic against the kings and mighty of the earth in the Parables of Enoch, a theme that seems to be of central importance for the work. In 1 En. 53:6, the kings and mighty have "hindered" the righteous, while in 46:8 they have persecuted them. Elsewhere, they have denied the Lord of Spirits, led astray those who dwell upon the earth (56:4), and have failed to recognize the Lord of Spirits as the source of their authority (46:5 and 63:4-7). In 46:7 they are accused of idolatry, and in 46:4-8; 48:10; and 62:12, the taunt-song against the king of Babylon from Is. 14 is used against them.

While most of these charges could have been placed against Herod the Great, they fit the Jewish perception of Gaius Caligula better. The characterization, "kings and mighty *of the earth*," seems to be more universal in scope than a local client-king, and 1 En. 46:7 likewise uses Is. 14 to picture the hubris of the kings as cosmic in extent. As the examination in chapter VI will show, in the traditional exegesis of scripture of the period, Is. 14 carries the symbolic value of a polemic against a king or emperor who has lost track of his true place in the cosmos and dares to claim equality with God.

With this understanding of the interpretation of Is. 14 in mind, the reign of Gaius Caligula suggests itself as a likely time in the first century A.D. for the composition of the Parables. This emperor made claims of divinity unprecedented for a *Roman* emperor, although they were, of course, based on Hellenistic and oriental philosophies of kingship. These claims will be examined further in chapter VI. The important event of his reign for the present discussion is the attempt to have his statue set up in the temple in Jerusalem in response to the actions of the Jews of Jamnia who had torn down a statue of the emperor set up by their Gentile neighbors. His attempt nearly instigated a popular revolt in Palestine, a revolt that was forestalled only by the emperor's assassination.[81] Philo's characterization of Gaius significantly alludes to Is. 14:

> What is this that you say? *do you a mere man seek to annex also ether and heaven,* not satisfied with the sum of so many mainlands, islands, nations, regions, over which you assumed sovereignty, and do you deem God worthy of nothing in our world here below, no country, no city, but even this tiny area hallowed for Him and sanctified by oracles and divine messages you propose to take away, so that in the circumference of this great earth no trace or reminder should be

left of the reverence and honour due to the truly existing veritable God?[82]
The allusion to the Zion tradition in 1 En. 56:5-8 may well be a response to the threat to the temple: the city of God's righteous ones will be a hindrance to the horses of the emperor's viceroy as he attempts to install the statue of Gaius. The period seems to be one in which the Jews in Palestine were close to the point of armed rebellion, and it must have had apocalyptic expectations and literature associated with it.

The above argument assumes that an apocalyptic work is generally composed in a time of crisis that epitomizes the problems reflected in the writing; however, the threat to Jerusalem could have been as much a matter of apocalyptic anticipation as imminent reality, and the offensive practice of emperor worship in non-Jewish areas of Palestine can be traced to the last quarter of the first century B.C. Herod the Great seems to have been in the forefront of the introduction of the cult of the emperor in the east. He rebuilt Samaria and renamed it Sebaste in honor of Augustus. He also built a new city at Straton's Tower, naming it Caesarea, likewise in honor of his patron. Both cities had in their midst a temple dedicated to the divinity of Augustus.[83] Resistance to Roman rule antedates Herod's nomination to the kingship; however, it intensifies in the revolts that take place after his death and in the time of Pontius Pilate, who caused a riot when he introduced standards into Jerusalem bearing the portrait of the emperor. The period between the death of Agrippa I and the beginning of the revolt against the Romans is marked by messianic movements, some of which appear to draw upon the symbolism of the Exodus tradition.[84] In chapter VI below, it will be noted that this tradition plays an important role in the symbolism of the Parables.[85] Gaius is the only emperor who attempts, in the period before 70, to force emperor-worship upon the Jews, and his reign is therefore the most likely time to which the Parables of Enoch could be dated; however, a case could be made for composition as early as the latter part of the reign of Herod the Great[86] or as late as the early years of the first revolt against the Romans.

On the basis of the typological examination of the ouranology and angelology of the Parables, its likely use by Matthew, and the examination of its relation to the events of the first centuries B.C. and A.D., it appears that the work was composed sometime between the last quarter of the first century B.C. and the fall of Jerusalem in A.D. 70. While the midst of the first century A.D. seems to be the most likely time of composition, that judgment does not carry a high degree of probability.

The Provenance of the Parables and the Enochic Literature

Greenfield's suggestion, that the Parables of Enoch belongs to a different Enochic strand of tradition than that represented by the Qumran manuscripts,[87] is a key insight in the discussion of the tradition history of material within the work. While the Qumran sect is not totally isolated from what might be called proto-Merkabah mysticism, it does seem to have lost its interest in Enoch prior to the period during which the Parables was produced. However, if the work belongs to another strand of the Enochic tradition, then the question of the relationship of the traditional material in it to the rest of the Enochic literature must be raised.

The tradition-historical problem is most acute in relation to the fallen-angel material in 1 En. 6-11 and the Parables of Enoch. The common elements in this material have usually been explained through reference to a common source, a hypothetical Book of Noah, which some claim to be an earlier work incorporated in the composition of 1 Enoch and others to be a later work interpolated into it.[88] The fragments of this work generally have been sought in 1 En. 6-11; 54:1-56:4; 60; 64:1-69:25; and 106-7. However, the various passages are too diverse in character to have been originally one source. One does not even mention Noah (1 En. 54:1-56:4), while in another he is mentioned only incidentally (1 En. 6-11). There are references to a Book of Noah in Jub. 10:13-14 and 21:10. The work involved there, however, seems to be one concerning medicine and healing[89] or the performance of sacrifice. What the passages in 1 Enoch do have in common is that they contain various versions of the traditions concerning fallen angels. The problem is to determine how these versions are related. The appropriate method with which to approach this problem is form criticism rather than literary criticism.

Sjöberg subjected the literary-critical attempts to distinguish various sources in the Parables to a thorough examination and concluded that there is insufficient evidence for sources behind the work[90] and that, if the connections between passages are seen as associative rather than logical,[91] the work can be read as a unity. The one major exception that he makes to his conclusion is the Noachic material.[92] He makes this exception mainly on the basis of the unanimity of the prior discussion on the presence of the Noachic material in 1 Enoch.[93] Part II below will question the unity of this hypothetical body of material through a form-critical examination of 1 En. 54:1-56:4 and 64:1-69:12. Part III will show that, if, as Sjöberg claims, the connections in the Parables are associative rather than logical in character, 1 En. 54:1-56:4 and 64:1-69:12 can be read as an integral part of the writing. The method involved will be a redaction-critical study of the thematic elements in the traditions used in the work and the way in which they fit into the traditional genre, *mašal*.

PART II

A FORM-CRITICAL EXAMINATION
OF 1 EN. 54:1-56:4
AND 64:1-69:12

INTRODUCTION TO PART II

It is possible to identify two distinct traditional units within the hypothetical Noachic material in the Parables of Enoch. These two units can be distinguished on the basis of the presence of two different genres, (1) a midrashic excerpt, based on Is. 24:17-23, that can be found in both 1 En. 54:1-56:4 and 64:1-68:1, and (2) two lists of fallen angels that can be found in 1 En. 69:2-12. The two units can also be distinguished on the basis of their use of scripture. The Is. 24:17-23 midrash is, obviously, an exegetical tradition based on that particular passage of scripture. The two lists of fallen angels are related to a Gen. 6:1-4 midrash, which is distinct from the other exegetical tradition. In addition, examination of the relationship of the two units to mythological patterns from the Ancient Near East and the Greco-Roman world indicates that there are structural differences between them. The units embody two distinct and coherent myths that attribute the origin of evil to heavenly beings. Each, however, views evil under different aspects: the one is concerned primarily with the abuse of authority by kings and angels, the other, with problems related to purity.

The two traditional units have been combined in 1 En. 6-11 in such a way that the two versions of the Is. 24:17-23 midrash in the Parables of Enoch cannot be dependent on chapters 6-11 as a source but must depend upon an earlier traditional interpretation of Is. 24:17-23, one that has survived at least into the first century A.D. Since 1 En. 6-11 is pre-Maccabean in origin, this tradition must extend back into the third century B.C. The survival of a tradition over this particular period is not an unreasonable hypothesis, since the third century seems to be the origin of the patterns of traditional scriptural exegesis that appear later in such diverse sources as Josephus, Philo, and the targumin.[1]

The procedure followed in Part II will be to establish the two genres, to determine the essential elements of the traditional unit for which each genre forms the nucleus, and to examine the way in which the two units have been combined in

1 En. 6-11. In addition, some attention must be paid to the *Sitz im Leben* of the two genres. The context in which these traditions are developed, preserved, and utilized will be of particular importance in Part III as a basis for a discussion of the relation between oral and written modes of expression in Judaism of the Hellenistic period as reflected by the Parables of Enoch.

CHAPTER III

THE IS. 24:17-23 MIDRASH

A comparative examination of 1 En. 54:1-56:4 and 64:1-68:1 with Is. 24:17-23 indicates that the former two passages embody a common exegetical tradition based on the latter passage. It is possible to establish this relationship on the basis of both structure and content. Not only does the passage from the Isaiah Apocalypse (Is. 24-27) have a concave structure, which is duplicated by the two passages from 1 Enoch, it also has both a parallelism between the punishment of kings and angelic beings and a distinctive eschatology in common with the latter. However, before the comparative examination is undertaken, some attention must be given to two preliminary matters: the problem of midrash as a genre and the problem of the date of the Isaiah Apocalypse.

Excursus 1:
Midrash as a Method and a Genre

The term *midrash* is used to designate a number of different types of literature from the Rabbinic midrashim, which are composite works combining a number of different genres, to the Qumran pesharim, which quote scripture verse by verse and comment on it, and the Genesis Apocryphon, which attempts to rewrite scripture. In addition, the term *midrashic* can be used to refer to a method involving the interpretation or application of scripture. A greater degree of precision in the use of the term is needed.

Midrash as a genre. Addison G. Wright gives the following definition of midrash, using the Rabbinic midrashim as a touchstone:

> The basic midrashic structure, common to all forms that can be labeled midrash down to the smallest independent unit, is merely that one begins with a text of Scripture and proceeds to comment on it in some way. The midrashic unit must be so structured that the material contained therein is placed in the context of a Scripture text, and is presented for the sake of the Biblical text; it is a literature about a literature.[1]

As Wright uses this definition, it excludes works that anthologize a number of passages rather than interpret one primary text.[2] While other passages may be adduced in the process of interpretation, there must be one primary text to serve as the structural basis of the unit.

Types of midrash. Wright gives three classifications of midrash:[3] (1) exegetical midrash (verse by verse exposition of scripture), (2) homiletic midrash (exposition based on a particular passage of scripture but tending to concentrate on a verse or two within the unit), and (3) narrative midrash (rewritten and embellished scripture). Vermes makes similar distinctions,[4] but he considers homiletic midrash to be the earliest form.

Most of the midrashic excerpts in the Parables of Enoch fall under the category of homiletic midrash. They tend to concentrate on one or two verses from a passage, introducing allusions to other passages of scripture in order to interpret those verses, and they are parenetic in function: their purpose is to encourage the righteous to endure their present situation by depicting their future reward and the punishment of their oppressors. Rather than quoting scripture precisely, these units are allusive in style, the result, most likely, of the use of oral-formulaic language in the composition of the units.[5] Some of the midrashic units in the Parables represent narrative midrash, or rewritten scripture. These units include the Is. 24:17-23 midrash, the unit under discussion, which embellishes that passage by expanding the details of the punishment of the kings of the earth and the host of heaven and by introducing traditional material associated with the interpretation of the flood narrative in Genesis.

Composite and component types. For midrash to serve as a designation of genre, a work, either literary or traditional, must be concerned with the interpretation of a particular passage of scripture at its highest level of organization. The Rabbinic midrashim are composite works that are midrashic at this level, although they include a number of component types within their structure. In the Parables of

Enoch, a number of component units are midrashic excerpts derived from the traditional cycles of the interpretation of scripture. Vermes makes a distinction between midrashic fragments as component elements in other types of compositions and the original traditional context:

> Haggadic extracts figuring as examples in homiletic works, . . .are not to be confused with authentic exegetical tradition. These are severed from their scriptural context, and although in most cases they echo the old Haggadah, they are definitely extraneous to it and secondary to what may be called, in the broadest sense, targumic exegesis.[6]

"Haggadic extracts," however, are frequent in Jewish and Christian literature of the period, and their observation frequently provides the essential clues to the structure of thought.[7] Many of these short units are obviously concerned with the exegesis of one particular passage of scripture, adducing others for the purpose of the interpretation of the central one.[8] Some designation is needed for these units *as component types*, and, while *midrashic excerpt* might be more accurate, *midrash* will be used throughout this dissertation in this limited sense.

Midrash and tradition. What Vermes terms "targumic exegesis" is obviously a traditional rather than a literary type in the Hellenistic period. From the standpoint of a discussion of midrash as a component type it is important to recognize that, although "haggadic extracts" may be secondary to true "targumic exegesis," their primary relationship in most cases is to that body of traditional interpretation rather than to other works of literature. In other words, these units are part of an oral tradition rather than a literary tradition.[9] A clear distinction between oral and written "literary" types will be of importance in the next chapter.

Midrash as a method of understanding. Ultimately, midrash is central to the cultural epoch that begins with the formation of Judaism in the post-exilic period. The older national era derived its self-understanding directly from its epic cycles of traditions, which were pliable and could be readily shaped to meet current needs. In the subsequent period, these traditions have been deposited, and to a certain extent ossified, in the form of scripture, and the

determination of the meaning of existence now requires a
hermeneutic. It is now the traditional interpretation of
scripture that represents a pliable means of dealing with
current need.[10] Even when fragments have become detached from
the traditional body of material, their use in new contexts
represents a natural continuation of the use of midrash as a
method of understanding the present or future.

Excursus 2:
The Date of the Isaiah Apocalypse

The Isaiah Apocalypse (Is. 24-27) has been the subject
of much discussion during this century, and it is beyond the
scope of this dissertation to examine the history of its
interpretation in any detail. Key points of disagreement
include the date, unity, and purpose of the passage. It is
necessary, however, to make some comments concerning the date
of the material, since its *terminus ad quem* is close to the
terminus a quo of the related Enochic traditions with which
this dissertation is concerned.

While a pre-Exilic date has long been out of the
question for the Isaiah Apocalypse, dates that extend into the
latter part of the second century B.C. have been proposed.
The discussion of the date has generally revolved around the
identity of the city whose destruction is predicted in the
material.[11] The results of this discussion have been inconclusive since the information provided in the apocalypse is
insufficient to permit historical identification. It is more
likely that, as Otto Kaiser indicates, the passage is "not
meant to refer at all to the destruction of a particular city,
but to the eschatological end of city life altogether."[12]

Kaiser argues that the latest stratum of the passage,
Is. 25:8a and 26:19, contains references to the resurrection
of the dead and is therefore possibly contemporary with the
book of Daniel,[13] although he admits that such an argument
must be used with caution. He places the next latest stratum,
Is. 24:21-23--part of the passage with which this dissertation
is concerned--and 25:6-8, somewhere in the first third of the
second century B.C. on account of its "more advanced apocalyptic speculation."[14] Kaiser distinguishes two other strata

that contain material dealing with the eschatological judgment
and eschatological songs of thanksgiving. His theory of
composition is almost certainly too mechanical in that it
attempts to find a logical order where one ought to expect an
associative one. He presents no convincing reason for reading
the passage as anything other than a unity. His *terminus ad
quem* rests solely on the comparison with Daniel, although it
is certainly presumptive to assume that the idea of the
resurrection of the dead originates in the Maccabean revolt.

Nickelsburg, in a study of the question of resurrection
in intertestamental Judaism, argues that Dan. 12:2 is dependent
upon Is. 26:19 because, while Is. 26:19 speaks only of the
resurrection of righteous Israelites in order that they might
be vindicated (cf. Is. 26:14), Dan. 12:2 speaks of a resurrection of both the righteous and the unrighteous for the
purpose of judgment and either reward or punishment.[15]

> For Isaiah the resurrection of the righteous is *in
> itself* vindication for the righteous. For Daniel resurrection is *a means* by which both the righteous and the
> wicked dead are enabled to receive their respective
> vindication or condemnation. Thus Daniel has gone
> beyond Isaiah. There will be punishment for the wicked
> who are already dead.[16]

While Nickelsburg does not raise the question of the date of
the Isaiah Apocalypse, it is fairly clear that it need not be
contemporary to Daniel, particularly if Dan. 12:2 treats it
as scripture.

In addition, Is. 24:17-23 can not be so easily treated
as obviously late on the basis of its "more advanced apocalyptic speculation"[17] since it is related to other passages of
scripture that have their roots in the mythology of the
Ancient Near East: Is. 14:12-21; Ezek. 28:1-19; and Ps. 82.
Kaiser's judgment here should have been based on a typological
examination of proto-apocalyptic writings. The two scholars
who have made such an examination have come to different
conclusions. Otto Plöger[18] compares the Isaiah Apocalypse to
several other apocalyptic passages from the prophetic books
and attempts to specify the beginning of the reign of Antiochus
the Great, 223-187 B.C., through relation of the eschatology
of the passage to the beginning political struggle between the
Ptolemies and the Seleucids for the control of Palestine, a

more concrete suggestion than is warranted by the nature of the evidence. Paul Hanson[19] assigns the Isaiah Apocalypse, along with Third Isaiah, to disciples of Second Isaiah and dates it in the late sixth century B.C. on the basis of the similarity of its mythic pattern to that of Second Isaiah. The Isaiah Apocalypse is not of great interest to Hanson in *The Dawn of Apocalyptic*, and he reserves final judgment for a comparison of the passage with Zech. 12 and 14.

Ultimately, any attempt to date the Isaiah Apocalypse must take into account the time at which the entire book of Isaiah would have been complete and held in such regard that major additions would have been unlikely. There is a *terminus ad quem* in Sir. 48:22-25, which presupposes the association of Second Isaiah with chapters 1-39.[20] Sirach belongs to the beginning of the second century B.C., and the existence of the complete book of Isaiah at that time is confirmed by the great Isaiah scroll from Qumran, which can be dated in the second century.[21] Sirach appears to indicate that not only Isaiah but also the *Nebi'im* were complete at the beginning of the second century. Sir. 48:22-49:12 mentions Isaiah, Jeremiah, Ezekiel, and the book of the Twelve Prophets in that order with various quotations from or allusions to those books; Sir. 39:1 seems to mention the three divisions of scripture, *Torah*, *Nebi'im*, and *Kethubim* (here, "the wisdom of all the ancients"), although the last certainly can not be considered a fixed collection at that time; and Jesus ben Sirach's grandson, who translated the work into Greek toward the end of the second century, not only clearly takes the *Nebi'im* as a specific collection alongside the *Torah*, but also assumes that his grandfather did:[22]

> Whereas many great teachings have been given to us through the law and the prophets and the others that followed them, on account of which we should praise Israel for instruction and wisdom; . . . my grandfather Jesus, after devoting himself especially to the reading of the law and the prophets and the other books of our fathers, and after acquiring considerable proficiency in them, was himself also led to write something pertaining to instruction and wisdom.[23]

While the grandson may have idealized the centrality of the law and prophets for his grandfather, Sir. 45-49 uses the *Torah* and both the former and the latter prophets in a way that

suggests that they are considered normative collections at the
beginning of the second century B.C. This conculsion implies
that the book of Isaiah must have been completed some time
earlier in order to be regarded as part of a definitive
collection of *scripture* at that time. While the date of the
composition of the Isaiah Apocalypse and the close of Isaiah
itself can not be fixed with any certainty, it is clear that
the book is regarded as scripture, and therefore an appropriate object for midrash, at the time of the composition of
1 En. 1-36, which contains the earliest example of the tradition that, it is here argued, is based on Is. 24:17-23.

*1 En. 54:1-56:4 and 64:1-68:1 as
Midrashim of Is. 24:17-23*

1 En. 54:1-56:4 and 64:1-68:1 are related in both
structure and content to Is. 24:17-23, and a comparative
examination establishes the former as midrashim of the latter.
In terms of structure, the passages from the Parables of Enoch
reflect the concave structure of the passage from the Isaiah
Apocalypse. In terms of content, the three passages parallel
the punishment of heavenly beings with that of the kings of
the earth. In addition, they have in common a distinctive
eschatology that introduces a period of imprisonment for the
host of heaven and the kings of the earth prior to the
eschaton. An incidental use of flood imagery in the depiction
of cosmic catastrophe in Is. 24:18c leads to the use of Noah's
flood as a prototype for the eschaton in 1 En. 54:1-56:4 and
64:1-68:1. The latter two passages, together with 1 En. 6-11,
provide evidence that Is. 24:17-23 formed the basis of a traditional unit in Judaism of the Hellenistic period.

The Structure of the Midrashic Unit

(A)

(Is. 24:17) Dread and the pit and the trap are upon you,
    inhabitant of the earth.
(18) And if one flees from the sound of the dread,
    he will fall into the pit,
And if he comes up from the midst of the pit,
    he will be caught in the snare.

(B)

For the windows of the height are opened,
  and the foundations of the earth are shaken.
(19) The earth is completely broken;
The earth is tossed to and fro;
The earth totters.
(20) The earth staggers like a drunkard,
  and is shaken to and fro like a shack;
And heavy upon it is its rebellion,
  and it falls and rises no more.

(A_1)

(21) And on that day, Yahweh will call to account
  the host of the height upon the height,
  and the kings of the earth upon the earth.
(22) And they will be gathered together,[24]
  prisoners in a cistern [or pit],
  and be shut up in a dungeon,
And after many days, they will be called to account.
(23) Then the moon will be abashed,
  and the sun ashamed,
For Yahweh Ṣeba'oth reigns on Mount Zion and in Jerusalem,
  and his glory [reigns] before his elders.

This passage may be divided into three parts: Is. 24:17-18b, 18c-20, and 21-23. The first section appears independently at Jer. 48:43-44, where it is directed against Moab rather than the inhabitants of the earth (cf. also Lam. 3:47). This change, taken with the cosmic implications of the catastrophe in Is. 24:18c-20, represents a profound change in application of material that was once part of an oracle against a specific nation. The three sections present three different images of catastrophe or judgment that are increasingly cosmic and mythological in character. They have little in common that would suggest that they circulated as a unit prior to the composition of the Isaiah Apocalypse, and the relationship of Is. 24:17-18b with Jer. 48:43-44 and Lam. 3:47 suggests that the three sections were, in fact, independent traditional units that were associated in the composition of the larger unit.[25]

Although the three sections were probably not a unit prior to the composition of the Isaiah Apocalypse, the midrashic use of the passage in the Parables of Enoch treats them as a unit with a more or less concave structure. There is a section (A) concerned with the catastrophe awaiting the inhabitants of the earth at the beginning and a section (A_1) concerned with the imprisonment and judgment of the host of heaven and the kings of the earth at the end. While these two sections are not precisely parallel, they both involve in part judgment and punishment of earthly begins, the inhabitants or the kings of the earth. In the center is a contrasting section (B) that describes a cosmic catastrophe first in terms of the world-flood and second in terms of a severe earthquake. It is possible that the association of certain words led to the combination of the three sections. Verses 18c and 21 place the height (מרום) and the earth in parallel, and, although the words are different, "pit" (פחת) in verse 17 and "cistern" (בור) in verse 22 could have been associated. In the Parables of Enoch, it will be argued, the "A" and "A_1" sections are elaborated in terms of the punishment of the kings and mighty of the earth and the host of Asael, while the allusion to the flood in section "B" gives rise to the use of traditional material dealing with the flood.

The treatment of the passage in Targum Jonathan also suggests that, in traditional interpretation, Is. 24:17-23 was seen as a coherent unit. In the MT, the passage follows an eschatological hymn of thanksgiving in verses 14-16a and a transitional section, verse 16b-c, that represents the prophet's anguish at the contrast between the cosmic hymn, which celebrates Yahweh as the creator and ruler of the universe, and the suffering of the Jews at the hands of the treacherous. The transitional section leads into verses 17-23, which represent a vision of judgment in which God ends the contradiction between divine power and present reality by the imprisonment and punishment of the rebellious powers. The Targum removes the question of theodicy from verse 16b-c and transforms it from a transitional section to an introduction to verses 17-23. The following are the MT and targumic versions of the verse 16b-c:

(MT)

ואמר רזי־לי רזי־לי אוי לי בגדים בגדו
ובגד בוגדים בגדו:

But I say, "I pine away,
I pine away. Woe is me!
For the treacherous deal treacherously,
the treacherous deal very treacherously."[26]

(Targum)

אמר נביא רז אגר לצדיקיא איתחזי לי
רז פורענו לרשיעיא אתגלי לי

רי לאנוסיא דמתאנסין
ולבזוז בזוזין דהא מתבזיז:

The prophet says, "The secret of the reward of the righteous has been shown to me; the secret of the punishment of the wicked has been revealed to me. Woe to the oppressors, for they will be oppressed, and to the plundering of the plunderer, for he will be plundered."

The Targum has interpreted the enigmatic רזי-לי by relating it to רז, "secret," and has made that secret explicit through reference to the reward of the righteous[27] and the punishment of the wicked. Note the way in which the repetition of the phrase in the Hebrew requires the mention of two secrets in the Targum. It then transfers the anguish from the prophet to the wicked and transforms the verse into an eschatological judgment saying. The process of interpretation in the Targum is quite obvious, and it is equally apparent that it interprets verse 16b-c as the introduction to verses 17-23. The oppressors and the plunderer are the host of the heights and the kings of the earth of verse 21.

1 En. 54:1-56:4 can also be divided into three sections corresponding to the structure of Is. 24:17-23. In this case, the two outer sections, 1 En. 54:1-6 and 55:3-56:4, deal with the punishment of the host of Asael and the kings and mighty of the earth, while the middle section, 1 En. 54:7-55:2, deals with the world-flood without even mentioning Noah.

(A)

(1 En. 54:1) And I looked and turned to another part of the earth and saw there a deep valley where a fire was burning. (2) And they brought the kings and the mighty and were casting them into that deep valley. (3) And there my eyes saw that which they were making their instruments:[28] iron chains that were beyond weighing. (4) And I questioned the angel of peace who accompanied me, saying, "For whom are these bonds[29] prepared?" (5) And he said to me, "These are being prepared for the host of Asael that they [the angels of punishment, cf. 1 En. 53:3 and 54:2] might take them and cast them [into] the abyss of every punishment and cover their jaws with jagged rocks, as the Lord of Spirits has commanded. (6) And Michael, and Gabriel, and Raphael, and Phanuel will seize them on that great day, and they will cast them into a blazing furnace on that day in order that the Lord of Spirits might punish them because of their iniquity in that they became servants to Satan and caused those who dwell on the earth to sin."

(B)

(7) And in those days the punishment of the Lord of Spirits will come forth, and he will open all the storehouses of the waters that are above the heavens[30] and those of the fountains that are beneath the earth. (8) And all the waters will be mixed with[31] the waters: that which is above the heavens is male, and the water that is beneath the earth is female. (9) And they will blot out all who dwell upon the earth and who dwell beneath the ends of the heavens. (10) For they [will] have recognized their iniquity, which they have done on the earth, and because of it [the iniquity] they will be destroyed. (55:1) And afterward, the Head of Days repented and said, "In vain did I destroy everyone of those who were dwelling on the earth." (2) And he swore by his great name, "Never again shall I treat like this all those who are dwelling upon the earth, and I shall place a sign in the heavens, and it will be a pledge between me and them forever, so many days as the heaven shall remain over the earth, and that is according to my command."

(A_1)

(3) "When I desire to grasp them by the hands of the angels on the day of affliction and distress before this,[32] my punishment and my wrath will dwell upon them," says God, the Lord of Spirits. (4) "Mighty kings who dwell [upon] the earth, you will be forced to see my Elect one, for he will sit on the glorious throne and judge Asael and all his associates and all his host in the name of the Lord of Spirits." (56:1) And I saw there various hosts of angels of punishment going and bearing whips and chains of iron and bronze. (2) And I questioned the angel of peace, who was accompanying me, saying, "To whom are these ones going who are bearing whips?" (3) And he said to me, "[They are going] to their [the host of Asael's] elect and their loved ones that they might cast [them] into the deep fissure of the valley. (4) And then that valley will be full of their elect and loved ones, and the days of their lives will be ended, and the days of their sin from then on will cease to be numbered."

1 En. 64:1-68:1 presents the same pattern; however, it has elaborated sections "B" and "A_1" to deal with the flood and the punishment of the angels and kings in more detail. The reasons for these expansions will be examined later in this chapter and in chapter VII.

(A)

(1 En. 64:1) And I saw other forms hiding in this place. (2) I heard the voice of the angel saying: "These are the angels who descended upon the earth and who revealed secrets to the children of men and led the children of men into error[33] so that they sinned."

(B)

(65:1) In those days Noah saw how the earth tottered so that its destruction was near. (2) And he set out from that place and went to the ends of the earth and cried out to his grandfather Enoch, and Noah said three times with a bitter voice: "Hear me, hear me, hear me!" (4)[34] And immediately there was a great disturbance upon the earth, and a voice was heard from heaven, and I fell upon my face. (5) And Enoch my grandfather came to me, and he stood beside me and said to me: "Why do you call upon me with a bitter cry and lamentation?" (3)[34] And I said to him: "Tell me what it is that is happening upon the earth that the earth is thus weary and shaken, lest I perish with it."

(6)[35] And an edict has gone forth from the presence of the Lord concerning those who dwell upon the earth, that their destruction is imminent because they have learned all the secrets of the angels and all the violence of the satans, and all their most secret powers, and all the powers of those who make potions, and the powers of [those who make] charms, and the powers of those who cast molten images throughout the whole earth. (7) And how silver is produced from the dust of the earth, and how lead comes to be upon the earth, (8) because tin and lead are not produced from the earth like the former, there is a fountain that produces them, and an angel stands in it, and that angel is swift.[36]

(9) And afterwards my grandfather Enoch grasped me by my hand and lifted me up and said to me: "Go, because I have asked the Lord of Spirits about this disturbance that is upon the earth. (10) And he said to me: 'On account of their iniquity, their judgment is fixed and will not be withheld[37] in my presence; on account of the sorceries[38] that they have sought out and learned, the earth will be destroyed and whoever dwells upon it.' (11) And there is no place of refuge for these [the angels] forever, because they have shown them what is secret, and they are condemned; but as for you, you my son, the Lord of Spirits knows that you are pure and innocent from this blame concerning the secrets. (12) And he has established your name in the midst of the holy ones, and he will preserve you from amongst those who dwell upon the earth, and he has destined your seed of righteousness for kingship and great magnificence, and from your seed a fountain of righteous and holy ones will come forth, and they will have no number forever."

(66:1) And after this, he showed me the angels of punishment who are poised to come forth and set free all the powers of the waters that are beneath the earth that they may serve as judgment and as destruction for all who live and dwell upon the earth. (2) And the Lord of Spirits commanded the angels who were going forth that they should hold back, because those are over the powers of the waters. (3) And I went away from before the face of Enoch.

(67:1) And in those days the word of God came to me, and he said to me: "Noah, your lot came before me, a lot that has no reproach, a lot of love and righteousness.

(2) And now the angels are building a wooden [vessel], and when they have finished this task, I shall place my hand upon it and preserve it, and the seed of life will come forth from it, but let a change occur lest the earth remain destitute. (3) And I shall establish your seed before me for ever and ever, and I shall disperse those who dwell with you; it [Noah's seed] will not be unfruitful upon the earth, and it will be blessed and multiply upon the earth in the name of the Lord."

(A_1)

(4) And he will imprison those angels who revealed iniquity in that burning valley that my grandfather Enoch formerly showed me in the west amid the mountains of gold and silver and iron and lead and tin. (5) And I saw that valley, in which there was a great disturbance and a disturbance of the waters. (6) And when all this happened, from that molten metal and their [the waters'] disturbance the odor of sulphur was produced in that place, and it was associated with those waters, and that valley of the angels who led astray was burning beneath that region. (7) And through its valleys streams of fire will come where those angels will be punished who led astray those who dwell upon the earth.

(8) And in those days those waters will serve the kings and the mighty and the exalted and those who dwell upon the earth for the healing of the flesh and the punishment of the spirit; and their spirit is filled with desire, so that their flesh will be punished because they have denied the Lord of Spirits; and they see their punishment throughout the whole day and do not believe in his name. (9) And as the burning of their flesh increases so their spirits will undergo a change for ever and ever, because there is no one before the Lord of Spirits who utters a vain word. (10) For punishment will come upon them because they continue to believe in the desires of their flesh and to deny the spirit of the Lord. (11) And these very waters in those days will undergo a change, because when those angels are punished in those waters, those springs of water will be changed in regard to their heat, and when the angels come forth, those waters, which are springs, change, and they become cold. (12) And I heard Michael replying and saying: "This punishment [with] which the angels are punished is a witness to the kings and mighty who rule the earth. (13) For these waters of judgment are for the healing of the flesh of the kings[39] and for the desire of their flesh, but they do not see or believe that these waters will change and become a fire that burns forever."

(68:1) And afterwards my grandfather Enoch gave me the explanation of all the secrets in the book and the parables[40] that were given to him, and he joined them together for me in the discourse of the book of Parables.

While the basic pattern of Is. 24:17-23 has undergone development in terms of the legendary material used to elaborate the unit, it is still present even in 1 En. 64:1-68:1.

The intrusive appearance of the material in 1 En. 54:7-55:2 and 65:1-67:3, which has given rise to literary-critical attempts to establish the existence of sources behind the material in 1 Enoch, can now be explained on form-critical grounds as the elaboration of the flood motif in a midrashic pattern based on the passage from the Isaiah Apocalypse.

Parallels in Content between Is. 24:17-23 and the Midrashic Tradition in the Parables

Parallelism of the punishment of angels and kings.
Not only do these passages share a basic structure, they also have certain elements of content in common. The first of these elements is the parallelism of the punishment of the kings of the earth and the heavenly host.[41] While Is. 14:12-21 may use a Canaanite astral myth as a prototype for the fall of the king of Babylon, depending upon what one does with *Helel ben Shaḥar*,[42] in Is. 24:21 the host of the height and the kings of the earth are mentioned in *parallel*, and in verse 22 they are both to be shut up in a pit or dungeon. In 1 En. 54:1-6 the imprisonment of the kings and mighty is paralleled with that of the angels, and they are to be imprisoned in a valley or "the abyss of every punishment." This place should be compared to the pit (בור) in Is. 24:22, where the term is a synonym for Sheol.[43] In 1 En. 55:4 the "mighty kings" are forced to witness the judgment of the host of Asael, and, although this particular verse shows signs of the special concerns of the Parables in making the Elect one rather than the archangels responsible for the judgment (cf. 1 En. 54:6 and 61:8-9), the judgment of Asael and his associates is certainly a part of the tradition.

The parallelism of the punishment of angels and kings is also preserved in 1 En. 56:1-4. The "elect and loved ones" of the host of Asael who are punished there are more likely the kings and mighty than the giants of 1 En. 6-11. Charles[44] interprets *ḫeruyān wa-fequrāna zi'ahomu*, "their elect and loved ones," in light of 1 En. 6-16, where the giant offspring of the fallen angels and women are termed *fequrānihomu*, "their [the angels'] loved ones." The Greek version reads τῶν ἀγαπητῶν [αὐτῶν] in 1 En. 10:12 and τῶν υἱῶν ὑμῶν τῶν ἀγαπητῶν in

1 En. 14:6. While it is difficult to determine precisely the original language behind *fequrān*, a look at possible Hebrew and Aramaic equivalents is helpful. A comparison of citations of *fequr*[45] with Old Testament passages indicates that the word is generally the equivalent of דוד or ידיד. These words do not seem to be used to express the feelings of a parent toward a child. The word דוד has several quite specific meanings: (a) "son of a father's brother as customary husband," (b) "father's brother" (paternal uncle), (c) "cousin," (d) "love (lust)," and (e) the name of a god.[46] ידיד is found in the Old Testament six times: four times (Deut. 33:12; Ps. 60:7; 108:7; and 127:2) it refers to the beloved of Yahweh, once (Is. 5:1) it refers metaphorically to Yahweh himself, and once (Ps. 84:2) to the temple. On the few occasions when the feelings of a parent for a child are expressed *verbally*, a finite form of the verb אהב is used (cf. Gen. 22:2; 25:28; 37:3-4; and 44:20) rather than a passive participle. In Aramaic, חביב seems to correspond to דוד and occasionally to ידיד, while רחם corresponds to אהב.

Some changes in usage are found in the Hellenistic and Roman periods. In 1 En. 99:5, *fequrānihomu*, "their beloved," refers to children, and the examples in 1 En. 10:12 and 14:6 have already been noted. In the New Testament, the passages in which Jesus is termed ὁ υἱός μου ὁ ἀγαπητός, Mk. 1:11; 9:7; and 2 Pet. 1:17, are the result of exegetical traditions that combine Ps. 2:7, where the king is addressed as God's son, with the *LXX* of Is. 44:2, in which Israel is addressed as παῖς μου Ιακωβ καὶ ὁ ἠγαπημένος Ισραηλ, ὃν ἐξελεξάμην (cf. Is. 42:1).[47]

The last case suggests the correct province of the parallelism of "elect" and "loved ones" in 1 En. 56:3-4. It represents the language of God-man relationships rather than that of parent and child. The idea of "elect" or "chosen" obviously belongs to the expression of a divine-human relationship rather than that of a parent and child, and if *fequr* reflects an original ידיד or חביב, which seems to be the most probable alternative, the second member of the pair of epithets also should belong to the same realm of discourse. The relationship between the host of Asael and their elect and

beloved is being characterized as in some way comparable to
that between God and a man. The "elect and loved ones" of the
host of Asael are the "kings and mighty of the earth," and this
expression of their relationship is in itself an implicit
indication of the way in which the angels have led men astray:
through idolatry or the worship of the host of heaven (cf.
1 En. 46:7; 65:6-7; and 68:4). The interpretation of Is.
24:17-23 in the Targum points in the same direction when it
suggests in Is. 24:23 that it is those who worship the sun and
moon who will be ashamed at the revelation of the kingdom.[48]

The parallelism of the host of heaven and the kings
of the earth in Is. 24:21-23 and the close association of the
fallen angels and the kings and mighty in 1 En. 54:1-6; 63:1-
64:2; and 67:4-13 is further indication that the kings and
mighty should be identified as the elect and beloved of the
host of Asael in 1 En. 56:3-4. In chapter VI below it will be
argued that the parallelism between the punishment of the
angels and the kings is the primary reason for the use of this
traditional unit in the Parables and that it is introduced at
comparable points in the second and third parables when, in
each case, the eschatological punishment of the kings and
mighty is depicted. Since the punishment of the kings is the
major topic, it would be strange to find the punishment of
the giants, who are not mentioned elsewhere in the Parables,
of central importance in section "A_1" of 1 En. 54:1-56:4. It
should also be noted that the fetter motif, begun in 1 En.
53:3-5 and 54:2 in connection with the kings and the mighty,
is continued in 1 En. 56:1 in connection with the elect and
loved ones of the host of Asael. In contrast, the giants
in 1 En. 6-11 are punished and destroyed by being sent into
battle against each other. The reference to the kings in 1 En.
55:4 likewise suggests that in 56:1-4 the poet has returned to
the parallelism of the punishment of the kings and mighty and
the fallen angels. It should therefore be concluded that both
the "A" and the "A_1" sections of 1 En. 54:1-56:4 parallel the
punishment of kings and angelic beings.

The punishment of the angels and the kings and mighty
of the earth is also paralleled in 1 En. 64:1-68:1. 1 En.
64:1-2 appears to be transitional material intended to lead

from the punishment of the kings and mighty to that of the angels. Verse 1 refers to 1 En. 54:4-5 as well as to 63:10-11, where the kings are apparently sent to Sheol for punishment, and it seems to imply that the angels are already imprisoned and awaiting punishment, although 67:4 places that event in the future. The inconsistency in time is probably the result of an attempt to reconcile the time of the context, which is concerned with the *eschatological* judgment, with the antediluvian time of the midrashic tradition, in which the flood serves as a *prototype for the eschaton*. The use of the Is. 24:17-23 midrash introduces several eschatological problems into the Parables, and these will be examined in more detail later. However, it is important to note here that the connections in the Parables are associative rather than logical. The imprisonment of the kings in Sheol in 1 En. 63 leads to the related motif of the imprisonment of the angels in chapter 64. The traditional association of motifs leads the poet to parallel the punishment of the kings and angels in 1 En. 64:1 by assigning the same place of torment to both; the temporal problems are of secondary concern.

1 En. 67:4-13, the "A_1" section of the Is. 24:17-23 midrash in 1 En. 64:1-68:1, also deals with the punishment of the kings and mighty in parallel with that of the angels. In this case, a folktale that connects a thermal spring with the punishment of demons underground seems to have been utilized to develop the relationship between the punishment of the angels and that of the kings. In 1 En. 67:4-7, the punishment of the angels is related to the vulcanic activity--streams of fire (lava), the smell of sulphur (gases), and a disturbance of the waters (geysers)--that is associated with the thermal spring. This folktale could have been related to any of several sites of thermal springs along the Jordan rift, sites that were used as baths.[49] In 1 En. 67:8-13, the use of this spring as a bath by the kings and mighty is related ironically to their punishment on the day of judgment. While the precise details of the passage are no longer clear, it seems that, while the warm waters heal and comfort the body, they also dull the spirit through the incitation of lust. The dulled spirits make the kings and mighty insensitive to the

demands of the Lord of Spirits, thus insuring the punishment
of their flesh and spirits (cf. verse 9) when the waters change
to streams of fire at the eschaton. The idea is perhaps
comparable to Ex. 14:17-18, where Yahweh hardens the heart of
Pharaoh in order to get glory over him, and it also should be
compared to the concept of the ironic punishment in texts
like the Apocalypse of Peter, a parallel that suggests
Hellenistic concepts of the punishment of the damned.[50]
Another Hellenistic overtone might be the idea of psychic
torment which James M. Reese finds in Wsd. Sol. 17:2-21:

> In hellenistic times the treatment of these descents
> [into Hades] became the vehicle for the speculation of
> moralists and jurists, who were developing new theories
> about criminal punishment to conform to advances in psy-
> chology. The new theories were applied even to the escha-
> tological punishments of those condemned in Hades, and the
> crude examples of the early myths were reinterpretated as
> signifying *the psychological torture that vice produces
> upon an evil personality.* For example, the Danaïdes
> trying to fill their leaky vessels were interpreted as
> symbols of the frustrations experienced by men who give
> themselves over to a life of pleasure-seeking.[51]

In 1 En. 67:8-13, the vice which produces the psychological
torment is "the desire of their flesh," which, through the
baths, serves to transform the spirits of the kings: "And as
the burning of their flesh increases so their spirits will
undergo a change for ever and ever, because there is no one
before the Lord of Spirits who utters a vain word."[52] The
irony is doubly compounded, for not only are the kings punished
by the medium to which they resorted for healing but also the
instrument of their torment is associated with the punishment
of their cosmic counterparts, the angels, who, apparently,
have led them astray.

   The burning valley in which the angels are imprisoned
in 1 En. 67:4 is also a counterpart to the pit or cistern of
Is. 24:22, the place of imprisonment of the host of the height
and the kings of the earth. The association of the valley with
the metallic mountains ties the passage to 1 En. 52-54 and the
previous use of the Is. 24:17-23 midrash.[53] It is also
apparent from the description of the prison of the fallen
angels that the word *valley* is not to be taken in the usual
sense of that word as a depression on the surface of the earth.
1 En. 67:6 describes the place as "that valley of the angels

who led astray. . .burning *beneath* that region," and the
association with a thermal spring likewise suggests a sub-
terranean region. The place is described in 1 En. 54:5 as the
"abyss of every punishment" and in 56:3 as the "deep fissure
of the valley." The word valley in this context should be
taken as a metaphor for Sheol, cf. 1 En. 63:10; however, it
has already been noted that בור in Is. 24:22 has similar
implications.

The flood. The allusion to the flood in Is. 24:18c
results in the use of Genesis and related material to elaborate
the "B" section of the Is. 24:17-23 midrash. However, it is
interesting to note that 1 En. 65:1-67:3 turns to Is. 24:19-20
rather than to Genesis for material descriptive of the crisis
that faces Noah. In 1 En. 65:1, Noah sees "how the earth
tottered [*'aǧnanat*][54] so that its destruction was near." In
verse 3, he asks Enoch "what it is that is happening upon the
earth that the earth is thus *weary* [*sarḥat*] and *shaken* [*'anqal-
qalat*]." Verse 9 likewise refers to a disturbance upon the
earth. The verbs are quite close to Is. 24:19-20; however, a
similar tradition is found in 1 En. 83, where Enoch has a
vision in which he sees the heavens collapse upon the earth and
the earth sink into the abyss. This motif is independent of
the flood tradition; Enoch *averts* the impending disaster by
prayer. A similar motif is found in the *Viṣhṇu Purāṇa*, a
Hindu work to be examined in the next chapter in connection
with 1 En. 6-11, where the earth, in danger of sinking into
the abyss because of the combined weight of all the demons on
it, averts the disaster by praying to the gods for relief.
The motif may also be related to the earthquake, which Hartman
treats as a distinct eschatological motif.[55] The narrative
in 1 En. 65-66 is dependent upon 1 En. 83 or a similar tradition: both Enoch and Noah go to their grandfathers for
information about the impending disaster, and 1 En. 83:8-10
probably explains the forbearance motif in chapter 66, a motif
that otherwise does not fit well into the flood tradition.
Since the "collapse of the earth" is independent of the flood
tradition, its use as a sign of the impending flood in 1 En.
65-66 is probably to be explained by Is. 24:18c-20, where the

flood and the collapse of the earth are associated. In
addition, the language of 1 En. 65:1 and 3 is closer to Is.
24:19-20 than it is to 1 En. 83.

Eschatology. The use of the flood tradition in Genesis
is also important in order to understand the unique eschatology
represented in the traditional unit. The reference to the
deluge in Is. 24:18c is a metaphor, an invocation of the flood
tradition intended to suggest the cosmic dimensions of the
catastrophe that is to overtake the inhabitants of the earth.
The details of the following two verses, Is. 24:19-20, are
more appropriate to an earthquake than a deluge, and, as
has been noted, they seem to represent a tradition distinct
from the flood. In Is. 24:21-22, the kings and the host of
the height will be called to account "on that day" (ביום ההוא),
which seems to coincide with the cosmic catastrophe of verses
18c-20. They will then be imprisoned, *"and after many days"*
(ומרב ימים) they will be called to account. This latter day
of judgment appears to coincide with the reign of Yahweh in
Jerusalem of verse 23. Israel is now to be governed by Yahweh
rather than by the rulers of the nations. The sun and moon
will be ashamed at that time either because they are in some
way associated with the host of the height or because their
glory will be exceeded by that of Yahweh (cf. Job 25:5 and
31:26-28).

What was, in the Isaiah Apocalypse, basically metaphor
intended to deal with the problem of life under foreign rule
rather than the direct rule of Yahweh has become in the later
tradition behind 1 Enoch a more concrete eschatological scheme.
The cosmic catastrophe, which was *interpreted* in the Isaiah
Apocalypse through a reference to the flood, is now *identified*
with it, and the period represented by "after many days" has
become the period between the deluge and the eschaton. In
1 En. 54:5, the host of Asael are to be bound and cast into
"the abyss of every punishment" and their jaws are to be
covered with jagged rocks. In 1 En. 54:6 they are to be seized
and cast into a blazing furnace "on that great day," apparently
the day of the last judgment (cf. Is. 24:22, ומרב ימים), which
may be echoed by "on that great day"). The imprisonment in
"the abyss of every punishment" and the punishment in a furnace

"on that great day" correspond to the imprisonment in the pit and the judgment "after many days" in Is. 24:22.

The version of the tradition in 1 En. 54:1-56:4 does not make the relation between the flood and this eschatological scheme completely clear. The temporal reference in 1 En. 54:7, the verse that introduces the flood section, is imprecise: "And in those days the punishment of the Lord of Spirits will come forth. . . ." Are "those days" the eschaton of the previous verse or the earlier imprisonment of the angels in verse 5? Unless "that great day" of 1 En. 54:6 is something other than the eschatological judgment day, the reference in 54:7 must be to the imprisonment of the angels in verse 5.

From the other two examples of the tradition in 1 En. 6-11 and 64:1-68:1, however, it is clear that the scheme identified the deluge with the time of the imprisonment of the angels and the eschaton with the time of their punishment (cf. also 1 En. 86:1-89:9 and 90:20-27, where the Apocalypse of the Animals spells out the scheme in detail). In chapter 10, Uriel is sent to warn the "son of Lamech" of the coming flood. Then in verses 4-6 Raphael is given the following commission:

> Bind Asael by [his] feet and hands and cast him into the darkness, and lay open the wilderness that is in Dadouel and cast him there. And place him under jagged and sharp stones and cover him over with the darkness, and let him dwell there until the [new] age [εἰς τοὺς αἰῶνας]. And cover up his face and let him not see the light. And on the great day of judgment he will be led away to the conflagration.

In verses 11-13 Michael is given a similar commission for Shemiḥazah, and the time of imprisonment is given there as seventy generations. The fallen angels are to be imprisoned at the time of the flood and consigned to the flames on the great judgment day.

The similarity in the details of the imprisonment and judgment in 1 En. 10:4-6 and 54:5-6 indicates that the same tradition and time structure lie behind both, although the lists of archangels are slightly different. However, while details of the content of the tradition based on Is. 24:17-23, including the eschatology, are found in 1 En. 6-11, the structure of that tradition, based on the concave pattern of the passage of scripture, has been lost. The kings of the earth have been replaced by the giants, and a narrative has been developed using Gen. 6:1-4 as a starting point. Although the version of the tradition in the Parables is in a literary context from a later time, it must depend upon the traditional interpretation of Is. 24:17-23 rather than on 1 En. 6-11.

1 En. 64:1-68:1 also clearly identifies the time of imprisonment of the angels with the flood (cf. 1 En. 65:11 and 67:4-7), although in this version the angels are currently being punished. In this passage, the imprisonment of the kings is separate from that of the angels, since they represent the current enemies of the group in which the Parables was produced, and only their punishment in the thermal spring is associated with that of the angels.

The literal identification of Is. 24:18c-20 with the flood tradition from Genesis has created a problem when this material is used in the Parables. The work is concerned with *contemporary* opponents; therefore, the parallelism of the *imprisonment* of the host of heaven and the kings of the earth in Is. 24:17-23 does not precisely suit its purpose if the time of that imprisonment is identified with Noah's flood. As long as Is. 24:17-23, or a midrashic tradition based on it, uses the flood tradition as an allusion designed to describe the cosmic dimensions of the *coming* overthrow of the kings of the earth and their subsequent imprisonment with their angelic associates, no temporal problem exists. But when the allusion develops into an eschatological scheme that uses the flood story as a prototype for the eschaton, ambiguities result if the kings of the earth are then identified as contemporary kings. 1 En. 6-11 resolves these ambiguities through the use of Gen. 6:1-4, so that the giants, the offspring of the Sons of God and the daughters of men, take over the role of the kings of the earth. However, in 1 En. 54:1-56:4 the ambiguity is not resolved. There, the time of the imprisonment of the kings and mighty of the earth, who are the contemporaries of the group in which the Parables were produced, is identified with the imprisonment of the angels and the flood. The ambiguity is resolved in 1 En. 64:1-68:1 through use of the folktale concerning the thermal spring to retain the force of the parallelism between the punishment of the kings and the angels without the resulting temporal problems that the literal use of the Is. 24:17-23 midrash imposes on the Parables. 1 En. 64:1-68:1 therefore represents a significant advance over 54:1-56:4 in the use of the traditional unit in the Parables. It seems likely that the folktale was not part of the traditional unit based on Is. 24:17-23 but was introduced into the unit in the composition of the Parables to solve a specific problem.

Utilization of Other Passages of Scripture in the Is. 24:17-23 Midrash

In the discussion of midrash above, it was concluded that midrashic use of passages of scripture provided an important means for the articulation of thought in Judaism of the Hellenistic period. Important religious, social, and political ideas seem to be attached to certain passages of scripture, which serve as their carriers, and, as a result, to determine the structure of thought in Judaism of the period one must observe its exegetical basis.

The Is. 24:17-23 midrash does not represent the type of midrashic method used in the Qumran pesharim, where a number of different passages may be quoted to interpret one central passage. The most important passage of scripture used is the flood tradition from Genesis, and its function in the eschatology of the traditional unit has already been examined. It should be noted that the use of the flood tradition carries with it a certain amount of pseudo-scientific material from the period. The most notable evidence of this material is in the information in 1 En. 54:8 that the upper waters are male and the lower female, a tradition that has its origin in Babylonian notions reflected in the *Enuma elish* but continues to be associated with the flood in Talmudic traditions and particularly in Kabbalism.[56] The conjunction of the waters, male and female, in the destruction of the inhabitants of the earth thus carries with it creation symbolism. The flood is seen not merely as a means of punishment of mankind but as a re-creation of the cosmos.[57]

Another item of current pseudo-scientific material is the change from "windows" (ארבת) in Gen. 7:11 (cf. Is. 24:18) to "storehouses" (*mazāgebt*, probably אצרות in Hebrew, cf. Job 38:22; Ps. 135:7; Jer. 10:13; 51:16; and Sir. 43:14). This word has become a technical term in the astronomical material utilized in the Parables (cf. 1 En. 41:4-5; 60:12,19-21; 69:23). The presence of this material indicates that the Is. 24:17-23 midrash does not simply draw upon Gen. 6-9 for the interpretation of the passage from the Isaiah Apocalypse but rather upon the tradition of interpretation of Genesis. It also ties the midrash to an important strand of material in the Parables, the astronomical passages whose function is to demonstrate that beyond the chaos of history there is a divine order in the universe and that God must and will act to restore that order where it has been disrupted by the forces of evil, the kings and their angelic associates.[58]

The other element of the Is. 24:17-23 midrash that might be traced to scriptural exegesis is the depiction of the imprisonment and punishment of the angels and kings. Actually, it is difficult to determine whether these details are due to the use of scripture, allusion to non-Jewish material, or reflection of burial customs and common notions of the state of the dead in Sheol, and these may not be mutually exclusive options. Scriptural sources for this material will be considered here and non-Jewish parallels in the next section.

The Is. 24:17-23 midrash elaborates the imprisonment and punishment of the kings and the host of Asael by reference to the fetters with which they are bound and the instruments of punishment. There are several passages in the Old Testament that speak of fetters or prisoners, passages that may be of importance for the development of this tradition. Ps. 107 represents what might be called a Yahwistic aretalogy in which Yahweh is praised for his goodness toward various wicked men who, when they repented, were shown mercy. Verses 10-11 describe one such group of men:

> [There are] those dwelling in darkness and gloom,
>   prisoners [אסירי, cf. Is. 24:22] of affliction
>   and iron [fetters];
> for they rebelled against the words of God,
>   and scorned the plan of the Most High.

In 1 En. 54:1-5, the kings and the host of Asael are to be bound with "iron chains that were beyond weighing," and the kings and mighty of the earth in the Parables are those who have denied the name of the Lord of Spirits and failed to acknowledge him as the true source of their power (1 En. 46:5 and 7). While, in 1 En. 67:6-7, the valley of imprisonment has become a burning valley, in the earlier parallel, in 1 En. 10:4-5, it is a place of darkness consistent with older traditions concerning Sheol. Job 36:7-12 speaks of kings who are bound in fetters on account of their arrogance, although there the reference seems to be to actual adversities without the symbolic overtones of Sheol. Lam. 3:6-9 provides another parallel:

> He [Yahweh] has caused me to dwell in dark places,
>   like the ancient dead;
> he has built a wall about me, and I cannot go out;
>   he has made my bronze [fetters] heavy.
> Although I cry out and call for help,
>   he turns aside my prayer;
> he has walled up my way with stone blocks,
>   and my paths he has twisted.

1 En. 54:2 is interested in the weight of the chains. Ps. 2:3, in which the kings of the earth threaten to burst the fetters of Yahweh and his messiah, and Ps. 149:8-9, where Yahweh binds the kings and nobles of the nations with fetters and executes judgment upon them, should also be noted. Behind these passages there seems to be a common tradition, associated with a genre, which Eissfeldt terms a "sentence of judgment,"[59] that deals with the imprisonment of kings on account of their arrogance, violence, or rebellion against Yahweh,[60] and it is quite possible that this tradition has had, in one way or another, an impact on the Is. 24:17-23 midrash.

Another detail of interest is the placing of stones on Asael in 1 En. 10:5 and on the host of Asael in 54:5. While Lam. 3:9 might seem to be related, it specifies hewn stone, while those in 1 Enoch are clearly rough, jagged ones. A better parallel is found in a burial custom reflected in Lam. 3:53:[61]

> They have silenced my life in the pit,
>   and have cast stones upon me.

The burial of Absalom in 2 Sam. 18:17 describes the actual custom: "And they took Absalom and tossed him in a thicket, into a large pit, and they piled up a very large heap of stones upon him." This apparently ignominious end is then contrasted in 2 Sam. 18:18 to the memorial that Absalom had planned for himself. Similar burials are given to Achan, who broke the institution of חרם (Jos. 7:26), and to the king of Ai (Jos. 8:29), who was hanged after resisting the Israelites. The purpose of the custom seems to be to provide for the proper separation of the living and the dead: the ghost of the corpse placed under the stones would not return to revenge his execution. In 1 En. 10:5 and 54:5, the angels are being treated in their imprisonment in Sheol like executed criminals in the grave. The piling of stones on Asael in 1 En. 10:5 and the placing of stones on the jaws of the host of Asael in 54:5 are intended to insure that their spirits remain in the "abyss of every punishment." Both variants of the custom are attested in European folklore as means of laying a ghost.[62]

While the treatment of Asael in 1 En. 10:4-5 is similar to that of Absalom in 2 Sam. 18:17--both are cast into a pit in the wilderness and covered with stones--it is also possible that either the fetters or the rocks reflect continued traditions or customs rather than scriptural exegesis. Judaism of the Hellenistic period is in a transitional stage in which the written versions of the old traditions are becoming, or in many cases have become, the normative expressions of the tradition. Given the role of scripture in Jewish culture of the period, it is better to assume that language that reflects scripture in most cases represents some level of scriptural exegesis. On the other hand, the customs of a culture, like burial practices, would probably be more resistant to change than oral tradition and thus more likely to serve as a source independent of the exegesis of scripture for the details of a narrative. On the other hand, the proper burial of a criminal could well have been a topic of halakic exegesis. Even where practices or traditions have continuity with the past, Jews of the Hellenistic period would probably have had an awareness of relationships to the texts of scripture.

Mythological Patterns in the Is. 24:17-23 Midrash

While the midrashic traditions may form the most important means of the articulation of thought in Judaism of the Hellenistic and Roman periods, it would be rash to conclude that the structure of thought is solely midrashic. It has become clear that patterns of thought based on mythic traditions common to the ancient world were present in Israelite thought from the beginning and continued to penetrate Jewish thought in the Hellenistic period, even in Palestine.[63] Apocalyptic literature is full of such material, and it is difficult at times to determine whether a specific tradition that seems to be related to material known from elsewhere in the ancient world has been a part of Israelite and Jewish traditions for some time or whether it has recently penetrated the Jewish world. Ultimately, questions about the essence and continuity of a religious tradition are raised by the examination of apparently foreign material in a native tradition.[64]

Like midrashic traditions, mythic structures of various origins are used as means of the articulation of thought in Judaism of the Hellenistic period. A case in point is the use of apocalyptic patterns that have no specific basis in scripture but that, upon examination, are found at various times and places in the ancient world.[65] These structures are at times integrated into Jewish tradition through identification with the interpretation of specific passages of scripture[66] so that it can become difficult at times to determine if a motif has been borrowed from the Hellenistic world or is based on the exegesis of the Old Testament. However, it is clear that in the definition of a traditional unit, which ultimately represents a pattern of thought, one must pay attention to the presence of mythological structures as well as to patterns of scriptural exegesis.

Were this dissertation primarily concerned with the tradition history of the myth of the fallen angels, it would be necessary to examine the mythological patterns in the Is. 24:17-23 midrash in some detail in order to determine their relationship to non-Jewish mythological traditions. However, since the primary concern is with tradition and redaction in the Parables, the emphasis will be upon establishing the

existence of mythic patterns of thought as a means toward the
isolation of distinct patterns or units of thought rather than
upon tracing the origin of each motif. Comparison with other
traditions from the Ancient Near East or the Hellenistic world
is therefore not intended to establish a direct historical
relationship in each case but is rather a part of a phenomenological attempt to establish the structure of the symbolism in
the traditional units involved.

Several different myths from the ancient world seem to
be in some way reflected in the Is. 24:17-23 midrash. They
include (a) "war in heaven," (b) Prometheus, (c) anti-royal
traditions, and (d) the late Babylonian cosmogony and eschatology known from Berossus.

War in heaven. While this myth is known in several
different cultures,[67] the closest version to the material in
1 Enoch is the Battle of the Titans from Greek mythology.[68]
While the material in 1 Enoch is actually closer to the Prometheus myth in the way in which it treats the theme of rebellion against divine authority,[69] the imprisonment of the Titans
in Tartarus is comparable to that of the host of Asael in
Sheol. Parallels between 1 En. 10 and 54:1-56:4 and Hesiod's
account of the fall of the Titans are interesting:

> And amongst the foremost Cottus and Briareos and Gyes
> [the allies of the Olympians] insatiate for war raised
> fierce fighting: three hundred rocks, one upon another,
> they launched from their strong hands and overshadowed
> the Titans with their missiles, and hurled them beneath
> the wide-pathed earth, and bound them in bitter chains
> when they had conquered them by their strength for all
> their great spirit, as far beneath the earth as heaven is
> above earth; for so far is it from earth to Tartarus.[70]

While the parallels between the Is. 24:17-23 midrash and the
Battle of the Titans are obvious, there is one important
difference: the kings and the angels are not defeated in a
battle with the archangels but rather are seized by them and
cast into a valley where they are bound with chains and
weighted down with rocks. If there is a relationship between
Hesiod and the earliest levels of the tradition behind 1 Enoch,
it may well be found in the common roots of both Greek and
Israelite traditions in the culture of the Ancient Near East.
It seems likely, however, that a Greek account of the Battle
of the Titans has influenced another version of the myth of

the fallen angels in 1 Enoch, a version that is otherwise
heavily dependent on 1 En. 6-11. In the Apocalypse of the
Animals, 1 En. 85-90, one of the archangels *stones the fallen
angels from heaven* before they are seized, bound, and cast
into the abyss (see 1 En. 88:3).

Gaster, in commenting on Is. 24:21-23, also relates
the imprisoned host of heaven to the vanquished gods of the
Enuma elish, gods that are known elsewhere in Akkadian literature as "'the bound (or, chained) gods.'"[71] They too are
imprisoned, although, after a time, Marduk shows them mercy.
Gaster observes that Is. 24:22c can be translated in two ways:
"'And they shall be deprived of a large number of their days,'"
or "'And after many days they shall be visited.'"[72] He takes
the visitation in a positive sense and suggests that it may be
a parallel to the Babylonian myth, where Marduk in the end
shows mercy to the vanquished gods. He points to 1 En. 21:3-6,
where seven stars are to be imprisoned for ten thousand years
for transgression of the divine laws concerning the proper
time for their appearance.

It should be noted that פקד, "miss," when understood
as "visit," can have either a positive or negative sense and
that in Is. 24:22c it may also be translated "call to account."
Thus, Gaster's argument, that the phrase may reflect the
Babylonian myth, is difficult to maintain on the basis of Is.
24:22c alone.[73] The tradition of interpretation of the passage
in Judaism and early Christianity is ambivalent.[74] The account
of the imprisonment of the seven stars is found in both 1 En.
18:12-19:2 and 21:1-10, where, in both cases, it is paralleled
with a version of the tradition concerning the fallen angels
based on 1 En. 6-11. The places of imprisonment of the stars
and the angels are paralleled, but it is interesting to note
that, while the stars' imprisonment is limited to ten thousand
years, the angels are to be imprisoned forever. 1 En.
10:12-13; 12:5-6; and 16:4 likewise imply that the final
imprisonment and punishment of the angels will be forever.
However, the account of the harrowing of hell in 1 Pet. 3:19-
20, which seems to be based on 1 En. 6-11,[75] implies that the
"spirits" there imprisoned in the days of Noah have an
opportunity for forgiveness.

The imprisonment of the stars in 1 En. 18:12-16 and 21:1-6 seems to be related to Is. 24:21-23 in some way, although it is difficult to determine if it is a parallel tradition or if it represents a different tradition of interpretation than the Is. 24:17-23 midrash. In the case of the stars, the visitation of Is. 24:22c could have been taken in a positive sense, while in the Is. 24:17-23 midrash it has been taken in a negative one. In any case, the parallel treatment of the angels and the stars shows that the two traditions were perceived as related but at the same time distinct, providing additional evidence that traditions dealing with fallen angels in Jewish apocalyptic have a complex basis in tradition.

It appears that the Is. 24:17-23 midrash is a Jewish version of a common motif from the ancient world dealing with the judgment and imprisonment of rebellious gods, although it is impossible to specify the precise way in which this version is related to the others. The motif must be seen as distinct from the version of the myth of the fallen angels based on Gen. 6:1-4. The Is. 24:17-23 midrash is concerned with a cosmic power struggle (cf. 1 En. 68:4) rather than the corruption of creation through the intermixing of levels of existence.

Prometheus. The Prometheus myth is closer in structure to the Is. 24:17-23 midrash than the Battle of the Titans.[76] The god is a Titan and the creator and benefactor of man. He steals fire for man and teaches him all the human arts and sciences. He should thus be classified as a culture hero. For his concern on behalf of man, and for his action in tricking Zeus into accepting bones hidden in fat as the appropriate sacrifice, Prometheus is chained to a mountainside to have his liver continually eaten by an eagle. The myth is well-known, and it has a number of variants in the classical sources.[77]

The mythological pattern behind the Is. 24:17-23 midrash seems to be, to a great extent, an *inversion* of the Promethean myth. In leading mankind astray, the angels have introduced sorcery and idolatry (1 En. 65:6-8,11). For this reason they are imprisoned in Sheol. The difference is that, as far as man is concerned, Prometheus is a hero, while the

host of Asael are considered evil. Various explanations for
the differences are possible. If the myth did represent a
borrowing from the Greek myth, the inversion would be necessary
to fit it into Jewish theology, since, while Greek mythology
could tolerate conflict between two divine beings, Jewish
thought could not.

The inversion is more likely to be explained in terms
of the dynamics of the development of Judaism or by the conflict of Jewish and Hellenistic culture. With the increasing
transcendence of God, certain divine functionaries, whose
actions may have once been seen as beneficial, are now seen as
responsible for whatever is perceived as evil in the universe
in order to absolve God of the responsibility for evil (cf.
1 En. 10:8). Job 15:15 and 25:5 (cf. 31:24-28), which suggest
that even the holy ones or the moon and stars are not pure in
the sight of God, are, perhaps, earlier stages in this process.
Since the host of heaven or of Asael should probably be perceived as the forces behind the cosmos, the negative valuation
of their activity reflects a sense of alienation from the
cosmos that is paralleled by a sense of alienation from history
or a feeling of a lack of control over the national destiny
implicit in the polemic against the kings and mighty. The
treatment of the cosmic forces as powers independent of God,
to some degree, represents a step toward Gnosticism; however,
it should be noted that this step is not consistently carried
through, since, throughout the Enochic material, one is
constantly given visions of a higher cosmic order beyond the
apparent chaos of the present.

The inversion of the culture-hero motif is one element
that the Is. 24:17-23 midrash and the angel-list tradition
have in common, and it will be necessary to return to it in
the next chapter. At that point, attention will be given to
the role of cultural conflict in the inversion of the motif.
The teaching of the human arts and sciences, including those
of warfare, astrology, and magic, is more clearly detailed
in connection with the angel-list tradition, and, since these
are the elements of the traditions that most clearly reflect
cultural conflict, that discussion is best postponed,

Anti-royal traditions. Is. 24:17-23 and the midrashic tradition based on that passage bring together a polemic against heavenly beings with one against the kings of the earth. The latter is related to a number of passages (Is. 14; Ezek. 28; and Ps. 82,[78] for example) that deal with the king who, in some way, exceeds his authority in relation to God and is cast down from his glory into the depths of Sheol. This motif is related to the fetter motif examined above, and in chapter VI below the use of anti-royal exegetical traditions in the thematic structure of the Parables will be examined in detail. It should be noted, however, that there are parallels in the Hellenistic philosophy of kingship, which is itself undoubtedly based on oriental kingship ideology.[79] The king is recognized as belonging to the divine realm, and parallels are drawn between God (Zeus) as the ruler of the cosmos, the sun as the ruler of the heavens, and the king as the ruler of mankind. The latter two reflect the glory of the former. At the same time, limitations are placed on the status of the king in the cosmos. He is only a reflection of divinity--the God manifest to man--and, while he is not subject to law, he must be self-ruled. Ordinary mortals are incapable of living in the reflection of divine glory and "are blinded, and prostrated with vertigo if they try to usurp royal prerogatives."[80] Lucian gives the following dialogue between Menippus and the natural philosopher Empedocles, who is the former's guide on a satirical cosmic trip:

> ". . .the eagle so far surpasses all the other creatures in strength of sight that he alone can look square at the sun, and the mark of the genuine royal eagle is that he can face its rays without winking an eye." "So they say," I replied, "and I am sorry now that when I came up here I did not take out my own eyes and put in those of the eagle. As things are, I have come in a half-finished condition and with an equipment which is not fully royal; in fact, I am like the bastard, disowned eaglets they tell about. . . ."[81]

The eaglet that is unable to gaze directly at the sun is cast out of the nest, according to the tradition. The myth is obviously royal in character--a coin from Armenia has been found that pictures two eagles gazing at the sun embossed on a crown worn by a king[82]--and it has an implicit polemic against kings who are not cut from royal material. The parallel between it and the Jewish anti-royal traditions is not precise, but it is obvious that they both move in the same world of thought. The Jewish anti-royal tradition is perhaps sharpened by nationalism and an even greater conception of the transcendence of God so that it would apply to any king who attempted to make himself equal to God and not merely to those unworthy of the reflection of divine glory. While neither Is. 24:17-23 nor the midrashic tradition based on it are specific about the crimes of the kings of the earth, the fall from glory implicit in their imprisonment suggests that they have forgotten their true place in the cosmos.

Babylonian cosmogony and eschatology. The distinctive eschatological scheme of the Is. 24:17-23 midrash may be related to traditions of Babylonian origin preserved in fragments of a work on the history of Babylon attributed to Berossus, a Babylonian priest of the third century B.C. Herman Ludin Jansen[83] argues that the cyclic worldview contained in these fragments, in which epochs are alternatively ended by destruction of the cosmos through flood or through fire, is responsible for the eschatology of what this dissertation has termed the Is. 24:17-23 midrash, in which the flood serves as a prototype for the eschaton and in which the eschaton involves the punishment of the angels and kings through fire. While such traditions could have had some minor role in the formation of the Is. 24:17-23 midrash by suggesting the relationship of the flood and the eschaton, the punishment of the angels and kings by fire is an idea distinct from the world conflagration and is probably related to Hellenistic ideas of the torment of the damned in Hades.

Summary. This survey suggests that the Is. 24:17-23 midrash draws upon motifs from several different mythological patterns known from the ancient world, combining them in its own way to meet its own needs. The passage of scripture upon which the midrash is based plays the formative role making it difficult to determine how direct the connection is between these motifs and various versions of the myths known from the ancient world. The midrash combines three mythological structures that are best seen as distinct but closely related in thematic value: (a) the Prometheus myth in which the

culture-hero motif has been inverted, (b) the imprisonment of
the Titans, and (c) anti-royal traditions. These three motifs
are related in that each deals with the fall and punishment of
of a god or king who has in some way rebelled against ultimate
authority. The similarity of the symbolic value is important.
C. Kerényi[84] observes that to the Greeks the Titans symbolized
boundless pride (ὕβρις) and violence or insolence (ἀτασθαλία).
The kings of the earth have a similar symbolic value in Jewish
tradition, as Is. 14:13-14; Ezek. 28:2,5,6,9; Ps. 2:2-3;
2 Macc. 9:4,7-8; and 1 En. 46:7 and 63:7 make clear. The
central theme of the Is. 24:17-23 midrash is the fall of the
mighty. It deals with angelic beings who take upon themselves
the role of God (cf. 1 En. 68:4) in revealing false forms of
worship to men, along with sorcery, and with kings who, if the
context of the Parables is any indication, have lost track of
their true status in the cosmos. The parallel imprisonment
and punishment of the host of heaven and the kings of the
earth is therefore a key element of the midrash. The
parallelism is related to a perception of the nature of evil as
both political and cosmic: a perception that is entirely
consistent with an apocalyptic worldview.

The Sitz im Leben *of the Is. 24:17-23 Midrash*

The *Sitz im Leben* of midrash is generally said to be
in the schoolhouse and the discussions of the Rabbis or in the
preaching of the Synagogue service.[85] The sectarian[86] groups
also provide an appropriate *Sitz im Leben* for midrash, and,
in chapter VII, Philo's description of the public assemblies
of the Essenes and the Therapeutae will be examined as a clue
to the context of the material in the Parables. The political
implications of the Is. 24:17-23 midrash point to a sect outside the theocratic establishment of the period; however, this
observation does little more than exclude the Sadducees. The
Is. 24:17-23 midrash should be seen as an excerpt from the
traditional interpretation of scripture of some Palestinian
religious group within Judaism, and its *Sitz im Leben* in that
community would be in the "public" exposition of scripture.

CHAPTER IV

THE LISTS OF FALLEN ANGELS

The two lists of fallen angels in 1 En. 69:2-12 also represent a distinct genre, the list or catalog, and form the basis of a traditional unit that carries with it a distinct relationship to the interpretation of scripture and a characteristic mythological structure.

The two lists or catalogs in 1 En. 69:2-12 have parallels in 1 En. 6:7 and 8:1-3. The first list in the Parables, 1 En. 69:2-3, is the same list, with some variations, as the one in 1 En. 6:7. The lists in 1 En. 69:4-12 and 8:1-3 are parallel in function--they both list angels along with an indication of what each angel taught mankind in leading them astray--but the names in each list are different. In 1 En. 8:2 men are led astray into godlessness and fornication, while in 1 En. 69:4-6 Jeqon and Asbeel lead the sons of God astray with the daughters of men, causing them to defile themselves with them, and Gadreel leads Eve astray. In general, 1 En. 8:1-3 is basically concerned with astrology and related arts while 1 En. 69:4-12 tends toward blacker uses of the magic arts (cf. 69:12).

It is not much use to spend time speculating about the original forms of the names of the angels until the Enoch manuscripts from Qumran Cave 4 are published.[1] In their present state, the two versions of the same list in 1 En. 6:7 and 69:2-3 are more or less in the same order with greater agreement toward the beginning than toward the end.[2] 1 En. 8:1-3 and 69:4-12, which have different names but the same function, present greater difficulties. The names in the latter are unique in Jewish angelology;[3] the names in the former are more or less identical with those in 1 En. 6:7 and may well represent an assimilation to the more familiar names in that verse. If this is the case, the unique names in 1 En. 69:4-12 should be seen as the original form of the tradition--or at least an indication of the use of a traditional catalog rather than a literary source--and the names in 8:1-3 as the result of redactional assimilation to the first list.

The traditional unit under consideration here seems to involve a *pair* of lists, one, 1 En. 6:7 and 69:2-3, a list of twenty leaders of the fallen angels and the other, 1 En. 8:1-3 and 69:4-12, a list of angels and what they taught mankind. The pair of lists stands side by side in the Parables but has been worked into a coherent narrative in 1 En. 6-11.

The list of angels should be treated as a genre in Judaism of the Hellenistic and Roman periods. These lists appear often enough that they should be familiar to anyone conversant with apocalyptic Judaism; however, they are so familiar that they have received little attention. The most frequent type encountered are lists of archangels;[4] however, other types, with or without specific names, are known.[5] These lists can function in a number of ways. They can be used to structure a heavenly vision, as in 1 En. 40. They can structure a narrative involving the action of angels, as in 1 En. 10, where the four archangels are given individual tasks to rid the earth of the fallen angels and the giants. The names of the archangels can even be listed on the implements of war in the War Scroll from Qumran, apparently to symbolize the presence of the angelic army in the eschatological battle.[6] In general, they can be said to perform an *ornamental* function that is consistent with the use of lists in popular literature in other cultures.[7] The implications of the use of the lists of fallen angels for the type of literature represented by the Parables of Enoch as a whole will be examined in chapter VII below.

The Sitz im Leben *of Angel Lists*

Josephus, in describing the Essenes, gives some information regarding the things that a candidate for admission must swear to carefully preserve and transmit:

> He swears, moreover, to transmit their rules exactly as he himself received them; to abstain from robbery; and in like manner carefully to preserve the books of the sect and the names of the angels [καὶ συντηρήσειν ὁμοίως τά τε τῆς αἱρέσεως αὐτῶν βιβλία καὶ τὰ τῶν ἀγγέλων ὀνόματα].[8]

The injunction, to preserve (συντηρήσειν) the books and the names is ambiguous. Does it mean to keep them intact or to keep them secret? In any case, the Qumran evidence shows that the sectarian rules and the library of the community were of great importance. To mention the names of the angels in the same context indicates that they were also of great importance. There is obviously a *Sitz im Leben* in sectarian Judaism for the preservation and transmission of angels lists.

It is difficult to determine from Josephus whether the names of the angels were a matter of written or oral tradition. The association with the books of the sect suggests that they were written lists; however, if that were the case, they would have been part of the books of the sect, and there would have been little need to mention them separately. In addition, no angel lists as such seem to have been found in the Qumran library. They are always part of a larger work of literature like the War Scroll or the angelic liturgy, and even there, with the exception of the names of the archangels, the sectarians never become very specific about the actual names. The angelic liturgy lists the princes by number, and, in the War Scroll, the phrases that seem to be expanded versions of angel names[9] may be intended to hide the actual names. It seems likely, therefore, that the names of the angels were a matter of oral teaching but that they could be used in various ways, including, with certain limitations, the production or ornamentation of narratives or other literary forms.

The angel lists in 1 Enoch go back to the third century B.C. and thus antedate the origin of the Essenes and the Qumran sect. Therefore, it is necessary to look beyond the Essenes of the second century and later to determine the original *Sitz im Leben*. The list in 1 En. 6:7 and 69:2-3 is composed of angels who were set over the natural phenomena, their names being etymologically related to their function.[10] In the list in 1 En. 8:1-3, each teaches the branch of knowledge appropriate to his name. The angel list should be related to an older genre known from the Egyptian wisdom tradition: an onomasticon, or name list, that tries to organize unexplained natural phenomena by listing them in some order. Von Rad argues that such a list lies behind God's questions in Job 38-41, and he comments that Enoch often hints that he has been given the explanations to phenomena that Job is unable to explain.[11]

In 1 En. 33:4, Enoch is given a writing that seems to belong to this tradition: "He [Uriel] showed everything to me and wrote it down for me, and he also wrote their names for me along with their laws and their companies." Actually, the mention of writing probably refers to the astronomical book in 1 En. 72-82, which is separated from 1 En. 33-36 only by the intrusive Parables of Enoch and to which chapters 33-36 seem to be an introduction. The journeys to the four quarters in chapters 33-36 seem to be intended to explain how Enoch received the knowledge recorded in chapters 72-82. In addition, 1 En. 81:5-6 seems to represent the end of the heavenly journey begun in chapter 21. The *seven* archangels in 81:5 are also a peculiar characteristic of 1 En. 20-36. In Judaism of the period the archangels are almost always four in number. One exception is 1 En. 85-90, which is based on chapters 1-36, and which preserves the variant traditions concerning the number of archangels in the latter section by organizing them into two groups, one of four archangels and one of three, in 1 En. 87:2. Elsewhere in 1 Enoch, chapters 12-13 seem to represent a narrative designed to explain how the sage obtained a previously existing writing, chapters 14-16 (cf. 1 En. 14:1 with 72:1), and the vision in 1 En. 83 seems to be intended to explain the existence of the prayer in chapter 84 (see 1 En. 83:10, where Enoch writes the prayer down for later generations). Both the similarity in content and the similarity in compositional technique suggest that the writing in 1 En. 33:4 is 1 En. 72-82. That work indicates a beginning interest in relating the cosmic order to angelic beings, since in 1 En. 82:10-20 it assigns names that have the form of angel names to the sidereal phenomena.

The original *Sitz im Leben* of the angel lists should be seen in the lore of scribal circles for whom Enoch, the heavenly scribe, would have been a hero.[12] They are the heirs of the wisdom tradition. Within that tradition, the onomasticon of natural phenomena has developed into angel lore that explains the natural phenomena by reference to the angels that control them. The companies of the angels explain the orderly nature of sideral reality.

Like the angel lists, the onomasticon of natural phenomena served an ornamental function in literature. It could be used in liturgy and prayer as well as in the discussions of sages to elaborate various motifs (see Ps. 104, 135, 136, and 148, Job 38-41, Sir. 43, Song of 3 Y. 35-60, and 1QH 1:8-15). Where the onomasticon gave rise to hymns of thanksgiving like Ps. 148, the angel list is reflected in the angelic liturgy and the angelology of Revelation.

*Exegesis of Scripture
and the Angel Lists*

The two versions of the angel-list tradition are associated with the interpretation of Gen. 6:1-4. The chief angel of the traditional unit is Shemiḥazah (cf. 1 En. 6:3,7 and 69:2), who is assigned responsibility for leading the sons of heaven astray with the daughters of men (cf. 1 En. 6:3; 9:7-8; and 10:11-12). In addition, the second of the two lists in the Parables (1 En. 69:4-12) refers to Gen. 6:1-4, although it assigns responsibility to a different angel:

> (1 En. 69:4) And the name of the first one was Yeqon, the one who led astray all the sons of the angels [*daqiqa malā'ekt*][13] and caused them to descend upon the earth and led them astray through the daughters of men. (5) And the second, his name was Asbeel; that one taught evil counsel to the sons of the holy angels [*la-daqiqa malā'ekt qedusān*] and led them astray so that they defiled their flesh with the daughters of men.

This tradition represents a particular interpretation of Gen. 6:1-4, an interpretation that is found in the form of a narrative in 1 En. 6-11. Since the latter version is more complex, much of the following examination of the relation of the angel lists to scriptural interpretation and to mythological patterns will concentrate on it.

It is frequent practice to interpret Gen. 6:1-4 in light of 1 En. 6-11 as an ancient myth involving the fall of heavenly beings through intercourse with human women;[14] however, the emphasis in Genesis is on human attempts to transcend man's limitations, and the punishment meted out in

Gen. 6:3 is a limitation on the length of human life. Punishment of the sons of God is not mentioned.[15]

The elements of the tradition about the sons of God and the daughters of men in Gen. 6:1-4 include the following:
1. daughters are born to the increasing human population on earth
2. the sons of God see that they are beautiful and take wives from their number
3. the length of human life is limited, apparently to prevent the sons of God from transferring immortality to their offspring
4. children are born to the wives, and they become the legendary mighty men

Only the last point presents serious problems, thanks to the tortured syntax of Gen. 6:4.

הנפלים היו בארץ בימים ההם וגם אחרי־כן אשר יבאו בני האלחים
אל־בנות האדם וילדו להם המה הגברים אשר מעולם אנשי השם:

> The *Nephilim* were in the land in those days, and also thereafter, when the sons of God were going into the daughters of men and begetting [children] for themselves; these were the mighty ones of old, men of renown.

It is not clear if the pronoun, המה, refers to the *Nephilim* or to the children of the sons of God. A related problem is whether the *Nephilim* and the offspring of the sons of God and the daughters of men are identical. It seems more likely that the offspring of the Sons of God are the mighty ones of old and that the *Nephilim* are a distinct but comparable group of legendary warriors that could be mentioned in the same breath as the "*Gibborim*." Gen. 6:4 seems to imply that the *Nephilim* were already present at the time of the birth of the latter. However, there may have been variations in the traditions. Ezek. 32:27 mentions a class of warriors prepared to greet Pharaoh in Sheol, the "mighty ones, the fallen ones of old" ($gibbôrîm\ nôph^el\hat{i}m\ m\bar{e}\ ^\epsilon\hat{o}l\bar{a}m$),[16] who lie in state with their weapons as aristocrats of Sheol. The participle, $nôph^el\hat{i}m$, could easily have been pointed $n^eph\hat{i}l\hat{i}m$. Ezek. 32:27, therefore, not only suggests that *Nephilim* should be derived from נפל, "fall," in the sense of those fallen in battle, it also suggests an association of the *Gibborim* and the *Nephilim*. Both are related to the Greek demigods, which, in a myth to be examined below, were the offspring of gods and women and were sent into battle by Zeus to destroy one another. In 1 En. 10:9 and 12, the giants are to destroy each other in battle, a detail that suggests that the interpretation of Gen. 6:1-4 in 1 En. has preserved at least some older traditions that did not find their way into the text of scripture.

The Ugaritic Poem of the Gracious Gods likewise suggests that the *Gibborim* and the *Nephilim* are the Hebrew parallels to the Greek demigods and that the giants of 1 En. 6-11 reflect some old traditions related to them. In the poem,[17] two insatiable demigods, Dawn and Sunset, are born as the result of intercourse between El and two human women, and their activities are suggestive of those of the giants in 1 En. 6-11. It is therefore possible that Gen. 6:1-4 is the Hebrew version of the Poem of the Gracious Gods. Since Yahweh has been identified with El of the Canaanite pantheon, the sons of Elohim could have been substituted for El to make the myth acceptable in a Yahwistic context. This substitution could explain why, in Gen. 6:3, Yahweh is concerned that "*my* spirit" should remain in man. The story fits into the Yahwist's antediluvian history because the possession of the divine spirit implied by the myth leaves man in a position to further exceed his human limitations. The myth is concerned with human sin rather than with any transgression on the part of the sons of God.

While Gen. 6:1-4 and 1 En. 6-11 share elements of older traditional material, in one central aspect the structure of the Enochic version has been changed so that it is very much an *interpretation* of (or narrative midrash on) Gen. 6:1-4. The focus has been shifted from man to the sons of God, or angels, and the myth has become the myth of the origin of evil for certain Jewish apocalyptic circles. Evil in some way results from the incursion of heavenly beings into the earthly realm.

In the angel-list unit in the Parables of Enoch, Asbeel is said to have led the angels astray "so that they defiled their flesh with the daughters of men" (1 En. 69:5, cf. 7:1; 9:8; and 10:11). It is interesting to note that these heavenly beings have flesh, or bodies, that can be defiled, apparently, through contact with the women's menstrual blood. 1 En. 15:4 suggests this mode of defilement;[18] however, there are also several other possible concepts of impurity involved. The following passage from Josephus' description of the Essenes might be relevant:

> They are divided, according to the duration of their discipline, into four grades; and so far are the junior members inferior to the seniors, that a senior if but touched by a junior, must take a bath, as after contact with an alien.[19]

While the idea may be that one must purify oneself after contact with someone whom one can not be certain is ritually pure, it is also possible that there is a concept here that mixture of ranks, or orders of being, renders the higher rank unclean.[20] It also seems likely that the laws concerning mixed fruits[21] or the offspring of illegitimate degrees of marriage (*mamzerim*)[22] have been applied at the cosmic level in the tradition of interpretation of Gen. 6:1-4 behind 1 Enoch. In 1 En. 10:9, the giants that resulted from the mixture (μειγέντας, cf. 1 En. 10:11)[23] of the angels and the women are called *mamzerim*--the word is transliterated as μαζήρεοι!--and 1 En. 15:3-10 is greatly concerned with what is proper and natural to the human and the angelic realms. In other words, the angels have defiled themselves by mixing with a lower order of being as well as by coming in contact with whatever impurity that sexual intercourse might carry with it.

The giant offspring of the angels and women are neither fish nor fowl, so to speak, as a result of the illegitimate mixture of two realms. Therefore, they have unnatural appetites that cannot be satisfied (cf. 1 En. 7:3-5 and 15:11). These appetites are the way in which the mixture of two realms unleashes evil upon the world--evil in the form of violence, which pollutes the earth itself through bloodshed, thereby calling for the purification of the earth through the waters of the flood (cf. 1 En. 7:3-5; 10:7,18-22). The Qumran Enochic manuscripts and later survivals in Manichaeanism indicate that the giant motif took on a life of its own.[24]

The other way in which the angels introduce evil into the world is through the teaching of the human arts and sciences to their human wives. The secret knowledge that they reveal includes magic, which the Enochic tradition considers appropriate only to the heavenly realm, cf. 1 En. 16:3. It is interesting that the angel-list tradition in the Parables of Enoch is interested only in this means of the introduction of evil. The giant motif is carefully avoided, although intercourse between the angels and women is mentioned. This lack is probably to be explained on the grounds that the Parables is not interested in the problems raised by the version of the myth of the fallen angels based on Gen. 6:1-4. It uses the angel-list tradition only to ornament its own account, which is based on the Is. 24:17-23 midrash.

It can be concluded that the tradition of interpretation of Gen. 6:1-4, with which the angel-list tradition is associated, has subjected that passage to a thorough reinterpretation. The following are the basic elements of that tradition, and they can be compared to the elements of Gen. 6:1-4 above on p. 78:

1. the angels descend from heaven, led by one of their number, to go astray through the daughters of men
2. they defile their flesh through contact with the women, begetting giant children with insatiable appetites who introduce violence into the world
3. they reveal secret arts and magic to mankind
4. men are perishing as a result of the revelation of secret wisdom and the violence of the giants
5. the flood is necessary in order to cleanse the earth from the pollution caused by bloodshed

The tradition obviously interprets Gen. 6:1-4 in its context as the introduction to the flood narrative. It has changed the focus of the passage of scripture, however, from a concern for man's attempt to transcend his human limitations to the introduction of evil into the world through the angels' incursion into a realm to which they do not belong. While much of the above was established through reference to 1 En. 6-11 as a whole, all of the above elements except the second half of number 2 and number 5 are explicitly associated with the angel lists in 1 En. 69:2-12.

Mythological Patterns
and the Angel Lists

It is obviously impossible to discuss the relationship between the angel-list tradition and scripture without impinging upon the problem of mythological traditions known from the ancient world. Gen. 6:1-4 raises such problems. Therefore, what follows to a certain extent represents a continuation of the above discussion.

Marriages of gods and humans. Intercourse between gods and humans is known from other mythological traditions than the Hebrew and Canaanite ones. Gaster makes the following comment on Gen. 6:1-4:

> The story is based on the widespread notion that sexual intercourse can convey the qualities of the one partner to the other. Hence, such intercourse between gods and mortal women, or between goddesses and mortal men, is discountenanced and taboo, lest the divine thus become human, and the human divine. It is the latter possibility, involving the acquisition of immortality, that alarms Yahweh, and he therefore deals promptly with the situation by arbitrarily limiting the span of human life.[25]

Gaster considers the motif of the birth of heroes from the intercourse of gods and human women as a late literary development from earlier popular accounts concerning local gods and goddesses or nymphs. If he is correct in this judgment, it should still be noted that, in the ancient world, the motif appears in Greek, Canaanite, and Hebrew literature from the epic period and that it plays an important role both in Ancient Near Eastern royal ideology, as Gaster notes, and in popular and literary legends about heroes and great men in the Hellenistic period.

An earlier Greek myth, found in Hesiod's *Eoiae*, illuminates both Gen. 6:1-4 and 1 En. 6-11:

> Now all the gods were divided through strife; for at that very time Zeus who thunders on high was meditating marvellous deeds, even to mingle storm and tempest over the boundless earth, and already he was hastening to make an utter end of the race of mortal men, declaring that he would destroy the lives of the demi-gods, that the children of the gods should not mate with wretched mortals, seeing their fate with their own eyes; but that the blessed gods henceforth even as aforetime should have their living and their habitations apart from men. But on those who were born of immortals and of mankind verily Zeus laid toil and sorrow upon sorrow.[26]

The text goes on shortly to tell of the destruction of the race of heroes in battle, apparently a reference to the Trojan war. The "storm and tempest" can be taken as a

parallel to the flood tradition, although here it results in
the destruction of crops rather than in the inundation of the
land in order to destroy or decimate man. The storm is
associated with a myth that deals with the birth of heroes or
demigods from the marriage of gods and mortals in a way that
reinforces the suggestion above that the *Nephilim* are those who
have *fallen in battle*. The destruction of the demigods in the
sight of their parents corresponds to the punishment of the
giants in 1 En. 10:9-10,12 and 14:6. This myth also provides
confirmation for the position that Gen. 6:1-4 is a myth about
the limitation of human life, not the fall of the sons of God.
The "blessed gods" are to henceforth have their habitations
apart from men, but there is no indication that they will not
remain *blessed* gods. The myth of the fallen angels as such is
a creation of Judaism of the Hellenistic age. The fall of the
angels is not derived from Genesis but is the result of the
interpretation of Genesis under the impact of other influences
that will be examined shortly.

The inversion of the culture-hero motif. Both
versions of the angel-list tradition claim that the angels led
mankind astray by teaching them various arts and sciences,
including magic (cf. 1 En. 8:1-3 and 69:4-12). This element of
the tradition represents an inversion of the Promethean or
culture-hero motif, which has already been examined above in
chapter III in connection with the Is. 24:17-23 midrash. If
one looks closely at the inversion of this motif, it reveals
an ambivalence in the scribal tradition toward secret knowledge
and magic. The knowledge that some Alexandrian scribe claims
for Solomon in Wsd. Sol. 7:17-22 is quite similar to that
taught by the angels in 1 En. 8:1-3:

> For it is he [God] who gave me unerring knowledge of
>   what exists,
> to know the structure of the world and the activity
>   of the elements;
> the beginning and end and middle of times,
> the alternations of the solstices and the changes
>   of the seasons,
> the cycles of the year and the constellations of the stars,
> the natures of animals and the tempers of wild beasts,
> the powers of spirits and the reasonings of men,
> the varieties of plants and the virtues of roots;
> I learned both what is secret and what is manifest,
> for wisdom, the fashioner of all things, taught me.[27]

Here, Wisdom is responsible for teaching what the fallen angels teach in 1 Enoch. In the tradition, Enoch, the heavenly scribe, plays the role of a culture hero. According to Jub. 4:17, he introduces writing, wisdom, and the knowledge of the signs of heaven to men. It is therefore interesting to discover in 1 En. 69:8-11 that one of the fallen angels is blamed for introducing widsom and the art of writing to men. In 1 En. 16:3, when the final sentence is passed against the angels, they are told that there are even deeper secrets than the worthless ones that they had been shown--secrets in which the story-teller may well have been interested.

The ambivalence toward wisdom, and magic, suggests that there may have been a tradition within Jewish wisdom circles of the period, a tradition that celebrated the angels for the introduction of secret knowledge in much the same way that Wisdom personified does in Wsd. Sol. 7:17-22 quoted above. The role of angels in magic and their revelatory function in apocalyptic literature points in the same direction. The inversion of the culture-hero motif in the angel-list tradition should be taken as a reaction to the role of the angels in another segment of the scribal or wisdom tradition. Hengel[28] makes a similar argument in relation to the sons of Seth who, according to Josephus (*Ant*. 1. 69-71), were responsible for the discovery of astronomy and its preservation for the generations after the flood. In this particular case the culture-hero motif has not been inverted. Hengel relates the ambivalence to cultural conflict between Hellenism and Judaism within the latter. The secrets taught by the angels are taken by the Ḥasidim as elements of Hellenistic culture.

An examination of the coherent names in the lists in 1 En. 6:7; 8:1-3; and 69:2-3 indicates that by and large they are etymologically related to natural phenomena over which they have been placed; there is, therefore, nothing in the list of names itself that suggests that it is a list of fallen angels. A distantly related version of the list is to be found in 3 En. 14:3-4. The angels in that list functioh as the rulers of the world, but in trembling before Metatron, along with the rest of the heavenly host, they display their obedience to divine authority. It is therefore likely that the list in 1 En. 6:7 and 69:2-3 was not originally a list of fallen angels but has been assigned that role as a result of some development of thought that has taken place in certain Jewish circles of the Hellenistic period. The association of the angels with the natural phenomena suggests that the culture-hero motif is attached primarily to the angel-list tradition rather than to the interpretation of Gen. 6:1-4 and that the latter tradition gains this motif by appropriation of the lists.

The complaint of the earth. Wilhelm Bousset[29] and Hans Dieter Betz[30] have related the complaint of the earth in 1 En. 7:6 and 9:2 to a myth found in a Hermetic document, the *Kore Kosmu*.[31] In that work, souls are created by God and assigned their places "in the intermediate region of the universe."[32] They are then assigned the task of creating the race of animals, and, proud of their achievement, they begin to overstep their bounds, breaking the divine law and thinking themselves the peers of the gods in heaven. For this sin, they are imprisoned in the bodies of men dwelling on earth. So far, this myth represents a common Hellenistic cosmology and anthropology with its roots in Orphic teachings that can be found reflected in the classical period in Plato. Philo, in *Gig.* 6-8, uses this material in interpreting Gen. 6:1-4. The one new element, perhaps, is the specific reason for the imprisonment, the souls' creation of animals, which leads to hubris. In the *Kore Kosmu*, the souls, having been imprisoned in the bodies of men, quarrel, and men begin to kill each other. Their bodies, unburied, pollute the four elements, Earth, Air, Fire, and Water, who complain to God. God resolves the problem by introducing the mysteries of Osiris and Isis to civilize men.

If the complaint of the Earth in 1 Enoch is related to the complaint of the four elements in the *Kore Kosmu*, it would explain why the interpretation of Gen. 6:1-4 in 1 En. 6-11 has shifted the center of interest from the *Nephilim* and mankind to the sons of God or the angels. The angels have been identified with the souls of daemons--as Philo does in his interpretation of Gen. 6:1-4[33]--and their audacity is seen as the origin of evil. There are, however, two important

differences. First, 1 En. 6-11 is not simply another version
of the Hellenistic myth but a Gen. 6:1-4 midrash that uses the
Hellenistic myth to interpret the passage of scripture.
Traditions about the giants as violent men are probably one
of the points of contact between the tradition behind the *Kore
Kosmu* and the interpretation of Genesis, and it is the giants
who are responsible for the bloodshed that pollutes the earth.
In addition, the hubris of the angels is seen as a lust for
the daughters of men rather than a desire to be equal to the
gods in heaven. For their transgression, they are imprisoned
in Sheol, like the Titans, rather than in flesh, like the souls
of the *Kore Kosmu*. This last element is found in 1 En. 6-11,
where it may be due to the use of the Is. 24:17-23 midrash,
which follows motifs related to the Titans or the "chained
gods" of Babylonian tradition.

Second, while the concept of *mixture* is to be found
in the *Kore Kosmu*, it is based on Greek philosophical ideas
that make it the *sine qua non* of creation, which is seen as
the good work of God himself. In 1 En. 6-11, the concept
of mixture becomes the way of explaining how evil originates
through reference to Jewish laws dealing with mixed fruits
and *mamzerim*.[34] The mixture of two realms, the heavenly and
the earthly, which are originally good in and of themselves,
produces evil results.

While it seems likely that there is some relationship
between the tradition behind the *Kore Kosmu* and the interpretation of Genesis in 1 En. 6-11, it is difficult to specify
the exact nature of that relationship or the origin of the
traditions. A similar myth is found in Hinduism in an early
text, the *Vishṇu Purāṇa*, which might conceivably contain
traditions contemporary to the Hellenistic period.[35] The
fifth book of that writing sets out to tell of the birth of
Kṛshṇa and begins by telling of a complaint that the earth
makes to the gods:

> At that time, Earth, overburdened by her load,
> repaired to mount Meru to an assembly of the gods,
> and addressing the divinites [*sic*], with Brahmā at
> their head, related in piteous accents all her
> distress. . . . [There follows a description of
> the participation of all things, including the gods,
> in Vishṇu. This description, in some way, seems to

THE LISTS OF FALLEN ANGELS

be parallel to the prayer of the archangels in 1 En. 9, which is intended to raise the question of the responsibility of God for what has happened.] "At this present season [the Earth continues] many demons, of whom Kálanemi is the chief, have overrun, and continually harass, the region of mortals. The great Asura Kálanemi, that was killed by the powerful Vishṇu, has revived in Kansa, the son of Ugrasena, and many other mighty demons, more that I can enumerate [the text goes on to list a number of names!], . . . are born in the palaces of kings. Countless hosts of proud and powerful spirits, chiefs of the demon race, assuming celestial forms, now walk the earth; and, unable to support myself beneath the incumbent load, I come to you for succour. Illustrious deities, do you so act that I may be relieved from my burden, lest helpless I sink into the nethermost abyss."[36]

The deities respond to the Earth's request by going to "the northern coast of the milky sea"[37] to report her complaint to Vishṇu. He responds by plucking two of his hairs, which are to descend to earth as Kṛshṇa and Balaráma, who will relieve Earth of her burden. He also sends the gods themselves to earth to fight the Asuras and destroy them.

While the nature of Earth's distress is different—she is unable to support the weight of the demons instead of being polluted by bloodshed—there are other parallels in the Hindu version, parallels that are closer to 1 En. 6-11 than the one in the *Kore Kosmu*. In 1 En. 6-11 and in the *Vishṇu Purāṇa* mankind is troubled by either giants or the demons; in the *Kore Kosmu* it is man who is the problem. In 1 En. 6-11 the Earth's complaint ascends to the archangels, who in turn take it before God, while in the *Vishṇu Purāṇa* the Earth appeals to the gods and the gods to Vishṇu; in the *Kore Kosmu* the elements go directly to God. In the Hindu version, the gods are dispatched to earth to fight the demons; in the Jewish version, the archangels are commissioned to imprison the angels and punish them. However, in the *Kore Kosmu*, Isis and Osiris are sent to introduce religion to man. The Hindu version also singles out and names a chief demon and lists his associates, a parallel to the role of Shemiḥazah and the angel lists in 1 En. 6-11. The point is not that 1 En. 6-11 is dependent upon a Hindu myth but rather that the myth must have been fairly widespread in the Near and Middle East in the Hellenistic and Roman periods and is quite possibly eastern rather than western in origin. The source of the contact between the Hindu and the western versions could be in the Greek kingdoms that were established in India after the time of Alexander.

The myth in 1 En. 6-11 could also be examined from a purely phenomenological standpoint. The Guarani Indians of South America anticipate the destruction of the world, and their shamans report visions of a prayer of the Earth:

> Die Medizinmänner, wenn sie in ihren Träumen bei *Ñanderuvuçú* waren, haben es häufig genug selbst gehört wie die Erde diesen bittet: "Ich habe schon zu viele Leichen gefressen, ich bin es satt und müde, mache ein Ende, mein Vater!" Ebenso ruft das Wasser zum Schöpfer, er möge es ausruhen lassen und so auch die Bäume, die das Brennholz und Baumaterial liefern und die ganze übrige Natur.[38]

Here the earth is tired of consuming corpses; in 1 Enoch she has been polluted by bloodshed. In the Guarani tradition, the motif is eschatological in function, while in 1 Enoch the flood that results from the pollution of the earth serves as a prototype for the eschaton. While it is likely that there is a historical connection between the Hindu, Jewish, and Hermetic versions of the complaint of the earth, the existence of the Guarani parallel indicates that the motif can appear in eschatological contexts as a distinct element and that it must be examined in the role it plays in each context. Historical relationships between motifs in religious traditions explain little more than the source of the material. Even where similarities exist in the association of several motifs in different traditions, the particular way in which the motifs are structured in each tradition must be examined in terms of the structure and dynamics of development of that particular tradition.

In making the connection between the tradition behind the *Kore Kosmu* and the complaint of the earth in 1 En. 6-11, Betz argues that Jewish apocalyptic is Hellenistic in character and that there is a radical discontinuity between it and the older Israelite tradition.[39] To a certain extent, this insight is correct in that Jewish religion of the period must be seen in the context of the Hellenistic world. It uses material derived from its environment and deals with many of the same problems as other national groups in the period. In this connection, it is important to recognize that 1 En. 6-11 is

not a fuller version of Gen. 6:1-4 but a new *Gestalt* formed
in a specific time and place. The passage may use various
older mythological motifs as well as traditions derived from
the Hellenistic world, but it is the way in which these motifs
are combined to meet current needs that is important. The
combination must be seen as taking place under factors introduced by the contemporary environment.

At the same time, in relating Jewish apocalyptic to
Hellenistic religion, it is misleading to see a *radical* discontinuity with the past. The Jewish writer would have been
conscious of writing in his national tradition as he understood it. Therefore, in relating Jewish apocalyptic to
Hellenistic religion, it is important to develop a concept
of the role of both continuity and change in a religious
tradition. Syncretism has always been present in Israelite
and Jewish religion. The problem is to define what it is that
makes it a *tradition* in spite of the constant changes that
occur. An examination of 1 En. 6-11, the *Kore Kosmu*, and the
Viṣhṇu Purāṇa should not merely reveal that they have appro-
priated a common tradition; it should reveal that each has
used it in terms of its own tradition.

As in the case of the discussion of the exegesis of
scripture and the angel lists, it has been necessary to examine
the relationship between the lists and mythological patterns
in light of 1 En. 6-11 as a whole, omitting those elements
of that passage that can be attributed to the exegesis of
Is. 24:17-23, which also seems to have been used in the composition of that passage. While not all of the elements of
1 En. 6-11 show up in the traditions associated with the angel
lists in 1 En. 69:2-12, the interpretation of Gen. 6:1-4 found
in 1 En. 69:4-5 presupposes an exegesis of that passage that is
at least similar to that found in 1 En. 6-11. The defilement
of the flesh of the angels in 69:4-5 results from the connection of the angel list with the interpretation of Gen. 6:1-4,
while the nature of the angel lists themselves probably
accounts for the culture-hero motif and its inversion. While
the parallel in the *Viṣhṇu Purāṇa*, which lists a chief demon
and a number of subordinates, suggests that the interpretation of Gen. 6:1-4 in light of the complaint of the earth

tradition suggested the use of a traditional Jewish angel list to ornament the narrative, the angel lists themselves have a distinct impact on the form of the tradition. Both the interpretation of Gen. 6:1-4 and the inversion of the culture-hero motif are present in 1 En. 69:2-12, although the giant traditions seem to have been intentionally suppressed.

The exegetical tradition of Gen. 6:1-4 is important in that it seems to have formed the basis for a myth of the origin of evil, a myth that displaced the Adamic myth in certain apocalyptic circles. 4 Ezra is the only major Jewish apocalypse that depends entirely upon the Adamic myth, and it should be noted that it is written after the catastrophe of A.D. 70, when the Jewish nation has newly become obsessed with its own sin as an explanation for the tragedy. Of course, the Adamic myth remains a viable alternative throughout the period, since the Adam literature extends back into the Hellenistic age. However, the myth of the origin of evil based on the interpretation of Gen. 6:1-4 found in 1 En. 6-11 meets the need of a Judaism concerned with the purity of the nation under pressure from the impact of a new and powerful alien culture, a problem first raised, apparently, by Ezra, but one that remains of importance throughout the Persian, Hellenistic, and Roman periods. This myth projects the concern for racial and cultural purity on the cosmic level and sees the mixture of the levels as the cause of evil. It is likely that this myth of the origin of evil is a Ḥasidic polemic against an increasingly Hellenized aristocracy reflected in the Tobiad family history preserved by Josephus.[40] The violence of the giants would therefore reflect the growing class struggle found in Sirach.[41]

CHAPTER V

THE ESSENTIAL ELEMENTS OF THE IS. 24:17-23
MIDRASH AND THE LISTS OF FALLEN ANGELS

On the basis of the distinction of the two genres and on the basis of the analysis of the role of the exegesis of scripture and of the use of mythological patterns in the two traditional units, it is possible to establish the basic elements of the Is. 24:17-23 midrash and of the lists of fallen angels. The comparison of the two sets of basic elements will reveal that the two traditions represent two distinct *Gestalten*.

The Is. 24:17-23 Midrash

Genre and exegesis of scripture. This unit is an exegetical tradition based on Is. 24:17-23, from which it derives its structure. The basic passage of scripture is interpreted through reference to the flood tradition from Genesis and by elaboration of the details of the parallel punishment of the host of heaven and the kings of the earth. In the two versions of this unit in the Parables, the only possible reference to Gen. 6:1-4 is the allusion to the elect and beloved of the host of Asael in 1 En. 56:3-4; however, this phrase is more correctly seen as a reference to the kings and mighty of the earth, and the reference to the giants in 1 En. 6-16 as the beloved sons of the fallen angels should be taken as a coincidence. The midrash can, therefore, be distinguished as a unit on the basis of its use of scripture.

The name of the leader of the fallen angels. The Is. 24:17-23 midrash lacks a concern with listing the names of the angels. One version characterizes them only as the host of Asael; the other version in the Parables mentions no names. The lack of names may be an accident; however, the fact that the unit apparently considers Asael the leader corresponds to the situation in 1 En. 6-11, where he is taken as one of the two leaders of the angels. Literary criticism based a two source theory on the two names in chapters 6-11, and, while its method of explanation may be in need of revision, the recognition of the distinction between the two names does seem to be correct.[1]

The sins of the angels. In the Is. 24:17-23 midrash, the sins of the fallen angels are characterized as the introduction of idolatry and sorcery. There is no suggestion that they have gone astray after the daughters of men and fathered giants. This distinction, of course, corresponds to the lack of the use of Gen. 6:1-4 with its concern with the sexual union of the heavenly beings with the daughters of men.

The punishment of the angels. The midrash parallels the punishment of the kings of the earth with that of the angels. In doing so, it brings together two different strands of traditions from the ancient world: one dealing with the hubris of royalty and the other dealing with the rebellion and punishment of heavenly beings or gods. The punishment of the kings and angels is associated with a distinct eschatology, based on Is. 24:17-23, that places the initial imprisonment of the angels and kings at the flood and their punishment at the eschaton.

Mythological patterns in the unit. It has already been noted that the midrash brings together traditions dealing with kings and others concerned with the rebellion and punishment of gods or heavenly beings. It thus produces a tradition that serves well as a polemic against the abuses of power and delusions of personal status common among royalty in the Hellenistic and Roman periods. It is for this reason that the tradition has been used in the Parables. It should also be noted that the midrash shares the inversion of the culture-hero motif with the angel-list tradition. The fact that the two units have this motif in common is probably due to the understanding of the role of angels in Jewish apocalyptic: they have taken over the role of Wisdom personified as revealers of knowledge to the sage. An inversion of this motif can thus be assumed as a means of explaining as magic, sorcery, and idolatry the knowledge of the enemies of the sect.

ESSENTIAL ELEMENTS   93

The Lists of Fallen Angels

Genre and exegesis of scripture. This traditional unit contains two angel lists. The first is a list of angels placed over the elements of the cosmos and was probably not originally a list of *fallen* angels. The second is related to an interpretation of (or narrative midrash on) Gen. 6:1-4 and, in addition, contains an account of the revelation of secret knowledge to men. As a genre, the angel list is best suited to perform a function known from popular literature in other cultures, that of the ornamentation of a narrative. It provides a traditional list that can be drawn upon in various situations to embellish a story. The two lists perform that function in both 1 En. 6-11 and the Parables of Enoch.

The name of the leader of the fallen angels. The angel-list tradition seems to treat Shemiḥazah as the leader of the fallen angels. He heads the first list in both the Parables and 1 En. 6-11, and the latter passage clearly assigns him the responsibility for leading the angels astray after the daughters of men, a detail that corresponds to the association with the interpretation of Gen. 6:1-4. Asael appears as the tenth angel in both versions of the first list, and the fact that he heads the second list in 1 En. 6-11, found in 8:1-3, may well represent redaction. Chapters 6-11 clearly understand both Shemiḥazah and Asael as leaders of the angels, and the latter name could easily have been placed at the head of the second list to carry that understanding through. It has already been suggested above that the second list, 1 En. 8:1-3, is suspect as redaction in its present form since it repeats names found in the first list in 1 En. 6:7.

The sins of the angels. While the traditions associated with the angel lists understand the sins of the angels to include the introduction of idolatry and sorcery, as well as false wisdom, their chief crime is marriage with human women. This motif is central to the narrative in 1 En. 6-11 in which the lists are set, a narrative that represents an interpretation of Gen. 6:1-4. The giant motif that is associated with the angel marriages in 1 En. 6-11 is absent from the version in the Parables, probably because of the special concerns of that work.

The punishment of the angels. There is no evidence that the tradition of interpretation of Gen. 6:1-4 associated with the angel lists reported the punishment of the angels, although it records the destruction of the giants, apparently an older traditional motif. In 1 En. 6-11, the punishment of the angels is derived from the Is. 24:17-23 midrash. In 1 En. 10:11-13, the punishment of Shemiḥazah and his associates is similar to that of Asael in 10:4-6 with the exception that the former are not weighed down with rocks. It is the punishment of Asael that is part of the Is. 24:17-23 midrash, and, since the punishment of Shemiḥazah even preserves the eschatology associated with that midrash, it seems likely that chapters 6-11 have used the Is. 24:17-23 midrash to supply the account of the punishment of the angels lacking in the earlier interpretation of Gen. 6:1-4. It has been noted that the latter passage was not originally concerned with the sin and punishment of heavenly beings, and, if its reinterpretation in light of the tradition dealing with the complaint of the earth was based on a version of that motif similar to the one in the *Kore Kosmu*, the focus of its concern would have been shifted from humans and giants to the angels as the ones responsible for the introduction of sin without supplying an account of the punishment of the angels in the process. In the *Kore Kosmu*, the souls are punished by being imprisoned in flesh, but the motif of the mixture of souls and flesh has been put to a different purpose in the Jewish version. It now explains the initial sin of the angels, leaving no part of the traditional pattern of either the traditions associated with the complaint of the earth or those associated with the interpretation of Gen. 6:1-4 to function as an account of the punishment of the angels. In 1 En. 6-11, the Is. 24:17-23 midrash has been drawn upon to supply the need for an account of the punishment of the angels.

Mythological patterns in the unit. As has been noted, the angel-list tradition has the inversion of the culture-hero motif in common with the Is. 24:17-23 midrash, and this particular element is associated primarily with the angel lists themselves. The lists represent traditional lists of angels placed over the phenomena of the cosmos, angels that have, in

certain circles, been identified as the sources of false and
dangerous wisdom. These lists have become associated with the
traditional interpretation of Gen. 6:1-4, a tradition that has
itself been reinterpreted in light of both a myth from the
larger Hellenistic world dealing with the distress and
complaint of the earth and Jewish laws concerning mixed fruits
and *mamzerim*. The resulting mythological structure is
concerned with the inner purity of the Jewish nation in its
struggle with what is perceived as the threat of the alien
culture of the Hellenistic world, while that of the Is.
24:17-23 midrash is directed outward toward the political and
religious threat presented to the nation by a world ruler who
has lost track of his true place in the cosmos.

The Tradition History of the Two Units

Most of the versions of the myth of the fallen angels
in Judaism are dependent in some way on the version in 1 En.
6-16, which represents a combination of the Is. 24:17-23
midrash and an interpretation of Gen. 6:1-4, including the
angel lists. It is necessary here to examine only 1 En. 6-11,
which provides evidence for the distinction between the two
units outlined above.

While 1 En. 6-11 is a fairly coherent narrative, structured according to the law of scenic duality,[2] it maintains
certain distinctions in assigning responsibility for the introduction of sin to two different leaders of the fallen angels.
These distinctions suggest that the passage is uniting two
different traditional units that have a separate existence
in the Parables of Enoch. The literary critics seized upon
the alternation of the names of the leaders of the angels to
argue that the passage was dependent upon two different cycles,
which they tried to reconstruct by literary-critical analysis
of 1 En. 6-11.[3] The literary-critical analysis of this
passage, however, is too mechanical to explain the composition
of chapters 6-11. The use of the law of scenic duality points
toward popular literature, although it does not necessarily
allow one to distinguish between oral and written composition
here. The story is told in a straightforward manner with a
certain amount of skill, not by using scissors and paste, so

to speak, to mechanically join two different cycles. The
doublets resulting from the use of two traditions fit well into
the pattern of the use of repetition for stylistic effect in
popular literature.

1 En. 6-11 makes Shemiḥazah the angel responsible for
leading the angels, or the "sons of heaven," astray after the
daughters of men, while Asael is charged only with the teaching
of forbidden arts and sciences. The opening verses clearly
establish the passage as a midrash on Gen. 6:1-4 and Shemiḥazah
as the leader:

> (1 En. 6:1) And it came to pass, when the sons of men
> increased, in those days beautiful and lovely daughters
> were born. (2) And the angels, the sons of heaven, saw
> them and desired them, and they said to each other, "Come,
> let us choose for ourselves wives from among mankind, and
> let us beget children for ourselves." (3) And Semeiazas,
> who was their leader, said to them, "I fear that you will
> not wish to do this deed, and I alone will be guilty of
> a great sin."

A folktale about an oath on Mt. Hermon follows, and then there
is found a list of the chiefs of tens of the angels with
Shemiḥazah at its head. After an account of the birth of
giants to the women, a second list of angels is found headed
by Asael:

> (1 En. 8:1) And Azael taught mankind to make swords
> and weapons and shields and coats of mail, [he taught them]
> the teachings of the angels, and he showed them the metals
> and their working, and armlets and adornments and eye
> shadow and eye-liner, and all sorts of choice stones, and
> dyes. (2) And much impiety arose, and they fornicated
> and went astray and were perverted in all their ways.

The charge stated here against Asael is that he taught men and
women various arts and crafts that led to their perversion.
While fornication is mentioned, it involves men and women, not
angels and women. Of course, the implication of the previous
part of the narrative, see 1 En. 7:1, is that Asael, along
with the other angels listed in 1 En. 6:7, was involved with
one of the daughters of men, but when the charges were specified against him, this one is omitted. It has been argued
above that Asael does not originally belong to the second list
but has been placed at its head since he and Shemiḥazah, who
heads the first list in 1 En. 6:7, are regarded as the two
chief leaders of the angels in 1 En. 6-11. The placement,
however, is thematically appropriate, since the Is. 24:17-23

midrash, with which Asael seems to be associated, shares the inversion of the culture-hero motif with the angel lists.

In responding to the complaint of the earth, the archangels make the following charges in their prayer to God:

> (1 En. 9:6) And you behold all things that Azael has done, who taught all the lawless things upon the earth and revealed the eternal mysteries that they practice in heaven, [and] mankind knew [them], (7) and Semiazas, to whom you gave the power to rule over the ones with him, (8) and they came to the daughters of the men of the earth, and they fornicated with them and were defiled, and they revealed all the sins to them.

The antecedent of ἐπορεύθησαν in verse 8 is τῶν σὺν αὐτῷ ἅμα ὄντων in verse 7. The original Aramaic conjunction at the beginning of verse 8 would have indicated simple sequence rather than the second half of a complex sentence structure embracing all three verses. An English translation that did not adhere so closely to the actual wording of the Greek text would read: ". . . the ones with him *who* came to the daughters of men. . . ." Again, Asael is held responsible for the revelation of secrets, and Shemiḥazah, as the leader of the angels who went astray with the daughters of men, is responsible for that sin.

Finally, the response of God to the archangels' prayer makes the same distinctions:

> (1 En. 10:8) . . .and all the earth was desolated, laid waste by the results of the teaching of Azael, and ascribe all sin to him.

> (10:11, Syncellus) And he [God] said to Michael, "Go, Michael, bind Semiazas and the others with him who mixed with daughters of men so that they were defiled with them on account of their uncleanness."

In chapter 10, not only do the distinctions in the charges against Shemiḥazah and Asael correspond to the other examples in chapters 6-11, they also correspond to the distinctions made above between the angel-list tradition and the Is. 24:17-23 midrash regarding the name of the chief angel and the sins with which the units are concerned.

It should also be noted that the imprisonment and punishment of Asael in 1 En. 10:4-6 corresponds more closely to that of the host of Asael in 54:4-6 than the punishment of Shemiḥazah in 10:11-13 does. These details have been examined on pp. 59-60 above and need not be pursued further here.

Chapter 10 has been structured so that each of the four archangels receives a commission: one is to warn Noah, one is to imprison Asael, one is to cause the destruction of the giants, or *mamzerim*, by sending them to fight against each other, and one is to imprison Shemiḥazah. Aside from using an angel list--that of the four archangels--to ornament a narrative, the structure seems to be intended to preserve the distinctions of the traditional units used in 1 En. 6-11. Elsewhere, the section displays similar techniques, which seem to preserve traditional variants through the use of doublets. An alternation between the complaint of the earth and the complaint of the souls of the dying appears in 1 En. 7:6; 8:4; and 9:2-3.

Not only does the analysis of 1 En. 6-11 indicate that the two traditional units are preserved there, it leads to the conclusion that the two units survive independently even after being joined there. Were the subsequent tradition totally dependent on chapters 6-11, it is doubtful that the Is. 24:17-23 midrash could have maintained its independence in the Parables. Since the passage is skillfully constructed on a pattern other than that found in the midrash, it does not seem likely that the poet of the Parables would have been able to reconstruct the Is. 24:17-23 midrash on the basis of chapters 6-11. The major point of interest in the latter passage is the interpretation of Gen. 6:1-4, and the Is. 24:17-23 midrash seems to have been used mainly to provide an account of the punishment of the angels and an eschatological scheme. Without the continued existence of an exegetical tradition based on Is. 24:17-23, it would be difficult to derive an account of the fall of the angels from chapters 6-11 that did not reflect the marriages of angels with women and the giant traditions but that did clearly reflect the concave structure of Is. 24:17-23.

While the fact that the two traditional units have both an association with the flood and an inversion of the culture-hero motif in common might suggest the conclusion that one gave birth to the other, it seems more likely that each arose in connection with the independent exegesis of the two passages of scripture involved. The flood seems to be initially an incidental allusion in the Is. 24:17-23 midrash, and the elaboration of the central part of the midrash in the two examples in the Parables does not introduce Gen. 6:1-4 into the material about the flood, nor is Asael charged with leading the sons of heaven astray after the daughters of men in 1 En. 6-11. In any case, adequate justification for treating Is. 24:21-23 as a myth dealing with the fall of heavenly beings can be found in the mythology of the ancient world. There is no need to explain the origin of the midrash on that passage by reference to the interpretation of Gen. 6:1-4.

There is likewise no need to attempt to explain the interpretation of Gen. 6:1-4, with which the angel-list tradition is associated, by reference to the Is. 24:17-23 midrash. The shift in the interpretation of this passage is more likely to be explained as the result of contact with the myth involving the complaint of the earth and the related Greek tradition concerning the imprisonment of souls in bodies. It has been noted above that Philo interprets Gen. 6:1-4 by reference to the latter material. In 1 En. 6-11, the Is. 24:17-23 midrash has been utilized to provide an account of the punishment of the angels; however, the pains that the teller of that tale takes to respect the two traditions as distinct variants indicates that both traditional units are well established at that time.

The inversion of the culture-hero motif is probably inevitable, given the role of angels in Jewish apocalyptic. If angels are seen as the source of esoteric knowledge, that knowledge can be taken as evil as well as good, particularly in a situation where cultural conflict might lead one to brand his opponent's knowledge as less than ultimate (cf. 1 En. 16:3). This motif should be considered as prior to both traditional units, and each has a point of contact with it. The Is. 24:17-23 midrash is concerned with the host of the height, or in slightly later terms, the angels who control the movements of sideral phenomena, and the targumic interpretation of Is. 24:23 as a reference to those who worship the sun and moon suggests that Judaism of the period sees the sin for which the angels are being punished as worship of the host of heaven.

As Franz Cumont[4] notes, astrology had the force of a religion in the Hellenistic age. Jub. 12:16-18 and Philo, *Abr*. 68-80, report how Abraham learned to look beyond the astrology and astronomy of the Chaldeans and find the God who controlled the stars. The concern in 1 En. 65:6-8 with sorcery and idolatry and the charge in 1 En. 68:4, which seems to be part of a transitional section attached to the Is. 24:17-23 midrash in 1 En. 64:1-68:1, that the angels act as if they were God, both suggest that the Is. 24:17-23 midrash is concerned with the revelation of knowledge of a *religious* nature, knowledge that is considered as less than ultimate and that could conceivably involve worship of the host of heaven.

The traditional interpretation of Gen. 6:1-4 also acquires this theme at the point at which lists of angels placed over the cosmic phenomena are used to elaborate the myth in that passage. This elaboration could have taken place under the stimulus of a version of the myth of the complaint of the earth that, like the version of the myth found in the *Viṣhṇu Purāṇa*, was concerned with listing the names of demons, or it could represent the exercise of the art of the teller of tales. Another possible explanation for the use of the angel lists and the inversion of the culture-hero motif in the interpretation of Gen. 6:1-4 is suggested by the version in the *Kore Kosmu*. There, Osiris and Isis introduce their mysteries to men in response to the complaints of the four elements, and this motif could have easily led, in the Jewish version, to the use of a list of angels responsible for the introduction of astrology and magic.

Conclusions

The roots of the myth of the fallen angels in Jewish apocalyptic are complex. While there seems to be a general theme present that treats the origin of evil as cosmic and external to man, it is realized in various ways through the exegesis of various passages of scripture and the use of various motifs.[5] Several passages of scripture are involved, each with its own distinct complex of ideas, and at points these passages can be combined with each other or with other passages to produce even more variants.

The association of non-Jewish myths or motifs with the exegesis of particular passages of scripture also produces variants, and in some cases the impact of such syncretism is probably too subtle to detect. It is possible that the accepted way to introduce a Hellenistic tradition into a Jewish context would have been to associate it with the exegesis of a passage of scripture. Philo's allegorical exegesis of scripture is a case in point; however, the process need not be limited to Alexandrian Jewish thought.

The key words in understanding the continuity of the Jewish religious tradition in the period are *scripture* and *traditional exegesis*. The interpretation of scripture is the source of meaning for the age. While the modern historian might make the distinction between the original meaning of the texts and their interpretation in the Hellenistic and Roman periods, the Jewish sage of the time would not have raised the problem. To him, scripture provided both a source of meaning and a framework for the ideas of his generation. Although the traditions dealing with fallen angels represent the thought of Judaism in the Hellenistic age, they would have been perceived as related to specific passages of scripture. The determination of the exegetical background of a complex of traditions is therefore of primary importance in understanding the history of these traditions.

The role of the traditional interpretation of scripture must also be seen as important. Modern scholars have been too ready to perceive a written version of a tradition as definitive. While a fluid division between scripture and non-scripture in the period may make it difficult at times to determine if a particular passage was seen as definitive, the frequent variants of traditions that appear in Jewish apocalyptic suggest a traditional process rather than a literary process behind the development of these variants. It is not that books and writing had no impact upon subsequent intellectual activity but rather that they may well have been of less importance than tradition in the composition of new works. An examination of variants of the version of the myth of the fallen angels found in 1 En. 6-11 would show that that passage is not simply being copied but that it--or the particular complex of traditions that produced it--has had its own impact on the traditional process.

In determining the meaning of the material, the variants that arise through such a process may be of greater value than the constants. The variations present and available in the traditions allow 1 En. 6-11 to base a concern for purity on Gen. 6:1-4 and the Parables of Enoch to base a concern with the abuse of royal power on Is. 24:17-23. The Parables can even draw upon the tradition of interpretation of Gen. 6:1-4 in the form of the associated angel lists to ornament its account; however, when it does so, it omits the giant traditions known to be popular elsewhere at the time. One segment of the Enochic writings, 1 En. 91-105, carefully avoids any version of fallen-angel material and stresses man's responsibility for sin (cf. 1 En. 98:4).

The traditional character of the fallen-angel material in the Parables of Enoch suggests that it is a mistake to explain its presence in that work as the result of the interpolation of a Book of Noah. The variations in the material assigned by literary criticism to this source do not suggest a single written source. What the material has in common is a concern with the introduction of sin, variously conceived, by heavenly beings and a concern with the flood tradition, both of which result from the exegesis of two different passages of scripture. However, if a source or interpolation theory is not an acceptable explanation of the presence of 1 En. 54:1-56:4 and 64:1-69:25 in the Parables, the role of these passages in the thought structure of that work must be examined. The following chapters undertake this task.

PART III

THE ROLE OF THE IS. 24:17-23 MIDRASH
AND THE LISTS OF FALLEN ANGELS
IN THE COMPOSITION OF THE
PARABLES OF ENOCH

INTRODUCTION TO PART III

The conclusion that the Is. 24:17-23 midrash and the lists of fallen angels are distinct traditional units requires a new examination of the way in which this material is used in the Parables of Enoch. The previous discussion has long treated these units as derived from a literary source, a hypothetical Book of Noah, which was either interpolated into or used by the Parables. The position that these units are traditional rather than literary in character leads to a new understanding of the relation between tradition and composition in the Parables.

Part III is a redactional-critical examination of the use of the Is. 24:17-23 midrash and the lists of fallen angels in the Parables. In chapter VI, the relationship of the Is. 24:17-23 midrash to other traditional units in the Parables will be examined. The work is interested in a polemic against the kings and mighty of the earth, and this concern is reflected in the choice of several midrashic traditions that are concerned with the downfall of royalty. The Is. 24:17-23 midrash has been chosen because it provides an account of the imprisonment and punishment of the kings of the earth, and it is used at the appropriate places in the structures of the second and third parables where such an account is in order.

In chapter VII, examination of the Parables as a whole points toward a new understanding of the relation between tradition and composition in that work. This section of 1 Enoch is composed of a collection of three parables, or mešalim, that shows signs of oral rather than literary composition. These mešalim are related to an older traditional genre, the mašal, which is known best as the designation of a type of proverb, but which also designated a longer type of composition that dealt with a vision of the fate of the righteous and the wicked, the central subject matter of the Parables of Enoch. The Is. 24:17-23 midrash is at home in such a composition, particularly when it is remembered that the taunt-song against the king of Babylon in Is. 14 is termed a mašal. In addition, the understanding of the basis

of the Parables in oral rather than literary composition
supports the conclusion of the previous chapters that the Is.
24:17-23 midrash and the lists of fallen angels are traditional rather than literary materials.

    Consideration is also given to the transformation
of an oral composition into a pseudepigraphon, a *literary*
type. A redaction-critical examination of the second example
of the Is. 24:17-23 midrash, 1 En. 64:1-68:1, illuminates this
process. The study of the relation between tradition and
composition in the Parables leads to an understanding of the
interplay between oral and written forms of composition in
apocalyptic literature.

CHAPTER VI

THE IS. 24:17-23 MIDRASH IN THE
THOUGHT AND STRUCTURE OF
THE PARABLES OF ENOCH

In the Parables, the enemies of the community are usually designated by some form of the phrase, "the kings and mighty of the earth." That epithet first appears in 1 En. 38:5, in the introduction to the first parable; however, it is the second and third parables that are primarily concerned with the kings and mighty and their fate.

The Second Parable: 1 En. 45-57

1 En. 46:4-8. The introduction to the second parable, 1 En. 45:1-6, mentions the judgment of the sinners by the Elect one, which is immediately interpreted in the following chapter by the midrash on Dan. 7:9-14, the first section dealing with "that Son of Man." 1 En. 46:1-3 is based on Daniel, but the description of the judgment of the kings and mighty in verses 4-8 is based on Is. 14:4-21:[1]

(1 En. 46:4) And this Son of Man whom you saw will *raise* up the kings and mighty from their *couches* and the strong from their thrones, and he will loosen the *reins* of the strong and break the *teeth* of sinners. (5) And he will *remove the kings from their thrones and their kingdoms* because they do not exalt him and glorify him and humbly confess whence kingship was given to them. (6) And he will cast down the faces of the strong and will fill them with shame, and *darkness* will be their dwelling place, and *worms* will be their bed, and they will not hope to rise from their beds, because they do not exalt the name of the Lord of Spirits. (7) And these are the ones who *judge the stars of heaven*, and lift up their hands against the *Most High*, and trample down the earth and dwell upon it. And all their deeds show forth iniquity, and their	*Is. 14:9*; 49:7(?) Job 17:13 Job 30:11 Ps. 3:7(MT, 8); 58:6! *Is. 14:9* Ps. 107:10; Lam. 3:6 *Is. 14:11*; Job 17:14; 21:26 *Is. 14:13-14* *Is. 14:14*

107

power [depends] upon their *wealth* and their trust is in gods that they have made with their hands, and they deny the name of the Lord of Spirits. (8) And they are persecuting the *houses* of his congregation and the faithful who depend upon the name of the Lord of Spirits.	Ezek. 28:4-5! Ps. 74:8

The above presentation is not intended as an exhaustive analysis of the relationship between 1 En. 46:4-8 and scripture. The purpose is rather to establish the passage as a midrashic tradition based on Is. 14, the taunt-song against the king of Babylon.

    Charles would have liked to have rewritten 1 En. 46:4-8;[2] however, even though the textual tradition does not always seem satisfactory, it is possible to read the passage as it stands. Charles treats verse 5a as a dittography of verse 4a, although, at the same time, he recognizes that verse 5a is closer to Is. 14:9 than the clause to which he claims it is a dittography. He explains this relationship by arguing that the reference to Is. 14:9 is not original and that it has been allowed to corrupt the Enochic textual tradition. Since, however, there are other allusions to Is. 14 in 1 En. 46:4-8, it is more likely that verse 4a is an intentional allusion to Is. 14:9 and that verse 5a should also be treated as original. The term "couch," *meskābāt*, suggests Job 17:13, and there may be overtones of Job 17:14 in 1 En. 46:6.[3] In Job 17:13, the poet speaks of spreading his couch in Sheol; in Is. 14:9, the kings already in Sheol are raised up from their thrones, which they apparently occupy there, to greet the newly-fallen king of Babylon, and the freedom with which the verse is used in the Parables of Enoch is suggestive of the freedom with which the Qumran pesharim treat their texts.[4] 1 En. 46:4-5 makes excellent sense as it stands. The action in verse 4 is obviously physical in character--something is done to the kings and the mighty--while verse 5a is a metaphor for a political action and is thus not redundant.

    Charles argues that *yek^wĕnnenu* in 1 En. 46:7a reflects ידינו, "judge," which he claims is corrupt for either יורידו or יפילו, "cast down," and that the reference is to Dan. 8:10.[5] He therefore suggests that Dan. 8:10 be used to rewrite 1 En.

46:7a-c, eliminating verse 7b and the end of verse 7c as superfluous. Another solution would be to read $k^wannana$ as "rule," a frequent meaning, rather than "judge"--a solution that would reflect the intention ascribed to the king of Babylon in Is. 14:13-14 in setting his throne above the stars. It is possible, however, that "judge" is an acceptable translation. One of the functions of the messianic figure, the Elect one, in 1 En. 61:8-9 is to judge the host of heaven. In addition, Wsd. Sol. 6:1 speaks of kings, βασιλεῖς, and judges of the ends of the earth, δικασταὶ περάτων γῆς, in parallel in the midst of a passage that deals with the judgment of kings who do not acknowledge the source of their power and consequently do not govern their kingdoms according to the law of God. Another possible parallel is the reference in Diodorus Siculus 2. 31. 4 to the twenty-four stars that are the "judges of the universe" (δικασταὶ τῶν ὅλων). These stars, along with the Zodiac, make up a group known as the counseling gods (βουλαῖοι θεοί),[6] who oversee both the affairs of mankind and those of the heavens (cf. 2. 30. 6).

The reports concerning Gaius Caligula suggest that, in his masquerades as various of the gods, he may well have been described as one who judged the stars. The truth of all the reports, or the emperor's personal attitude or supposed madness, need not be an issue here, since it is the Jews' attitude, reflected in the reports of Philo[7] and Josephus,[8] toward the cult of the emperor during his reign and toward the reports of his actions that is relevant for an understanding of the Parables. The emperor is said to have assumed in public the costumes of various gods--and goddesses--and to have conversed with Jupiter in terms at times either threatening or condescending.[9] More to the point is his motive in building a bridge across the gulf of Baiae. As Lindsay comments:

> Clearly the building of the bridge of boats, across which Gaius crossed and recrossed for two days, had some deep symbolic value for him. The first day, riding a richly-caparisoned horse, he wore a crown of oak leaves and a cloak of cloth-of-gold; he carried a battle-axe, a Spanish buckler, and a sword. The second day, he drove a two-horsed chariot, attended by a young Parthian hostage named Dareios. He seems to be making a solar and world-conqueror masquerade. . . . We can perhaps connect

the episode also with his behaviour in the northern wars. He "presented the companions and sharers of his victory with crowns of a new form, with a new name, having Sun, Moon and Stars depicted on them, and which he called *Exploratoriae*". On the Atlantic coast he drew up his engines of war (as if meaning to attack the Ocean) and bade his men fill their helmets and clothes with shells as "the spoils of Ocean due to the Capitol and the Palatium". Perhaps the image of world-conqueror and ocean-tamer was for him merged with that of Aquarius.[10] The identification with Aquarius, a sign of the Zodiac, suggests that the term of Diodorus Siculus for the related twenty-four stars, the judges of the universe, might in fact have some bearing on the charge in 1 En. 46:7 of judging the stars of heaven. The crowns with the sun, moon, and stars on them also indicate that Gaius wanted to masquerade as the ruler of the host of heaven. The episode at the Atlantic suggests the charge against Antiochus Epiphanes in 2 Macc. 9:8, that he was arrogant enough to think that he could command the waves. Both examples might be part of some otherwise forgotten piece of royal ideology. The masquerades certainly suggest that Gaius wanted to be thought of as the ruler of more than the Roman empire, and their symbolism suggests that 1 En. 46:7 makes perfectly acceptable sense in charging the kings and mighty with judging the stars of heaven.

1 En. 46:7 seems to be an allusion to Is. 14:13-14 without, however, quoting the exact language of that text. This style is typical of the Parables, and it is pointless to attempt textual criticism of the work with the assumption that it should reflect the exact phraseology of scripture. In the ancient world, a throne was connected with the act of judgment; setting one's throne above the stars therefore could well imply judgment of the host of heaven. In addition, the divine title *le'ul*, "Most High," is rare in the Parables,[11] appearing otherwise only at 1 En. 60:1. It is possible that 1 En. 46:7b, "and lift up their hands against the Most High," is a reference to Is. 14:14b, "I shall make myself equal to the Most High" (cf. 1 En. 68:4, where a similar charge is made against the fallen angels). It is interesting to note that, not only did Gaius address Jupiter as brother, he also threatened to set up his own statue in the temple at

Jerusalem.[12] Each represents a claim of equality, or identity, with the divinity.

Charles has pointed out several scriptural references in 1 En. 46:5-6 that take on added significance in light of a current understanding of exegetical traditions in Judaism of the period. In verse 5 the kings and mighty are to be removed from their thrones because they do not glorify the Lord of Spirits and acknowledge that he is the source of their authority. In verse 6 they have obviously been consigned to Sheol, to a bed of worms. These details should be compared to Is. 14, where in verse 11 the king of Babylon is to be brought down to Sheol, where maggots will be his bed and worms his covering, because of his attempt to claim equality with God. The account of the fall of Antiochus Epiphanes in 2 Macc. 9:1-29 is modeled on Is. 14:4-21.[13] There Antiochus is said to believe that he could command the waves (cf. Job 38:8-11; Jer. 31:35), weigh the mountains (cf. Is. 40:12), and touch the stars (cf. Is. 14:13-14). In this symbolism, the claim of a king, who calls himself the "god manifest," to equality with God is obvious. He is said to be on his way to Palestine to take further vengeance on the Jews for their insolence when he is smitten with abdominal cramps. His body swarms with worms, and he dies confessing, "It is right to be subject to God, and no mortal should think that he is equal to God" (2. Macc. 9:12). The account, of course, represents a Jewish anti-royal polemic rather than a historical version of the death of the king. The account of the death of Agrippa I in Acts 12:20-23 is similar:[14] the king is acclaimed by the people as a god, whereupon he is smitten by an angel and dies, eaten by worms, because he failed to give the glory to God. The account in Josephus, *Ant.* 19. 343-52, is similar: Agrippa appears in a silver garment, which is apparently symbolic of divine splendor, the people acclaim him as a god, he is smitten by abdominal pains, and confesses that

> I, a god in your eyes, am now bidden to lay down my life, for fate brings immediate refutation of the lying words lately addressed to me. I, who was called immortal by you, am now under sentence of death. . . .[15]

The illness of the king is also an important motif in the pattern of exegesis of Is. 14. In 1 En. 62:4-5, the kings and mighty are seized with pain like that of a woman in labor when they see the Son of Man on his throne. While here the pain is specifically described in terms of Is. 13:8, the motif is probably based on Is. 14:10, where חלית has been interpreted as "you are made *sick*" rather than "you are made *weak*." The illness motif has been attached to the worm motif, and it is interesting to note that in the Apocalypse of Peter, the persecutors of the righteous have an undying worm to consume their entrails.[16] A reference to the worms of Is. 14:11 is found in 1 En. 46:6, and the next clause, "and they will not hope to rise from their beds," may be a reference to the illness motif (cf. 2 Macc 9:18).

The evidence indicates that Is. 14:4-21 formed the basis of an exegetical tradition directed against tyrants who claimed divinity for themselves--a tradition that is to be found in 1 En. 46:4-8; 62-63; 2 Macc. 9:1-29; Wsd. Sol. 4-5; Acts 12:20-23; Josephus, *Ant*. 19. 343-52; and Philo, *Leg*. 347. The elements of the tradition include (a) failure to recognize that God is the source of the king's authority, (b) seizure by abdominal pains and worms, and (c) confession by the king that God is the true source of his authority.

1 En. 48:8-10. The Parables returns to the kings and mighty in 1 En. 48:8-10, and again the way in which scripture is used is important:

(8) In those days the kings of the earth and the strong who occupy the land through the deeds of their hands **will be** *downcast of face*, because on the day of their *distress* **and** their *trouble* they will not [*be able to*] *deliver themselves*. (9) And I [God] **shall** deliver them into the *hands* of my elect ones; like *straw in a fire* thus will they burn *before the face of the holy ones*; like *lead in water* [thus] will they be swallowed up *before the face of the righteous ones*, and *no trace of them will be found*. (10) And on the day of their distress there will be *rest* upon the *earth*, and before them [the righteous] they will *prostrate* [themselves] and *not rise*,	Ex. 15:14-16
	Is. 13:7-8
	
	Is. 46:2; 47:14
	Ex. 14:26-27
	Ex. 15:7; Is. 47:14;
	  Mal. 4:1 (MT, 3:19)
	Ex. 14:30; Is. 66:24
	Ex. 15:10
	Ex. 14:30; Is. 66:24
	
	Ex. 14:13,28; Is. 26:14
	
	Is. 14:7!; 2 Sam. 7:11
	
	Ps. 36:12; 140:10;
	  Is. 26:14; 49:7,23;
	  Ex. 14:30

and there will be no one who will
grasp them with his hands and
raise them up, because they have
denied *the Lord* of Spirits *and*   Ps. 2:2
his Messiah, and blessed be the
name of the Lord of Spirits.

Hartman is responsible for the recognition of most of the above parallels to Exodus.[17] The passage is obviously a midrash based on Ex. 14-15 with allusions to a number of other passages including, notably, Is. 14:7. In this particular case, Pharaoh becomes the archetype of the tyrant who fails to recognize the power of God.

1 En. 48:8-10 is peculiar in that, while elsewhere in the Parables of Enoch the Elect *one*, the Son of Man, or the angels are responsible for the punishment of the kings and mighty,[18] here they are delivered into the *hands* of "the elect *ones*." This peculiarity is probably to be explained by reference to Ex. 14:26-27, where the sea is controlled by the *hand* of Moses. In 1 En. 48:10, *wa-ba-qedmēhomu yewaddequ* could equally well be translated "and they will fall before them" or "and they will prostrate [themselves] before them." The phrase seems to be a double reference to the Egyptian army sinking into the sea and to the act of proskynesis, in which one falls on his face before a king expecting to be grasped and raised by the right hand of the one who is the object of worship (cf. Is. 41:13; 42:6; and 45:1). The kings have no one who will extend the hand of mercy to them.

1 En. 53:1-7. The Parables returns to the fate of the kings and the mighty in 1 En. 53:1-7, the passage that leads into the first example of the Is. 24:17-23 midrash in 1 En. 54:1-56:4.

(1 En. 53:1) There my eyes saw a valley, deep with open mouths, and everyone who dwells upon land or sea or the islands was bringing gifts and presents and tribute to it, but that deep valley did not become filled. (2) And their hands continually commit crimes, and everything that they produce through crime the sinners devour.[19] And the sinners will be destroyed from before the Lord of Spirits, and from the face of his earth they will be banished. And they will be destroyed[20] for ever and ever. (3) For I saw all the angels of punishment dwelling and preparing all the instruments[21] of Satan. (4) And I asked the angel of peace who was accompanying me for whom they were preparing these instruments.[21] (5) And he said to me, "They are preparing these for

the kings and mighty of this earth that they might be
destroyed in this way." (6) And after this the Righteous and Elect one will reveal the house(s) of his
congregation; thereafter they will no longer be
hindered on account of the name of the Lord of Spirits.
(7) And these mountains [cf. 1 En. 52:6] will not
remain before his righteousness as the earth [remains],
and the hills will be like a fountain of water, and
the righteous will rest from the affliction of the
sinners.

Charles[22] has observed that 1 En. 53 is based on Joel 3(MT, 4), which itself seems related to Is. 2:2-3. The idea of tribute or gifts in 1 En. 53:1 is related to Joel 3:3-8, and the reference to the plundering of the temple in Joel 3:5 could be what lies behind the problematic 1 En. 53:2a. The reference to the deep valley in 1 En. 53:1 corresponds to the valley of Jehoshaphat, the valley of the judgment of Yahweh, in Joel 3:2, 12. The use of the passage from Joel was probably suggested by relating 1 En. 52:8-9, where the appearance of God on the day of judgment will cause all the metals to melt, making weapons of war useless, to Joel 3:10, which has been read in light of Is. 2:4.

There are other passages that are related to 1 En. 53. In Is. 66:20, the nations will return the exiled Israel- ites to Jerusalem as a gift or offering to Yahweh, and Ps. 76:11-12(MT, 12-13) mentions the bringing of gifts to Yahweh in the context of the punishment of the kings of the earth:

(11) Make and pay your vows to Yahweh your God,
let all those about him bring tribute to the
feared one.
(12) He humbles the spirit of princes,
a terror to the kings of the earth.

Ps. 68:28-31; 76:12-13; and Is. 18:7 are similar. 1 En. 53:7 returns to the theme of 52:6, and both passages have a fairly rich number of references behind them (cf. Mic. 1:4; Nahum 1:5; Ps. 68:2; 97:5; Zech. 13:9; Mal. 3:2-3; Ps. 78:69; Ko. 1:4; Is. 14:4-7; and 2 Sam. 7:11).

With the use of Ps. 68 and 76, the Parables has drawn upon scripture passages that speak of the subjugation of the kings of the earth to the rule of Yahweh; however, in 1 En. 53, as in Joel 3, the attempts of the kings or nations to appease God through tribute is unsuccessful.[23] In Joel, their failure is attributed to their participation in the exile of

the Jews; in 1 En. 53, they seem to have restrained in some
unspecified way the righteous from the practice of their religion (cf. verse 6). In 1 En. 53:6, Charles claims that the
phrase *bēta mesteguba'a zi'ahu*, "the house of his congregation,"[24] refers to the *synagogues* of the righteous rather
than the temple: cf. Ps. 74:8 and 1 En. 46:8 where *'abyāt*,
"houses," is in the plural in the same phrase, suggesting that
bēt, "house," in 1 En. 53:6 should also be read as a collective. Charles also relates 1 En. 53:6 to 38:1 and 62:8, which
refer to the "congregation of the righteous [or the elect]."[25]
If Charles's interpretation is correct, the reference may be
to the reign of Caligula, when Jewish synagogues in Alexandria
were destroyed or profaned in anti-Jewish pogroms.

It seems fair to conclude that 1 En. 53 uses an exegetical tradition based on Joel 3, which has been interpreted in
light of a number of other passages of scripture. The tradition, like Joel 3, seems to be directed against nations or
sinners (cf. 1 En. 53:1-2,7) and it is likely that the Parables
applies it more specifically to the kings and mighty (cf.
1 En. 53:5) in light of Ps. 68:29 and 76:11-12, which relate
similar traditions to kings.

*The polemic against the kings and mighty and the
Is. 24:17-23 midrash in the second parable.* The unsuccessful
attempt of the kings and the mighty in 1 En. 53 to appease
the Lord of Spirits through tribute leads to the judgment
and punishment of the kings and mighty, along with the host
of Asael, in 1 En. 54:1-56:4, which has been examined above
in chapter III. The connection may have been suggested by
Ps. 68:2 and 76:11-12. The "instruments of Satan" in 1 En.
53:3 are identified in 54:3,5 and 56:1 as iron or bronze
chains, whips, and jagged stones, and the Is. 24:17-23 midrash,
to which these instruments belong, is used to depict the scene
of punishment. The parallel valleys in 1 En. 53:1 and 54:1
suggest that the valley of Jehoshaphat in Joel 3:2,12 has
been connected with the place of imprisonment, the pit or
cistern, in the Is. 24:17-23 midrash.

The distinctiveness in the Parables of the exegetical
tradition behind 1 En. 54:1-56:4 and 64:1-68:1 is apparent
when it is recognized that the work is not primarily concerned

with the fall of heavenly beings.[26] The kings and mighty of
the earth are its major target, and its critique of its royal
and powerful enemies has led to a tradition, the Is. 24:17-23
midrash, that describes the punishment of kings in parallel
with that of heavenly beings. However, the distinctiveness
of the exegetical tradition in the Parables should not lead
necessarily to the conclusion that it represents an intrusive
literary source. It is one of several different traditional
units that carry a polemic against tyrants, and it appears
at an appropriate point in the second parable for a description
of the judgment and punishment of kings. The analysis of the
next chapter will suggest that, in the thematic structure of
the Parables, the use of the Is. 24:17-23 midrash represents
the use of an element from another pattern to elaborate or
ornament one of the basic themes of the pattern behind the
Parables.

The Third Parable: 1 En. 58-69

In general, the third parable of the Parables of Enoch
has been produced through expansion, elaboration, and combination of materials that appeared in the first two sections
of the work. In some cases, fuller versions of the underlying
exegetical traditions may have been used, while in others
there is a combination of traditions that appeared independently in the second parable. While there is a degree of linear
progression from the beginning to the end of the Parables,
in that the Son of Man is at first named and later revealed,[27]
the basic literary structure in the work is that of recapitulation or recurrence as each parable elaborates the themes
of the last in more detail.

1 En. 61:6-13. The enthronement of the Elect one in
1 En. 61:6-13 is based on the heavenly ascent of Enoch in 1 En.
39:3-14. The latter passage contains an allusion to the presence of the Elect one in the heavenly scenario (cf. 1 En.
39:6-7), an allusion that is expanded in 61:8-9 by use of
material relating to the Elect one found in 1 En. 45:3; 49:4;
and 55:4. In addition, both passages contain the heavenly
Qeduššah scene (cf. 1 En. 39:9-14 with 61:9c-12). The

heavenly ascent motif found in 1 En. 39:3-8 is absent from
61:6-13; however, 60:1-6,25 may have been intended to serve
that purpose in the third parable.[28]

1 En. 61:6-13 is the other passage in the Parables,
aside from the two examples of the Is. 24:17-23 midrash and the
angel lists, that suggests that evil has a cosmic dimension.
In 1 En. 61:8-9, the Elect one is to judge the heavenly host
(cf. 1 En. 55:4). The contrast with the kings and mighty, who,
in 1 En. 46:7, are said to judge the stars of heaven, may be
intentional. In any case, unlike the kings, the stars know
whom to glorify (cf. 1 En. 61:9). Aside from this possible
contrast, 1 En. 61:6-13 is not of direct importance for the
polemic against the kings and mighty; however, it is of importance in establishing the compositional technique of recapitulation that is used in subsequent chapters of the Parables.

1 En. 62-63. In 1 En. 62, the Parables returns immediately to the enthronement of the Elect one. The initial
enthronement of the Elect one in 1 En. 45:3 is followed immediately by the midrash on Dan. 7:9-14 in 1 En. 46:1-3. 1 En.
62 begins with the enthronement of the Elect one in verses 1-3;
however, in 1 En. 62:5-63:12 the Elect one is displaced by the
Son of Man. The juxtaposition of the two traditions in 1 En.
45-46 has led to their conflation in chapters 62-63.

Nickelsburg has already recognized the verbal similarities between 1 En. 46 and 62-63:

> Enoch 46 anticipates the judgment scene in chapters
> 62-63. The Head of Days is accompanied by the Son of Man,
> who is the divinely appointed instrument for the judgment
> of the kings and the mighty. The description of their
> deeds and their punishment has a number of verbal points
> of contact with Enoch 62-63. The kings and mighty have
> persecuted the righteous (46:8/62:11). They have failed
> to extol God and acknowledge him as the source of their
> power (46:5bc,6f/63:7ab). Their power resides in their
> ill-gotten riches (46:7e/63:10). The Son of Man will
> put down the countenance of the strong (46:6a/62:5c).
> They will be filled with shame (46:6b/62:10c). Darkness
> will be their dwelling (46:6c/62:10d).[29]

Nickelsburg argues that "The points of similarity strongly
suggest that chapters 46 and 62-63 contain variants of a common
tradition, although the precise relationship between the two
passages is not clear."[30]

Further examination, however, suggests that 1 En. 62-63 represents a blending and recapitulation of various traditional units used in the second parable. These materials include (1) the enthronement of the Elect one as judge based on Is. 42:1-4 and found in 1 En. 45:3; 49:4; and 55:4, (2) the Dan. 7:9-14 midrash from 1 En. 46:1-3, (3) the Is. 14 midrash from 1 En. 46:4-8, (4) the naming of the Son of Man, which is based on Is. 49[31] and found in 1 En. 48:2-7, and (5) the midrash on Ex. 14-15, which is found in 1 En. 48:8-10. Nickelsburg has demonstrated conclusively that the structure of 1 En. 62-63 is derived from an exegetical tradition based on the servant song in Is. 52-53, a tradition that also lies behind Wsd. Sol. 2 and 4-5.[32] The tradition deals with the exaltation of a righteous man, and the punishment of those who formerly persecuted him is depicted in terms of the Is. 14 midrash. Thus, the Is. 14 midrash was part of a larger traditional unit; however, it also seems to have been an independent unit, and its use in 1 En. 46:4-8 may be what led to the use of the larger unit in 62-63. Aside from this one previously existing association, the interweaving of the various traditions used in 62-63 seems to depend upon their juxtaposition in the second parable.

Of the above material, the one association with scripture that has not been examined in relation to 1 En. 62-63 by the previous discussion is the use of Ex. 14-15, which is probably second in importance only to the tradition dealing with the exaltation of a righteous man. 1 En. 62:4-5 is clearly a reference to Is. 13:7-8;[33] however, it is possible that Ex. 15:14-16 also lies behind it. Both passages possess a number of key words in common that could have led to their association:

 ימס, "melt,"[34] Is. 13:7/נמגו, "be disheartened," Ex. 15:15
 ונבהלו, "be terrified," Is. 13:8; Ex. 15:15
 יאחזון, "seize," Is. 13:8/אחז, Ex. 15:14, and יאחזמו, Ex. 15:15
 יחילון, "have labor pains," Is. 13:8/חיל, "labor pains," Ex. 15:14

Ps. 48:5-6 is similar. In addition, 1 En. 62:5c is a reference to 48:8a, which, in the context of a midrash on Ex. 14-15, is probably a reference to Ex. 15:15: נמגו is from מוג, "to melt," or, in the *nifʿal*, "to wave to and fro" or "to be disheartened." 1 En. 62:8a, where the congregation of the elect is sown, is a reference to Ex. 15:17 (cf. also Ps. 44:2 and 2 Sam. 7:10), where Israel is planted (נטע) on Mt. Zion. 1 En. 62:11 is a reference to 54:1-56:4, but it may also reflect Ps. 78:49, a psalm that is based on the Exodus tradition. 1 En. 62:12a, which suggests that the righteous will be spectators at the punishment of the kings and mighty, is a reference to Ex. 14:30-31, where Israel witnesses the destruction of the Egyptian army. 1 En. 62:12b is a reference to the Song of Moses in Ex. 15:1-18, from which several of the references here and in 1 En. 48:8-10 were taken. 1 En. 62:13 is a reference to Ex. 14:13: in both verses the salvation of the righteous is associated with the fact that they will never again see their enemies. In light of the close relationship of 1 En. 62 and the Exodus tradition, it is also possible that 1 En. 62:7 is not only a reference to the servant of Yahweh in Is. 49:1-2,8 but also is a reference to the period Moses spent in the land of Midian hidden from Pharaoh. Note that Moses is frequently called the servant of Yahweh in the Deuteronomistic literature (cf. Deut. 34:5; Jos. 1:13; 8:31,33; 11:12; 12:6; 13:8; 14:7; 18:7; 22:2,5; 2 Kings 18:12; Wsd. Sol. 18:21). It is apparent that, in returning to material already developed in earlier portions of the Parables--in this case, 1 En. 48:8-10--the Parables does not limit itself to the contents of the previous passages but draws heavily upon the exegetical traditions that lie behind them. In fact, it would be more accurate to say that the poet reuses the same exegetical traditions rather than refers specifically to the passages from the previous two parables.

It is thus apparent that the exegetical background to 1 En. 62-63 is extremely complex. Since the framework is determined by the exegetical tradition based on Is. 52-53, 1 En. 62-63 could be classified as a midrash in that it has a central and structural relationship to one passage of scripture; however, since the association of exegetical traditions within it seems to represent to a significant degree the concerns of the Parables of Enoch, the passage must be seen as at least a step removed from the traditional targumic exegesis. Closer examination of the passage might prove fruitful;

however, it is sufficient here to establish the compositional pattern of the third parable to set the stage for the use of the Is. 24:17-23 midrash in that section.

The polemic against the kings and mighty and the Is. 24:17-23 midrash in the third parable. In the second parable, 1 En. 53 deals with the judgment and punishment of the kings and mighty following their unsuccessful attempt to appease the Lord of Spirits through the gift of tribute. This motif gives rise to the use of the Is. 24:17-23 midrash in 1 En. 54:1-56:4. In the third parable, chapter 63 contains material that deals with the judgment of the kings and the mighty following their unsuccessful plea for mercy. This material likewise gives rise, beginning in 1 En. 64:1, to a second block of material that is based, first on the Is. 24:17-23 midrash, and second on the angel-list tradition. In addition, just as the two valleys in 1 En. 53:1 and 54:1 seem to be coordinated to form the connection between the material in chapter 53 and the Is. 24:17-23 midrash, in 1 En. 64:1-2 the place of punishment of the angels is related to that of the kings in the previous chapter: "And I saw other forms hiding *in this place*. I heard the voice of the angel saying, 'These are the angels who descended upon the earth and who revealed secrets to the children of men and led the children of men into error so that they sinned.'" *The two blocks of material in the Parables of Enoch dealing with the imprisonment and punishment of angelic beings in parallel with that of the kings and mighty of the earth appear at similar points in the structures of the second and third parables, and in both places they are integrated into the structure of the section by the same compositional technique, coordination of the place of punishment of the angels with that of the kings.* Thus, it is highly unlikely that they represent interpolations. They should, instead, be treated as integral parts of the Parables of Enoch.

The Role of the Is. 24:17-23 Midrash in the Parables of Enoch

An important question that remains to be answered is why use a tradition dealing with the punishment of angelic beings when elsewhere the Parables does not seem to be concerned with fallen angels but rather with tyrants? A comparison with an allusion to the battle of the Titans in Hellenistic Judaism throws some light on this problem. The Titans were gods, but their imprisonment in Tartarus can become a prototype for the punishment of wicked men. Wsd. Sol. 17:1-21 uses the myth in describing the death of the first-born from the Exodus tradition:

(1) Great are thy judgments and hard to describe;
therefore uninstructed souls have gone astray.
(2) For when lawless men supposed that they held the holy
   nation in their power,
they themselves lay *as captives of darkness and prisoners
   of long night*,
shut in under their roofs, exiles from eternal providence.
. . . .
(14) But throughout the night, which was really powerless,
and which beset them from the recesses of powerless Hades,
they all slept the same sleep,
(15) and now were driven by *monstrous specters*,
and now were paralyzed by their souls' surrender,
for sudden and unexpected fear overwhelmed them.
(16) And whoever was there *fell down*,
and thus was kept shut up in a prison not made of iron;
(17) for whether he was a farmer or a shepherd
or a workman who toiled in the wilderness,
he was seized, and endured the inescapable fate;
for with one chain of darkness they all were bound.
(18) Whether there came a whistling wind,
or a melodious sound of birds in wide-spreading branches,
or the rhythm of violently rushing water,
(19) *or the harsh crash of rocks hurled down*,
or the unseen running of leaping animals,
or the sound of the most savage roaring beasts,
or an echo thrown back from a hollow of the mountains,
it paralyzed them with terror.
(20) For the whole world was illumined with brilliant
light, and was engaged in unhindered work,
(21) while over those men alone heavy night was spread,
an image of the darkness that was destined to receive them;
but still heavier than darkness were they to themselves.

The italicized parts seem to be allusions to the defeat and imprisonment of the Titans in Tartarus by Cottus, Briareos, and Gyes, the "monstrous specters" of verse 15. The imagery depicts symbolically the state of the Egyptians during the visitation of the angel of death.

In a discussion of the use of Hellenistic mythological symbols in Jewish art of the period, Erwin Goodenough comes to the conclusion that it is the value of the symbol which is borrowed and often interpreted in light of the Jewish tradition:

If Orpheus became for Christians a symbol of Christ taming the passions, he probably had been Moses or David, or some other Jewish figure, doing this for Jews when portrayed in a synagogue. The *value*, we see, is meaning in the connotational or associational realm. This remains constant in the migration of a symbol. The new religion will give new explanations of the symbol, precise verbalizations in the vocabulary of its own literal thinking. The historian of symbols has, then, the double task of finding the basic, unchanging values, together with the ever changing verbal explanations given by each new religion in adopting the old symbols.[35]

Goodenough's remarks are basically concerned with the problem of syncretism and thus are more appropriate to the analysis of Wsd. Sol. 17 than of the Is. 24:17-23 midrash, although, as the analysis in chapter III above indicates, there is the possibility of syncretism in the latter traditional unit. The concept of the *value* of a motif, or the theme to which it is related, is applicable to the use of parallel motifs from different traditional patterns within the same religious tradition. It is also relevant to narrative as well as graphic art. The value of the myth of the Titans is the divine punishment of the rebel against divine authority, and it can be Judaized by reference to Is. 14:4-21 or 24:17-23. Alexandrian Jews, like the author of the Wisdom of Solomon, can allude to the myth of the Titans freely to speak of the divine punishment of those persecuting them. The Palestinian author of the Parables, on the other hand, uses a midrash on Is. 24:17-23 for the same purpose. It is the *value* of the tradition that is important and not the precise identity of motifs. The structural examination of the Parables in chapter VII below will show that the reference to the judgment of *men* in 1 En. 41:1 is thematically parallel to the motif of the judgment of the *host of heaven* in 61:6-11.

It is clear from the Targum to Is. 24:16c, which was examined above in chapter III, that the *value* of the Is. 24:17-23 midrash was the secret of the reward of the righteous and the punishment of the wicked. The structural analysis of the Parables below will show that these themes are two of the important themes of the work. In fact, Sjöberg considers them *the* two important themes of the Parables.[36] He uses this observation as an argument for rejecting the hypothetical Noachic materials as a part of the Parables of Enoch, apparently because he misreads the thematic importance of what can now be recognized as the Is. 24:17-23 midrash; however, in light of the understanding of the passage in the Targum, that midrash is clearly related to the themes of the Parables of Enoch. It functions as a similar motif with the same thematic value, and it is used to comment on or to ornament the anti-royal polemic in the work. Its use adds a cosmic dimension to the wickedness and punishment of the kings and mighty of the earth; however, it seems to have been used more for the purpose of irony than for the myth of the origin of evil that it provides. The kings and the mighty of the earth are the heavenly beings, at least in their own minds or official ideologies, who have brought evil upon the earth.

CHAPTER VII

THE PARABLES OF ENOCH AS AN ORAL COMPOSITION
AND AS A PSEUDEPIGRAPHON

Examination of the style and structure of the Parables of Enoch suggests that the work was produced through the use of the techniques of oral composition, although the precise "mechanics" of this process are impossible to determine. An argument on the basis of style for this conclusion can only be provisional, since the Ethiopic version is probably a second generation translation and, in the last analysis, the work is too short to establish the use of formulaic language in any detail.[1] The recurrence of patterns and of exegetical traditions in the three parables, a phenomenon that has received some discussion in chapter VI above, is consistent with an oral style of composition. The genre of the Parables, the *mašal*, is also an oral type. Finally, there are hints within the Parables itself that it was originally spoken rather than written. The study will begin with a discussion of possibilities for understanding the role of oral composition in Judaism of the Hellenistic period, and it is intended to lead toward a new understanding of the relation between tradition and composition in the literature of that era.

Tradition and Literature
in Ancient Judaism

One of the legacies of literary criticism in the study of the Pseudepigrapha is the assumption that the books represent written documents, and that scholars must concern themselves with discerning who copied from whom. A corollary of this assumption is the belief that every ancient Jewish library contained a copy of the authorized edition of every book previously written by a Jewish author: an obvious projection into the past of a modern system for the publishing and distribution of books. In addition, there seems to be a tendency to assume that the most important version of a tradition for the ancient Jewish writer would have been the written one. While these assumptions are less and less representative of current scholarship on the Pseudepigrapha, they die slowly. Form criticism seems to have made greater inroads in the examination of canonical writings than noncanonical ones. Perhaps the most important development in recent years in understanding the literature of the period has been the relation of the targums to the traditional patterns of exegesis of scripture in the period and the recognition that these patterns have had their impact on other Jewish literature from the Hellenistic and Roman periods.

On the other hand, in examining the role of tradition in Judaism, it would be equally misleading to apply uncritically what has been learned about oral tradition and composition in nonliterate societies. It is quite obvious that the writing of texts of various types held an important role at that time. Jewish culture of the period seems to be in a transitional stage in which written and oral forms of expression exist side by side and seem to have an impact on each other. What is needed is an understanding of the distinct characters of these two modes of communication and of types of interplay that might take place between them.

The best indication of the relationship between oral and written modes of communication in ancient Judaism seems to be found in Philo's description of the Essenes and Therapeutae:

> But the ethical part [of philosophy] they [the Essenes] study very industriously, taking for their trainers the laws of their fathers, which could not possibly have been conceived by the human soul without divine inspiration. In these *they are instructed at all other times, but particularly on the seventh days*. For that day has been set apart to be kept holy and on it they abstain from all other work and proceed to sacred spots which they call synagogues. There, arranged in rows according to their ages, the younger below the elder, they sit decorously as befits the occasion with attentive ears. *Then one takes the books and reads aloud and another of especial proficiency comes forward and expounds what is not understood. For most of their philosophical study takes the form of allegory, and in this they emulate the tradition of the past.*[2]
>
> In each house there is a consecrated room which is called a sanctuary or closet and closeted in this they [the Therapeutae] are initiated into the mysteries of the sanctified life. They take nothing into it, either drink or food or any other of the things necessary for the needs of the

body, *but laws and oracles delivered through the mouth of prophets, and psalms and anything else which fosters and perfects knowledge and piety.* . . . The interval between early morning and evening is spent entirely in spiritual exercise. *They read the Holy Scriptures and seek wisdom from their ancestral philosophy by taking it as an allegory, since they think that the words of the literal text are symbols of something whose hidden nature is revealed by studying the underlying meaning.*

They have also writings of men of old, the founders of their way of thinking, who left many memorials of the form used in allegorical interpretation and these they take as a kind of archetype and imitate the method in which this principle is carried out. And so they do not confine themselves to contemplation but also compose hymns and psalms to God in all sorts of metres and melodies which they write down with the rhythms necessarily made more solemn.

For six days they seek wisdom by themselves in solitude in the closets mentioned above, never passing the outside door of the house or even getting a distant view of it. But every seventh day they meet together as for a general assembly and sit in order according to their age in the proper attitude, with their hands inside the robe, the right hand between the breast and the chin and the left withdrawn along the flank. *Then the senior among them who also has the fullest knowledge of the doctrines which they profess comes forward and with visage and voice alike quiet and composed gives a well-reasoned and wise discourse.* He does not make an exhibition of clever rhetoric like the orators or sophists of to-day but follows careful examination by careful expression of the exact meaning of the thoughts, and this does not lodge just outside the ears of the audience but passes through the hearing into the soul and there stays securely. . . .[3]

But when the guests have laid themselves down arranged in rows, as I have described, and the attendants have taken their stand with everything in order ready for their ministry, *the President of the company*, when a general silence is established--here it may be asked when is there no silence--well at this point there is silence even more than before so that no one ventures to make a sound or breathe with more force than usual--amid this silence, I say, *he discusses some question arising in the Holy Scriptures or solves one that has been propounded by someone else.* In doing this he has no thought of making a display, for he has no ambition to get a reputation for clever oratory but desires to gain a closer insight into some particular matters and having gained it not to withhold it selfishly from those who if not so clear-sighted as he have at least a similar desire to learn. *His instruction proceeds in a leisurely manner; he lingers over it and spins it out with repetitions, thus permanently imprinting the thoughts in the souls of the hearers*, since if the speaker goes on descanting with breathless rapidity the mind of the hearers is unable to follow his language, loses ground and fails to arrive at apprehension of what is said. . . . *The*

> *exposition of the sacred scriptures treats the inner
> meaning conveyed in allegory.* For to these people the
> whole law book seems to resemble a living creature with
> the literal ordinances for its body and for its soul the
> invisible mind laid up in its wording. It is in this mind
> especially that the rational soul begins to contemplate
> the thing akin to itself and looking through the words as
> through a mirror beholds the marvellous beauties of the
> concepts, unfolds and removes the symbolic coverings and
> brings forth the thoughts and sets them bare to the light
> of day for those who need but a little reminding to enable
> them to discern the inward and hidden through the outward
> and visible. . . .[4]

Behind Philo's obvious attempts to make Judaism look good in the context of Hellenistic culture and to describe the form of scriptural interpretation of the Essenes and Therapeutae in terms of his own methods of allegory, it is possible to discern the *Sitz im Leben* of midrash, pesher, and targum, and it does not stretch the imagination too much to describe these genres as allegory. In contrasting the banquets of the Therapeutae to those of Socrates described by Plato, Philo comments:

> I will describe in contrast the festal meetings of those
> who have dedicated their own life and themselves to
> knowledge and the contemplation of the verities of nature,
> following the truly sacred instructions of the prophet
> Moses.[5]

This method of learning seems formally parallel to Greek παιδεία, as a comment by Scholes and Kellogg makes clear:

> As long as Homer remained the only teacher of every
> subject, allegorical interpretation of his "hidden
> meaning" was the only avenue open to philosophical
> speculation.[6]

They see allegory as the first means of interpretation of the mythic patterns of oral poetic narrative--Homer, or, in Philo's case, Moses--

> when oral poetic narrative breaks down with the advent
> of literacy in the modern sense, or as a result of some
> other kind of radical cultural differentiation.[7]

According to Wright,

> The purpose of the midrashic literature was to make the
> Bible relevant and meaningful, to interpret it and draw
> out from it all of the lessons contained therein.[8]

While midrash as a genre may not be identical with Philo's allegorical interpretation, the interpretive impulse is identical. To paraphrase Paul Ricoeur, historically speaking, allegory--or, one might add, midrash--has served as "a modality of hermeneutics" rather than "a spontaneous creation of signs."[9] The main difference lies in the specific tools and styles of interpretation that midrash and allegory bring to the task of Biblical exegesis.

The "writings of men of old,"[10] in Philo's description of the Therapeutae, undoubtedly should be understood to include apocalyptic texts and other pseudepigraphon. The term μνημεῖον, "memorial," might indicate what modern scholarship terms a *testament*; however, it more likely is broader in application. 1 En. 68:1 records how the Parables was passed from Enoch to Noah, an important element of most pseudepigrapha and a feature that is shared with the narrower category of *testament*.

In what way the sect *imitates* the ancient writings is not clear. The phrase μιμοῦνται τῆς προαιρέσεως τὸν τρόπον could be translated "imitate the manner of conduct." F. H. Colson's translation makes the imitation that of the allegorical method found in the writings.[11] The following sentence has ὥστε with the indicative, which indicates a result or strong conclusion derived from the preceding discussion:

ὥστε οὐ θεωροῦσι μόνον, ἀλλὰ καὶ ποιοῦσιν ᾄσματα καὶ ὕμνους εἰς τὸν θεὸν διὰ παντοίων μέτρων καὶ μελῶν, ἃ ῥυθμοῖς σεμνοτέροις ἀναγκαίως χαράττουσι.

The imitation of the writings of the ancients must therefore have something to do with the composition of hymns, a suggestion that reinforces Colson's translation of the previous sentence and indicates that the allegorical, or midrashic, method used in the archetypes is also used in the composition of hymns. The Qumran hymns, which reflect the exegesis of scripture, are an obvious example.

It is not clear what is implied by the distinction between the composition (ποιοῦσιν) of the hymns and writing them down (χαράττουσι). Hymns and psalms are oral genres and their composition on the basis of midrashic patterns could very well have been oral.[12] In addition, the dative of manner, ῥυθμοῖς σεμνοτέροις, with the comparative adjective implies a distinction between the manner of composition and the manner of writing of the hymns. It is possible that the dative means "with the rhythms more *stately*," suggesting that the imperfections of oral composition are corrected in recording the hymn. While this interpretation of the passage is by no means certain, it suggests an interplay between oral and written forms of communication that corresponds to the obvious presence of the "allegorical method," midrash or scriptural exegesis, in both. That this "allegory" is a traditional art is suggested by *Quod Omn. Prob.* 82: "For most of their philosphical study takes the form of allegory, and *in this they emulate the tradition of the past.*" The context of this remark is the description of the Sabbath sermon.

Philo's descriptions indicate that there are two sources of authority for the interpretation of scripture, the president of the company, who is most skilled in allegorical interpretation or midrash, and the writings of the ancients, who are termed "the founders of their way of thinking." Of the two, the relative space that Philo devotes to the former and the terms of respect in which he describes his skills of exposition suggest that the living interpreter, and consequently the oral tradition of interpretation, held the most authority. The freedom with which the Qumran pesharim handle the text of scripture is likewise indicative of the authority of the interpreter.[13] In Philo's description, the answers to questions that perplexed the members, who obviously had access to the books of the ancients, were referred to the president of the assembly in the context of the Sabbath exposition of scripture. It therefore seems likely that the composition of books like the Parables of Enoch, which are primarily concerned with the perplexities of the present situation, takes place *primarily* in interaction with tradition and the on-going discussion, which are under the authority of the present leader of the group to which the poet belongs, and *secondarily* in interaction with older writings. This would particularly be the case if the style of composition reflected a close relationship to the traditional interpretation of scripture.

The Editorial Framework of the Parables

While the three parables in the Parables of Enoch appear to be visions of Enoch, the name of the sage does not seem to be firmly established in the work as a whole. It appears once in the introduction at 1 En. 37:1; in 39:2, which seems to be an interpolation; in 60:1, where Charles has suggested that the name of Noah should appear instead;[14] and in the material in 65:1-68:1, where, in 68:1, it is reported that Enoch gave the book of the Parables, along with its interpretation, to Noah. In addition, 60:8 refers to Enoch, apparently, without mentioning his name, and chapters 70-71 are two appended accounts of Enoch's translation. At the end of the work, however, the sage's name appears only in an editorial comment in 1 En. 69:29: "This is the third parable of Enoch."

The structure of the Parables of Enoch is marked by an introduction to each of the three parables that, in each case, attempts to indicate the content or topic of that parable, and a conclusion that seems to sum up the work as a whole (cf. 1 En. 38:1-6; 39:2b; 45; 58; and 69:26-29). These passages represent distinct structural elements, and they are all poetic in style. Two major elements of the Parables of Enoch that identify the work as Enoch's vision are to be found in the prose introduction in chapter 37 and the prose account of his translation in chapter 70. Both of these passages lie outside of the chief structural elements of the Parables and are in a contrasting style to the introductions to the individual parables and to the conclusion.

The other major passage in the Parables that indicates a relation between the visions and the sage Enoch is 1 En. 65:1-68:1, part of the second example of the Is. 24:17-23 midrash. In this case, 1 En. 68:1 contains information designed to tell the reader how the work was preserved through transmission from Enoch to Noah. Again, the style of the passage contrasts with the major part of the Parables: it is prose, and it represents an account in which the speaker is Noah rather than Enoch.

1 En. 68:1 is important to the Parables in that it represents an essential element of a pseudepigraphon, the transmission of the writing from the ancient worthy to whom it is attributed through his son or grandson to the present day. This theme is related to 1 En. 37:2-3, which is a part of the introduction to the entire work. In addition, in 1 En. 37:1-5; 65:1-68:1; and 70:1-4, the text begins with the third

person singular and within a few verses changes to the first
person singular, a pattern that seems to represent a compositional peculiarity of the editor of the work. It therefore
seems likely that 1 En. 37:1-5; parts of 65:1-68:1; and 70:1-4
represent a second structural element that has been imposed
upon an earlier one, the three parable structure. This element
is important to the nature of the present literary type of the
work, a pseudepigraphon. In these three passages the reader
is informed that the three parables represent visions of Enoch,
and that he passed them along to his "grandson" Noah before
his final translation. *However, if this secondary structure
is what makes the Parables a pseudepigraphon, it may not have
been one prior to the imposition of that structure, particularly since the name of Enoch is associated with the editorial
material.*[15] It is therefore possible that the double structure
of this work has resulted from a change in the basic nature
of the material: from an account of visions with a midrashic
content, produced, as it will be shortly argued, through the
techniques of oral composition, to a written pseudepigraphon.
This conclusion suggests that traditional material in a pseudepigraphon may be organized around other centers than the name
of a particular sage at the traditional level and that the
composition of a pseudepigraphon using traditional material
involves a change in the literary character of that material,
a change that may result in the fusion of originally distinct
structural elements.

  Part of the editorial work needed to transform the
three parables into a pseudepigraphon seems to have taken place
in 1 En. 65:1-68:1, part of the second example of the Is.
24:17-23 midrash in the Parables. While this material is
essential to the structure of the third parable, it would also
appear that part of it has been elaborated in the development
of the work as a pseudepigraphon to explain how the writing was
transmitted from Enoch to Noah and thence to the present day.

  1 En. 68:1 is the basic element of the transmission
motif. It also interrupts the orderly transition of 1 En.
67:12-69:1. 1 En. 68:2-5 is a heavenly monologue of Michael
"answering" Raphael concerning the punishment of the angels.
While it represents a distinct unit following 67:13, it seems

to have been suggested by Michael's speech in 67:12-13. In
this context, 68:1 is obviously intrusive.

1 En. 68:1, however, is related to the narrative in
65:1-66:3, where Noah is distressed by the tottering of the
earth and goes to the ends of the earth to inquire of Enoch
the reason for the disturbance. 1 En. 67:1-3 has a different
tradition that has God himself inform Noah of the coming flood.
This latter passage is a midrash on the flood narrative in
Genesis, like 1 En. 54:7-55:2 in the corresponding section
of the first example of the Is. 24:17-23 midrash.

Since 1 En. 65:1-66:3 is related to 68:1 and serves
to put Noah into contact with Enoch in order to explain the
transmission of the text, it must be seen as serving an
editorial function in the Parables. The passage, however, is
a complex unit, and it requires further examination.[16] It has
two basic structural elements. First, there is a narrative
structure in which Noah, in response to a strange event, goes
to the ends of the earth to seek an answer from Enoch.[17] This
structure is also found in 1 En. 106-7 and in the parallel
version of the birth of Noah in the Genesis Apocryphon in
which Methuselah goes to the ends of the earth to inquire of
Enoch concerning the birth of this strange baby. The narrative
pattern, however, is much older, being found in the *Gilgamesh
Epic* and the *Odyssey*, and since 1 En. 65-66 is not concerned
with the birth of Noah, it does not seem likely that it is
dependent on 1 En. 106-7 or the Genesis Apocryphon. A distinct
variant of this pattern in 1 En. 83:3-11 has Enoch turn to
his grandfather for the interpretation of a dream in which
the earth is swallowed by the abyss.[18] Second, Noah responds
to Enoch's appearance with the act of proskynesis. In 1 En.
65:4, he falls on his face, and in 65:9, Enoch raises him up
and places him on his feet. Proskynesis is the appropriate
response to a manifestation of divine or royal splendor and is
found in prophetic calls (Ezek. 1:28-2:1), revelatory scenes
(Dan. 8:18 and 10:9-10), and heavenly ascents (1 En. 14:24-
15:1).[19] The fact that it represents a distinct structural
element in 1 En. 65-66 is demonstrated by its absence from the
parallels to the journey motif listed above. Its presence in
1 En. 65, where the act honors Enoch, suggests that for the

group in which the Parables is produced the sage is considered
an important heavenly being, a reflection, perhaps, of the
apparent role of Enoch in chapter 71.

If these two structural elements are observed, some
order can be restored to 1 En. 65-66. First, it is obvious
that 1 En. 65:3 belongs after verse 5. Noah is disturbed by
the commotion of the earth; he goes to the ends of the earth
and calls on Enoch. It would make more sense if the question
in verse 3 were a response to Enoch's appearance and question
in verse 5. Second, 1 En. 65:6-8 seems to be intrusive in
its present context. The response to Noah's question in verse
3 comes in verse 9. There Enoch lifts up Noah in response
to the proskynesis in verse 4 and sends him on his way
with an answer to his question (1 En. 65:10-66:3). From the
standpoint of form criticism, the revelation, call, or answer
should come after the prophet or seer has been raised to his
feet (cf. Ezek. 2:1-7; Dan. 8:18-26; 10:10-14; 1 En. 14:25-
16:4; 60:4-6; and 2 En. 22:5-23:6). The answer in 1 En. 65:6-8
comes before Noah is raised to his feet; it has no element in
it that would fit it into the interchange between Noah and
Enoch; and it repeats material that is found later in 1 En.
65:10-11, which *is* tied into the structure of the passage. In
addition, like 1 En. 67:1-3, 65:6-8 does not use the usual
formula titles found in the Parables, and like both 67:1-3 and
54:7-55:2, it is concerned with the inhabitants of the earth
rather than with kings and angels. It therefore seems possible
that 1 En. 65:6-8 is part of the midrash on Genesis found in
1 En. 67:1-3 and is therefore part of the original version of
the Is. 24:17-23 midrash in 1 En. 64:1-68:1. This version of
the midrash should be seen as belonging to the third parable
prior to the transformation of the work into a pseudepigraphon,
and it would have included 1 En. 64:1-2; 65:6-8; and 67:1-13.

The remainder of the passage, 1 En. 65:1-5,9-12;
66:1-3; and 68:1, should be seen as a further elaboration of
the flood motif of the Is. 24:17-23 midrash in 1 En. 64:1-68:1.
Its purpose would be to place Enoch in contact with Noah and
explain how the writing was transmitted. It even implicitly
admits its editorial role by describing the transmission of a
book of which it is a part. It would be a mistake, however,

to term this material an interpolation. It is itself based, at least in part, on traditional materials; it fits properly into the thematic structure of the third parable in so far as it represents an elaboration of the flood tradition in the central portion of the Is. 24:17-23 midrash; and it was properly composed in that position in the editorial process that transformed the three parables into a pseudepigraphon. The editor seems to be conscious of the structure of the work and must, therefore, have been associated in some way with the composition of the three parables; however, in making Noah the speaker in a work attributed to Enoch, he has not shown the greatest possible degree of skill in composition.

The Three Parables as an Oral Composition: Formulas and Formulaic Language

The basic identification of oral composition is the presence of formulas and formulaic language, the building blocks of oral poetry. The performer uses a standardized pattern of speech that allows the rapid composition of verses according to a general pattern that dictates the traditional development of the material.[20] In the case of the Parables of Enoch, the sample is not extensive enough to produce sufficient evidence for a positive identification; therefore, only a provisional identification can be made. A second problem is the likelihood that the work is a second generation translation of the original Hebrew or Aramaic, making it impossible to identify metrical patterns associated with the use of formulaic language. In spite of these difficulties, some suggestions can be made concerning the presence of formulas and formulaic language in the Parables.

Formulas. The work is noted for its highly standardized and sometimes peculiar names and epithets, which are heavily used throughout the work. These include "Lord of Spirits," "Head of Days," "the Elect one," "that Son of Man," "the kings and mighty of the earth," and "the throne of his glory." "The Lord of Spirits" and "Head of Days" are particularly interesting. Both are designations for God based on a particular passage of scripture, but in each case the epithet is not identical with the original. The former is almost the exclusive term for God in the Parables,[21] while the latter is used as the result of the introduction of an exegetical tradition based on Dan. 7:9-14. "Lord of Spirits" is derived from יהוה צבאות of Is. 6:3 (cf. 1 En. 39:12), and "Head of Days" is from עתיק יומין of Dan. 7:9 (cf. 1 En. 46:1). One should assume that the poet was familiar with the original versions and that the alternates were used as the result of theological or traditional development; however, the poverty of other terms for God suggests that these have become formulas that fit the speech of the poet. It has already been noted that the Parables tends to allude to scripture rather than to quote it,[22] a detail suggestive of the presence of formulaic language, and the two peculiar divine titles may well fit into this tendency to fit the ideas of scripture into the standardized language of a particular group or poet.

Aside from the title formulas, there are other standardized phrases that appear. One is expected to "give thanks [or bless] and praise and exalt" in response to the manifestation of divine glory (cf. 1 En. 39:9-10; 47:2; 48:5; 61:7,9,12; 62:6; 63:2; 69:24,26; 71:11). The kings and mighty of the earth, or the sinners, have "denied the name of the Lord of Spirits" (cf. 1 En. 38:2; 41:2; 45:2; 46:7; 48:10; 63:7; 67:8,10). Because of this offense, and others, they are to be driven "from the face of the earth" (cf. 1 En. 38:1; 45:6; and 53:2).

Formulaic language. The Parables show some evidence of formulaic language, a technique of oral composition that involves a formula that can be combined with a number of different subjects or predicates to form a complete metrical unit. "To deny the name of the Lord of Spirits," mentioned above, seems to be such a unit. The full clause appears only when it seems to form one full line of poetry or when it is used in prose. In 1 En. 38:2, it has been shortened to form a new unit: "And where [will be] the place of rest of those who denied the Lord of Spirits?" A similar transformation is found in 1 En. 48:10: "Because they denied the Lord of Spirits and his Messiah." In each case, ". . . the name of . . ." has been omitted to allow a measure to be attached to either the beginning or the end of the line. "The name of the Lord of Spirits" can also be used with other verbs as in 1 En. 39:9; 47:2; 61:9; 63:7; and 69:24. The other formula listed above, ". . . from the face of the earth," is used with three different verbs.

The following examples become more problematic thanks to the uncertainties introduced by working with a translation, but each case seems to have some sort of formulaic pattern behind it. One example is the question and answer formula in the Parables of Enoch. It has two basic patterns, which, in the past, have given rise to source theories that Sjöberg has successfully rejected.[23] The formula appears in prose,[24] with one exception, and the form used seems to be dictated by the length of the question or answer that follows.

1. *wa-tas'elkwo la-mal'ak sa-yaḥawwer mesléya wa-k^{w}elo ḫebu'āta sa-yāre'eyani. . .*
   And I asked the angel who was accompanying me and revealing every secret to me. . .
2. *wa-tas'elkwo la-mal'aka salām sa-yaḥawwer mesléya. . .*
   And I asked the angel of peace who was accompanying me. . .

The first version is found in 1 En. 40:2; 43:3; 46:2; 52:3; and 61:3. The second one is found in 1 En. 40:8; 52:5; 53:4; 54:4; 56:2; and 60:24. There are variations, but the forms of the two versions given above seem to represent the essential patterns. The first and longer version seems to be used with shorter questions. The second is used with longer questions, so it has been shortened, but an extra word has been added to modify "angel."

Another formulaic pattern may lie behind 1 En. 56:4 and 58:3:

(1 En. 56:4)

wa-yetwēddā' ʿelata ḥeywatomu,
wa-ʿelata seḥtatomu 'emye'zē 'i-teth^{w}ēllaq^w.
And ended will be the days of their lives,
And the days of their sin thenceforth will not be numbered.

(1 En. 58:3)

wa-māḫlaqta 'albotu mawāʿla ḥeywatomu,
wa-[la-]qedusān ḫ^{w}alq^{w}a mawāʿel 'albomu.
And there will be no end to the days of their lives,
And for the holy there will be no enumeration of days.

It seems possible that the chiasmus present in 1 En. 56:4--

with "days of their lives" at the end of the first unit and "days of their sin" at the beginning of the next--has been destroyed in 58:3 in the process of translation. If so, the second line of 58:3 should read: *wa-mawāʿla qedusān ḫʷalqʷa ʾalbomu*, "And the days of the holy will have no enumeration." The implication of the two passages seems to be that, at the eschaton, the days of the sinners will *cease to be counted* while the days of the righteous will be *countless* (cf. 1 En. 58:6). Although the translation makes it difficult to determine the original with any precision, some formulaic expression seems to be present, an expression that can be applied with slight alteration to either the sinners or the holy ones.

Another type of formulaic language in the Parables of Enoch is to be found in the continuation of the older Semitic poetic style based on parallelism of line and thought.[25] This style is based on the use of pairs of words that are derived from traditional patterns of association. These pairs serve as the building blocks of couplets. One such pattern, which has its roots in older Hebraic usage, can be discerned in 1 En. 38:2:

> Where [will be] the dwellings [*maḥāder*] of the sinners?
> And where the place of rest [*meʿrāf*] of those who denied the Lord of Spirits?

In Ps. 132:7-8, the same parallel is represented by משכן and מנוחה and in 132:14 by מנוחה and the verb ישב. In the latter case, *māḥdar* and *meʿrāf* are the Ethiopic equivalents in that version of the Psalms, according to the citations in Dillmann's *Lexicon*. A similar pattern is found in 1 En. 39:4-5:

> And there I saw another vision: the dwellings [*maḥāder*] of the holy [*qedusān*],
> And the couches [*meskābāt*] of the righteous [*ṣādqān*].
> And there my eyes saw their dwelling [*māḥdar*] with his righteous angels [*malāʾekta ṣedqu*],
> And their couch [*meskāb*] with the holy ones [*qedusān*].

These two distichs contain a triple parallelism: (1) "dwellings"//"couches," (2) "righteous"//"holy," and (3) the larger parallelism between the two couplets that plays on the double meaning of "righteous ones" and "holy ones." Examples of the first pair can be found in scripture. In Ps. 132:3, אהל בית and ערש יצוע are paired; in Job 17:13, בית and יצוע are paired; and in Gen. 49:4, משכב and יצוע are parallels. A comparison with the scriptural references in each case suggests that the pairs in 1 En. 38:2 and 39:4-5 are the result of traditional word associations rather than of midrashic interpretation of those passages of scripture.

The possible examples of formulaic language given are fairly rudimentary, and the difficulties in such an examination presented by the translation are obvious; however, between the marked use of formulas for titles and epithets and the possibilities suggested by these examples, the stylistic evidence seems to be consistent with oral composition.

Poetry and prose. The recognition of the poetic character of much of the Parables of Enoch, which has been assumed above, must be attributed to Charles.[26] Unfortunately, he does not seem to have published an analysis of it. The poetic mode points toward a connection with oral literature, although it is not in and of itself definitive of it.

It is interesting to note that at times poetic passages in the Parables seem to be summarized in prose. 1 En. 69:22-24 is clearly a prose summary of part of the oath tradition in 1 En. 69:13-25. The continuation of the list of natural phenomena and their response to the divine power contained in the oath certainly must have been spelled out in the same style as 1 En. 69:16-21 in its original form. At other points in astronomical and narrative passages the text breaks into poetry, suggesting that the poetic elements may have been more extensive in the original form of the material (cf. 1 En. 41:7-8; 53:2,7; 56:4; 60:3; 65:12). Other prose passages seem to represent transitional material designed to link midrashic traditions, which are generally given in a poetic style[27] (cf. 1 En. 46:2; 52:1-5; 53:1; 61:1-2,6; 62:1,6; 63:1,10,12; 71:12). In other cases, the original tradition may have been in prose. Both of the heavenly *Qeduššah* passages, 1 En. 39:9-14 and 61:10-11, interrupt a poetic context with prose.

Structure and Oral Composition

In addition to the characteristic patterns of formulaic speech, oral composition is characterized by the use of patterns that serve as blueprints from which the composition is reconstructed each time the work is performed, or when the techniques of oral composition are used in the dictation or,

perhaps, in the written composition of a work. These patterns
are open to expansion, contraction, or alteration as the moment
demands, and they may be ornamented through the use of traditional lists or the introduction of similar motifs from other
patterns.[28] While it is not possible to examine in detail the
question of structure in the Parables as a whole, a glance at
the question of structure is helpful in the discussion of the
relation of the work to tradition.

Ideally, to analyze the structure of a work of oral
literature, one should have several different realizations of
the traditional pattern. There is only one version of the
Parables of Enoch; however, *the analysis in chapter VI above of
the role of the anti-royal polemic in the work has suggested
that a recurrence of pattern and content from parable to
parable is to be found in the Parables.* In the second and
third parables, the Is. 24:17-23 midrash is introduced at the
same point in the thematic progression of the units, and the
midrashic material used in the first two parables is recapitulated and intertwined in the third. Thus, the three parables
themselves make up in part for the lack of directly comparable
material elsewhere.

*The key to a structural analysis of the Parables of
Enoch is to be found in 1 En. 41:1-2 in a summary of things
that Enoch sees in his heavenly ascent, a summary that can
be directly compared to the order of 1 En. 60-63:*

(41:1) And afterward, I saw all the secrets of the heavens,	*1 En. 60:7-24*
and the kingdom, how it will be divided,	*1 En. 61:1-5;* cf. Ezek. 40-48, where the temple and land are measured; Is. 34:17; and Zech. 1:14-17 and 2:1-5 (MT, 2:5-9)
and the deeds of mankind, how they will be weighed with a balance.	*1 En. 61:6-11;* cf. especially 61:8
(2) And there I saw the dwellings of the elect, and the dwellings of the holy,	*1 En. 61:12-13;* cf. also 61:4 and 62:13-16 (see especially 61:12c)

and my eyes saw all the
sinners, who deny the name
of the Lord of Spirits,
being driven from there, and
they will be dragged [away],
and they will have no per-
sistence [wa-qawima ʾalbomu],
on account of the punish-
ment that will come forth
from the Lord of Spirits.

1 En. 62:1-63:12

The initial element of this pattern is to be found in the heavenly ascent and vision of the heavenly court in 1 En. 39:3-40:10, which corresponds to 60:1-6,25.

The comparison of 1 En. 41:1-2 and 60:1-63:12 yields the following thematic pattern:
1. the vision of the heavenly court
2. the secrets of the heavens
3. the division of the kingdom
4. the judgment of mankind (or the host of heaven)
5. the reward of the righteous
6. the punishment of the wicked

The heavenly ascent is associated with the vision of the heavenly court only in the first parable, probably due to the need of only one ascent in an apocalypse. The messianic motifs related to the Elect one and the Son of Man turn out to be subsidiary to at least four of the six themes. The Elect one is seen in the initial vision of the heavenly court in 1 En. 39:6-7, and as the work progresses, messianic material is related to the judgment, reward, and punishment themes. As it turns out, the messianic motifs represent a thread running through the whole work rather than a part of any one theme, although further examination might suggest that individual messianic motifs have associations with particular themes.[29]

It is more difficult to trace this particular pattern in the second parable. With the possible exception of the division of the kingdom,[30] the thematic elements are present, but there are several alternations between the various themes in chapters 46-53.[31] It is significant, however, that much of the midrashic material used in the alternations of the second parable is integrated into the pattern of 1 En. 41:1-2 in chapters 60-63. The way in which these traditions have been integrated in the third parable has been examined in chapter VI above. What seems to have happened in the composition of the work is that midrashic material appropriate to the themes has been *educed* in the second parable and subsequently *organized* into the thematic pattern in the third. A musical analogy best describes the compositional process: the themes are stated in the first parable, they are developed through the use of midrashic material in the second, and in the third they are recapitulated. This analysis suggests that there are two sets of structures of importance for the three parables: the thematic pattern used to construct the units and the midrashic patterns used in their construction. The latter may or may not have been associated prior to their use in the Parables.

    The following outline is a tentative analysis of the structure of the Parables based on the analysis above of the thematic pattern:

```
Introduction (1 En. 37)
First Parable (38-44)
   Introduction (38:1-39:2)
   Heavenly ascent (39:3-14)
      vision of the Elect one
      Qeduššah
   Vision of the heavenly court (40:1-10)
      the four archangels and their functions
   Thematic pattern summary (1 En. 41:1-2)
      the secrets of the heavens
      the division of the kingdom
      the judgment of mankind
      the dwellings of the righteous
      the punishment of the wicked
   The secrets of the heavens (41:3-9)
   Wisdom song (42)
      Wisdom's place before the throne
   The secrets of the heavens (43-44)
Second Parable (45-57)
   Introduction (45)
      mention of the Elect one
   The punishment of the kings and mighty (46)
      introduction of the Son of Man
   Vision of the heavenly court (47)
      the prayer of the righteous ascends
      the praises of the heavenly host
      the Head of Days is seated upon the throne
   The punishment of the kings and mighty (48)
      the naming of the Son of Man
      the kings and mighty repent to no avail
   The judgment of the wicked (49)
      the place of the Elect one before the throne
   The reward of the righteous (50-51)
      the Elect one is seated upon the throne
   The secrets of the heavens (52)
```

The punishment of the kings (53)
    they attempt to repent by bringing gifts to the valley
        of judgment
The Is. 24:17-23 midrash (1 En. 54:1-56:4)
    the punishment of the kings and the angels
    the flood motif
    the Elect one is seated on the throne to judge the
        hosts of Asael
Invasion of the Parthians and Medes (56:5-8)
Return from the Diaspora (57)
Third parable (58:1-69:25)
    Introduction (58)
    The secrets of the heavens (59)
    Vision of the heavenly court (60:1-6,25)
    The secrets of the heavens (60:7-24)
    The division of the kingdom (61:1-5)
    The judgment of the host of heaven (61:6-11)
        the Elect one is seated on the throne
            Qeduššah
    The reward of the righteous (61:12-13)
    The punishment of the kings and mighty (62:1-63:12)
        the Elect one/Son of Man is seated on the throne
        the kings repent to no avail
    The Is. 24:17-23 midrash (64:1-68:1)
    Brief vision of the heavenly court (68:2-69:1)
    The lists of fallen angels (69:2-12)
    The secrets of the heavens (69:13-25)
        the cosmological oath
Conclusion (69:26-29)
Translation of Enoch to heaven (70)
Revelation of Enoch as Son of Man (71)

The identifications in the second parable are based on a comparison of the midrashic material related to the pattern in chapters 60-63 with its source in the second parable. 1 En. 62:1-63:12, where the theme of punishment is found, draws upon midrashic material found in chapters 46, 48, and possibly 53. On the other hand, 1 En. 61:6-11, where the theme of judgment is found, draws upon material found in 39:6-7,9-14; 49:1-4; 51:1-5; and 55:4. To a modern eye, the distinction between the judgment and punishment themes seems unclear, since the latter also seems to involve judgment; however, it was apparently clear to the poet, since he associates different sets of traditional material with each theme.

One possible rationale behind the way in which the units in the second parable are ordered is their relationship to messianic motifs, which are probably the major *linear* element in the Parables.[32] The Elect one is first seen in the first parable (chapter 39), in the second parable he takes his place before the throne (chapter 49, cf. Wisdom in chapter 42) and then is seated on the throne in chapter 51. In chapter 55, he is seated on the throne to judge Asael and his host. Finally, in the third parable (chapter 61), he is seated on the throne to judge the host of heaven in a context very much like his first appearance in chapter 39.[33] The Son of Man, on the other hand, is first seen in the second parable in chapter 46 and then is "named" in chapter 48. The two messianic titles are finally identified in chapter 62, and in 1 En. 62:5 and 69:27 it is the Son of Man who is seated on the throne as judge. The seating of the Head of Days on the throne in 1 En. 47:3 is probably also an important part of this development. Much of the alternation of the themes of judgment and punishment in chapters 46-53 seems to be taken up with the development of the messianic motifs, which, therefore, should probably be seen as the rationale behind the order of the second parable. It is difficult to determine whether the messianic development achieved by the end of the third parable represents a new creation with the composition of the Parables or whether the awareness preserved in the Parables of the distinct exegetical basis of this development reflects the development of thought prior to the composition of the work. Given the traditional nature of the materials and patterns used in the composition of the work, the latter is probably the case, and, if so, it affords an interesting parallel to the development of Christology in early Christianity through the combination of exegetical traditions.[34]

While the linear element in the Parables may have provided a reason for producing three parables rather than one, the recurrence of pattern and content predominates and is the prime evidence for the use of the techniques of oral composition in the Parables. Northrop Frye uses the concept of recurrence as a central characteristic of what he terms *epos*, or the "genre of the spoken word and listener."[35] While he relates recurrence to "the regular pulsating metre that traditionally distinguishes verse from prose,"[36] the concept also seems valid at the level of structure. The recurrence of motifs, themes, and patterns in the Parables, as well as the possible presence of oral formulaic language, points toward a type of literature at home in the relationship between speaker and listener.

Ornamentation: Lists and Similar Themes from Others Patterns

The lists of fallen angels. Lord, in his study of Yugoslav singers of heroic tales, comments that lists are frequently used as ornamentation by any good oral poet to expand his narrative.[37] Such lists are not part of the basic thematic pattern of the poem, nor are they derived from written versions of the poems where these exist. They are, rather, conventionalized lists upon which a poet draws for a number of different purposes: to list the guests at a wedding or the heroes going off to battle. The singer will supply his own version of the list rather than memorize a version found in a written copy of the poem, or of a similar poem.

In the Parables, it is not as easy to demonstrate, on the basis of the material itself, that the lists of fallen angels in 1 En. 69:2-12 are dependent on tradition rather than directly on 1 En. 6-11 as it is to demonstrate that the Is. 24:17-23 midrash is dependent on tradition. In the latter case, the structure of the midrash was not preserved by 1 En. 6-11, and the presence of the two examples in the Parables must therefore have been derived from tradition. Aside from the divergence of the second list, however, the case for the lists of fallen angels is not as clear. On the basis of the comparative material derived from Lord's work, the lists should be treated as ornamentation derived from the poet's tradition. Josephus makes it clear that sectarian Judaism would have been concerned with the preservation of the names of the angels,[38] and it is more likely that these names were part of the oral lore of the sects. The situation of the angel lists is similar to the lists of ships in Homer, which scholars in the past have attempted to relate to written sources but which are more likely part of the traditional repertoire of the poets who produced the epics.[39]

The Is. 24:17-23 midrash. An oral composition may also be ornamented by use of an element of a different pattern that is similar to one of the elements of the work or performance

at hand.[40] The use of the Is. 24:17-23 midrash in the second
and third parables should be treated as such an ornament. It
is significant that, in the third parable, the poet turns to
the midrash at the point where the pattern common to 1 En.
41:1-2 and chapters 60-63 ends. The transition to the midrash
in both 1 En. 54:1 and 64:1-2, where the place of punishment
of the kings and mighty is related to that of the fallen
angels, is also indicative of the introduction of an ornamental
motif. The general lack of concern in the rest of the Parables
with the introduction of evil by, and the punishment of, angelic beings indicates that these motifs are not part of the thematic structure that lies behind the Parables but are used
because they in some way illuminate one of the themes of that
pattern.

The Genre of the Parables of Enoch

The question of the genre of the Parables of Enoch is
also relevant to the discussion of the work as an example of
oral composition. It could be classified as both apocalypse
and pseudepigraphon, but these categories are too broad to
serve as a designation of genre,[41] and they apply to the
written form of the work rather than to the three parables.
The work terms itself the "book of the parables," *maṣḥaf
za-mesālē*, in 1 En. 68:1 (cf. 37:5) suggesting that the genre
mašal might be an appropriate classification. However, the
work is obviously not a *mašal* in the sense of a proverbial
saying, nor is it a parable in the sense of most of the
parables of Jesus. Fortunately, the Old Testament does not
limit the use of the term *mašal* to short proverbs; a number of
longer compositions are so designated, compositions that are
relevant to the determination of the genre of the three
parables.

Among these examples are Ps. 49 and 78, both of which
should be classified as examples of oral composition. Ps.
49:4(MT, 5) is instructive here:

אטה למשל אזני אפתח בכנור חידתי:

    I will incline my ear to a proverb;
    I will solve my riddle with the zither.

The *kinnor*,[42] or zither, seems to have been a widely-known instrument in the ancient world: cf. Hittite, *kinirri[laš]*, and Sanskrit, *kinarī*. KB suggests a two to four stringed instrument, which seems similar to the *tambura*, one of the instruments used to accompany Yugoslav heroic songs.[43] In any case, it is clear that Ps. 49 belongs to an oral type of literature, termed a משל or חידה--these words also appear in parallel in Ps. 78:2; Prov. 1:6; Ezek. 17:2; and Sir. 47:17, and in the last case שיר is also a parallel--and that this type of literature could be performed to the accompaniment of the *kinnor*.

Ps. 49 is particularly interesting for the study of the Parables of Enoch since its theme is a comparison of the rich fool who, in the end, goes down to Sheol and the righteous man who, in the end, will be ransomed from the power of Sheol. The parallel reinforces Sjöberg's suggestion that the important themes of the Parables are the punishment of the wicked and the reward of the righteous.[44]

Other material in scripture labeled by the category *mašal* confirms this impression. The most important example is the taunt-song, or *mašal*, against the king of Babylon in Is. 14 (cf. also Mic. 2:4 and Hab. 2:6), which compares the heights reached by the king in his hubris to the depth of his fall into Sheol. This particular passage is the basis for the exegetical tradition behind 1 En. 46:4-8. A. R. Johnson compares the use of *mašal* to designate the taunt-song in Is. 14 to the use of the word to mean "byword": the king of Babylon is to become a byword or a public object of ridicule.[45] There also seems to be an element of comparison between the former and latter status of the king that is appropriate to the root meaning of *mašal*, a "likeness" or "comparison."

The oracles of Balaam are also termed *mešalim*, and Johnson observes that, in this case *mašal*

> denotes, not a parallel which already exists and thus serves as an example whereby its like may be avoided or brought into being, but one which is first pictured in the mind, possibly under so-called 'ecstatic' conditions, and then given colourful expression in words with a view to its corresponding appearance in actual life, i.e., *the pattern or shape of things to come as envisaged by the speaker in terms of Yahweh's purposeful action*.[46]

Johnson goes on to suggest that in this case the *mašal* assumes the role of a curse or blessing that functions in a magic or magico-religious fashion, and it seems possible that the phrase נשא משל על, "take up a parable against," in Is. 14:4; Mic. 2:4; and Hab. 2:6 has a similar idea in mind.

Johnson's description of this type of *mašal* fits the Parables of Enoch precisely. The introductions to the three parables, 1 En. 38, 45, and 58, confirm that the work concerns the righteous, the sinners, and the time at which God will act to punish the sinners and reward the righteous. The Targum to Is. 24:16c indicates that the Is. 24:17-23 midrash used in the Parables was concerned with the reward of the righteous and the punishment of the wicked.[47] In his discussion of the parables in the New Testament, Joachim Jeremias relates the parable of the last judgment in Mt. 25:31-46 to the Parables of Enoch.[48] It is significant that this particular parable, which seems different in style from the other parables of Jesus, is concerned with the punishment of the wicked and the reward of the righteous at the eschatological judgment. It was noted in chapter II above that the parable of the last judgment may, in fact, be dependent upon the Parables of Enoch, or a tradition related to it, for its treatment of the Son of Man.

The Parables of Enoch are related to what is clearly an oral genre, and that the *mašal* is something that one *speaks* is confirmed by the editorial material to the work. 1 En. 37:1 describes the work as a vision; however, 37:2-5 clearly presupposes that the three parables were words of wisdom that Enoch *spoke* to the men of old. Johnson's description, quoted above, of this type of *mašal* makes it apparent that the genre holds vision and speech in tension.

> (1 En. 37:2) And this is the beginning of the discourse of wisdom that I lifted up [my voice] to speak and to say to those who were dwelling on the earth: "Hearken, you of old, and behold, you of later times, the discourse of the Holy one that I shall speak before the Lord of Spirits." (3) It is better to speak [to] those of old, but [to] those of later times we shall not deny the beginning of wisdom. (4) Until now, there had not yet been given by the Lord of Spirits that which I have received, wisdom as I understand just as the Lord of Spirits desires, by whom the portion of eternal life has been given me. (5) And I received three parables, and I lifted up [my voice] to speak to those who were dwelling on the earth.

An editorial remark at the beginning of the third parable, in 1 En. 58:1, continues the same point of view: "And I began to speak the third parable concerning the righteous and elect." It is apparent that the editor of the Parables of Enoch considers the genre *māšāl* one that is to be spoken.

Oral Poet and Scribe: Types of Authorship

In oral composition, each time a work is presented it is composed anew on the basis of a pattern that is realized by use of a broad repertoire of formulaic expressions in the possession of the performer or poet. In a particular performance, the speaker may expand or contract the pattern to take account of inspiration or audience response. He may embellish his performance through the addition of material: lists and traditions from other patterns that may have an element in common with the pattern that he is re-creating.

When an oral composition is recorded, the artificial situation created by the need to write it down will generally affect the realization of the work.[49] In dictating to a scribe, the oral poet must speak slowly, thus disturbing the metrical flow of his composition. On the other hand, if a scribe were to attempt to compose a work on the basis of the techniques of oral composition--formulaic language and pattern realization--he would have to be versed in those skills himself. Scholes and Kellogg argue that, even where the poet and the scribe are identical, the distinction would be maintained between the styles of oral composition and the more inventive language of written composition:

> A "transitional text," one that represents a combination of oral and written composition, does not seem to be a possibility, much as some Homerists, medievalists, and others (including ourselves!) would like to believe in it. All the evidence of direct observation of living traditions points to the conclusion that even if the poet does his own writing, he will apparently compose in either the traditional oral-formulaic way (exhibiting all the hallmarks of oral composition) or in the literary way (exhibiting the originality of thought and phrase that characterizes literary composition).[50]

Albert Lord, on the other hand, suggests that it would be extremely difficult for an oral poet to compose in writing in the same way that he composes orally.[51] His position, however, is based on field observations in a culture that is not as literate as Jewish culture of the Hellenistic and Roman periods may be presumed to have been.

These comments, however, should not be allowed to rule out the possible appearance of *editorial* techniques in the recording of an oral composition, whether by a scribe or by the poet himself. Such techniques are required by the situation, since it appears from Philo's description that an oral interpreter of scripture could claim authority but that a written interpretation had to derive its authority through attribution to an ancient author. An oral composition that comes to serve as the basis of a written pseudepigraphon would require editing, and the editorial techniques involved must place an artificial distance between the poet and the ancient worthy to whom the text comes to be ascribed.[52]

Ultimately, it is impossible to determine if the Parables of Enoch was produced by dictation or by a poet serving as his own scribe. It might be suggested that a poet-scribe would be less likely to summarize poetic sections in prose; however, this distinction is not definitive since it is even possible that the summaries were introduced by later copyists. The number of inconsistencies in the work, which have given rise to various source theories, are probably in large part the result of an unskillful editor who attempted to attribute the Parables to Enoch by making Noah the speaker of a passage; however, this lack of skill could also point to a poet-scribe who was better versed in the skills of oral composition than in those of the editor.[53] Other inconsistencies that disturbed the literary critics, like the occasional use of a title formula in an apparently inappropriate context, are in fact characteristic of oral composition.[54] In the subsequent discussion, therefore, it will still be necessary to distinguish between poet and scribe, even if the two functions were represented by one person.[55] If the two were indeed one, the *writing* of the poet must still be seen as related to his performance in the traditional context.

1 En. 37:1-5, the introduction to the Parables, throws some light on the relationship between the oral situation and the writing of a pseudepigraphon. It distinguishes between

the manner in which the discourse is to be delivered to the ancients and to the moderns. The former are called upon to hearken, or to *listen* to the parables; the latter, to behold, or to *read* the supposedly ancient text. 1 En. 37:3, in declaring that it is better to *speak* to the ancients, may be expressing a preference for the authority of the spoken word over the written word, a preference that could correspond to the distrust of writing expressed in 1 En. 69:9-11. There seems to be a certain condescension involved in the writing of a pseudepigraphon.

If the claims of the introduction are taken as applying overtly to Enoch but covertly to the sectarian authority to whom the parables have been "given" (1 En. 37:5), the passage is illuminated by comparison to Philo's description of the one responsible for the exegesis of scripture on the Sabbath among the Essenes and Therapeutae. He has "especial proficiency"[56] or "the fullest knowledge of the doctrines which they profess."[57] Philo also comments that he does not selfishly withhold his greater understanding from those with lesser abilities:

> . . . he discusses some question arising in the Holy Scriptures or solves one that has been propounded by someone else. In doing this he has no thought of making a display, for he has no ambition to get a reputation for clever oratory but desires *to gain a closer insight into some particular matters and having gained it not to withhold it selfishly from those who if not so clearsighted as he have at least a similar desire to learn.*[58]

Read in this light, 1 En. 37:3-4 makes a rather expansive claim of authority for the poet of the Parables:

> It is better to speak [to] those of old, but [to] those of later times we shall not deny the beginning of wisdom. Until now, there had not yet been given by the Lord of Spirits that which I have received, wisdom as I understand just as the Lord of Spirits desires, by whom the portion of eternal life has been given me.

A similar claim is made in 1QH 4:27-29, although there without the fiction of a pseudepigraphon. It is interesting to note that the covert character of these claims nearly falls away in 1 En. 37:3 with the use of a first person *plural* verb: ". . . but [to] those of later times *we* shall not deny the beginning of wisdom."

The Sitz im Leben of Mašal and Pseudepigraphon

The Mašal. The *Sitz im Leben* of the *mašal* is to be found in the public exposition of scripture in sectarian Judaism. If Philo's description is followed, the precise context would be in the Sabbath sermon, although it is possible that a group devoted to the intense study of scripture would not limit its public exposition to the Sabbath.[59] The midrashic material in the Parables belongs to this context; however, it could be possible to question the relation of the astronomical and cosmological material to the Sabbath sermon. It must be observed, however, that the secrets of the heavens are an integral part of the structure of the work. In addition, the evidence from the Merkabah tradition, at a slightly later time, indicates that the heavenly ascent and the related secrets of the heavens were seen as related to specific passages of scripture.[60] The relation of the astronomical and cosmological passages to the exegesis of scripture is confirmed in the Parables by the version of the flood tradition in 1 En. 54:7-55:2, which is exegetical in character and contains allusions to such knowledge.

Pseudepigraphon. The *Sitz im Leben* of the pseudepigraphon is in the collection of writings of the ancients, the "founders of their way of thinking,"[61] which the sectarian would use in his closet for his study and meditation, if Philo's account is followed. This situation is confirmed, more or less, by the discoveries at Qumran, where a number of the sectarian writings, as well as books of scripture, were found scattered through caves that apparently served as living quarters for the monks. While Philo makes the writings of the ancients the archetypes for the other works, apparently the psalms and hymns, which he terms imitations,[62] if the relation between oral literature and writings developed in this dissertation is correct, the relationship between archetype and imitation runs in another direction. The archetypes are traditional interpretation of scripture, Philo's "allegorical interpretation," in the meetings of the sect and the use of other traditional patterns in the oral composition of psalms, hymns, and *mešalim*. It is the pseudepigraphon that imitates the traditional use of the interpretation of scripture, to the extent that such a work contains extracts from that tradition.

The pseudepigraphon must translate the authority of the oral exposition of scripture into another *Sitz im Leben*, the world of private study. The accepted convention used to establish the authority of a written work is to ascribe it to one of the ancients. The work that does not follow this pattern is the exception to the rule. The Wisdom of Jesus ben Sirach, which is the earliest Jewish writing that makes a claim of authorship that reflects the actual writer, and the Thanksgiving Hymns from Qumran, which use midrash in what seems to be an intensely personal way without, at the same time, ascribing the composition to one of the ancients, are such exceptions.

Conclusions

The role of tradition in the Parables. The form-critical examination of the Is. 24:17-23 midrash and the lists of fallen angels in part II above came to the conclusion that they were traditional units, rather than literary units, that have been included in the composition of the Parables of Enoch. An examination of the composition of the work itself confirms this conclusion. First, the Is. 24:17-23 midrash is only one of several traditional units used in the Parables of Enoch, units that serve as a polemic against kings, or a king, who has lost sight of his true position in the cosmos; it is therefore thematically compatible with the Parables. Second, the midrash is used at the same point in the development of the second and third parables and thus must be considered a part of the thought structure of the work rather than an interpolation.

Third, the Parables of Enoch represents an oral style of composition and as such must be considered to be related primarily to tradition rather than to the previous literary deposit. While, in the context of first century Judaism, it is possible that earlier writings have had an impact on subsequent oral tradition and writing, the units of a writing produced through the techniques of oral composition would have been drawn from oral tradition rather than from a literary source. It is therefore possible that 1 En. 6-11 has had an impact on the Parables, and particularly on the angel-list tradition, through the oral tradition or, possibly, through the earlier reading habits of the poet; however, the comparative study of oral composition[63] and the independence of the two versions of the second list in 1 En. 8:1-3 and 69:4-12 point toward the conclusion that the latter is the poet's personal list derived from tradition rather than from memorization of a written text. On the other hand, the Is. 24:17-23 midrash clearly represents a tradition that cannot have been derived from 1 En. 6-11. Both the Parables and chapters 6-11 are dependent on a traditional interpretation of Is. 24:17-23.

The hypothetical Book of Noah. Literary-critical attempts to explain the fallen-angel material in 1 Enoch through reference to a Book of Noah, or to Noachic fragments, must be discarded. The various units traditionally assigned to this body of material do not show sufficient unity to be explained by reference to one literary source, and they do not necessarily correspond to the description of the contents of the Book of Noah mentioned in Jubilees or to the Rabbinic midrash, the *Sefer Noaḥ*. What these units do indicate is a lively concern with the flood in the traditional exegesis of scripture, a concern that has found its way into various writings of the period. The use of the Is. 24:17-23 midrash and the lists of fallen angels are traditional rather than literary in character, and it should also be noted that the thematic pattern in 1 En. 60-63, which is related to 41:1-2, cuts right across one of the sections that Charles assigns to the Book of Noah, 1 En. 60.

The variations in style and usage in the Parables that have given rise to source theories are to be explained by the specificities of the individual midrashic traditions that have been used. A motif is frequently used for its thematic value rather than for its detailed agreement with other motifs in a work. These variations are not confined to the fallen-angel material. The *naming* of the Son of Man in 1 En. 48:2 depends on Is. 49:1, which indicates that the naming must be taken as a *primordial* act. In 1 En. 69:26-27, in the conclusion to the three parables, however, it is an

eschatological act that reflects the proclamation of the
throne name at the enthronement of a king. The Is. 24:17-23
midrash introduces a similar temporal problem with the
imprisonment of the kings at the time of the flood.

Other variations result from a remarkable fluidity
between heavenly beings and earthly ones in the Parables.[64]
In 1 En. 41:1, it is the deeds of *mankind* that will be weighed
in a balance, but in 1 En. 61:8, at the corresponding point
in the thematic pattern, it is the deeds of the *host of heaven*
that are weighed. The Elect one and the elect ones are
obviously related, and at points the latter are responsible
for the punishment of the kings and mighty rather than the
former (cf. 1 En. 48:9). The holy ones and the righteous ones
can refer either to men or angels. Likewise, the punishment
of the kings can be illuminated by reference to a tradition
that parallels the imprisonment and punishment of the kings
with that of angels. The hubris of the kings is cosmic in
dimension, and their punishment must be depicted in similar
terms. The Parables of Enoch obviously takes liberties in its
symbolism and should not be held to a modern idea of consistency in a work of literature. The value of the motif is of
more importance than the motif itself.

Pseudepigrapha and tradition. It is too soon to
generalize about the composition of pseudepigrapha on the
basis of the Parables of Enoch. Such works could also be produced through literary techniques. The Apocalypse of the
Animals in 1 En. 85-90 is a literary allegory based directly
on 1 En. 1-36. Not only does it reflect the eschatology of
chapters 6-11, it also reflects the shift from four to seven
archangels, a shift that takes place at 1 En. 20 (cf. 87:2).
However, when a conjunction of traditional material with the
techniques of oral composition is found in a pseudepigraphon,
that work should be examined primarily in the light of oral
tradition rather than literary tradition.

Attention needs to be given to the role that the name
of an ancient sage plays in the organization of traditional
units in oral tradition. With the exception of the editorial
material, the traditions in the Parables seem not to have
been associated with the name of Enoch in the oral tradition

behind the work. In addition, it is significant that, of
the material in 1 En. 1-36, at least chapters 6-11 seem to
have been independent of the name of Enoch prior to their
inclusion in an Enochic pseudepigraphon. They do not mention
the name of Enoch, and the sage must be introduced as having
been "hidden" previously in 1 En. 12:1. Perhaps the continued
association of themes and motifs with the name of Enoch in
writings attributed to the sage has its basis in the parallel
existence of literary and oral traditions within certain
groups. The oral traditions would be organized around the
traditional interpretation of scripture and would be the
responsibility of those concerned with the public exegesis of
scripture. The literary traditions would be those of the
scribes of the same groups who would tend to compose or edit
pseudepigrapha in the name of one particular sage. The
continuity that exists in the Enochic writings would therefore
be sociological in character. This "division of labor" is
reflected in the distinction of the traditional material from
the editorial material in the Parables. At the same time,
certain traditional material must have been associated with
the name of Enoch in the traditional exegesis of the appropriate passages in Genesis. Further work needs to be done on
the relation of pseudepigrapha and tradition, but it does seem
that literary tradition and oral tradition must be taken as
two distinct "literary" modes within Judaism of the
Hellenistic period.

CHAPTER VIII

THE PARABLES OF ENOCH AND THE
STUDY OF APOCALYPTIC

In the discussion of apocalyptic as a religious phenomena, there are two problems that arise from the examination of the Parables of Enoch. First, Betz, in relating the complaint of the earth in 1 En. 6-11 to a Hellenistic myth found in the *Kore Kosmu*, has argued that Jewish apocalyptic represents a discontinuity with the past in the Israelite-Jewish tradition.[1] While Betz's observation is important in understanding the role of Jewish apocalyptic in both the Jewish tradition and in the religion of the Hellenistic world, it raises the problem of the continuity of an important element of the Jewish tradition with its past. While some of the issues related to the problem of continuity and Hellenism are raised more acutely by 1 En. 6-11, the discussion of the Parables is relevant to the problem.

Second, the understanding of history and time in apocalyptic has been of interest in the recent discussion, and von Rad has concluded that apocalyptic is ahistorical in character.[2] An examination of the role of the kings and mighty in the Parables, however, is relevant to an understanding of the role that history plays in apocalyptic.

*Continuity, Hellenization, and
the Parables of Enoch*

The examination of the Parables of Enoch is of importance for the discussion of continuity and Hellenization in Jewish apocalyptic. While the study of the Is. 24:17-23 midrash and the lists of fallen angels in Part II above has suggested the possibility that Hellenistic traditions might have had an impact in the development of these two traditional units or in the traditional interpretation of Gen. 6:1-4, the key observation for this discussion is the major role played by exegetical traditions or midrashic excerpts in the Parables.

Midrash is an example of a mode of interpretation that appears when changes in the social situation of a tradition require a new mode of understanding the present.[3] When an "epic" tradition ceases to be a living tradition, it must become the object of interpretation as the community attempts to derive meaning for its new situation. Three elements of this process of reinterpretation can be distinguished: (1) the deposit of tradition, (2) the method of interpretation, and (3) new elements, which may be related to the older patterns of thought found in the deposit of tradition.

The deposit of tradition. The deposit of tradition in this case is the body of scriptures of the Jewish people. While all of the scriptures are not *epic* in the narrow sense of that word, they all function like an epic tradition as understood by Scholes and Kellogg:

> Epic also stands midway between sacred myth, a story whose events take place entirely outside of the profane world of historical men and events, and secular narrative, a story whose events take place entirely within the profane world of historical men and events, or within a fictional world whose operation is governed by the same laws as those that govern the actual world.[4]

The Jewish epic tradition involves the wedding of mythic patterns with legendary and "historic" material as part of a living oral tradition. This wedding is obvious, for example, in the account of the escape from the Egyptian army at the sea of reeds, where the mythic pattern of the creation narrative is used to interpret the traditional account of an event. Perhaps, to be more accurate, it should be said that the account of the event has impinged upon a previously existing mythic tradition.[5]

The use of this particular tradition in 1 En. 48:8-10 and 62:7-13[6] represents a second level of interpretation in which the earlier tradition has become a source for the derivation of meaning in a new situation. While there may be a parallel between the use of mythic tradition to interpret an event, the escape at the reed sea for example, and the use of scripture to interpret the present, the two methods of interpretation are in some way distinct as the result of the development of writing. The mythic tradition was an oral tradition, while the body of scripture that serves as the source of meaning in the tradition behind the Parables is a written tradition that has become a sacred text.

The method of interpretation. Scholes and Kellogg distinguish between the representational and illustrative aspects of myth. The former is found in *plot* and the latter in *theme*.[7] In the breakdown of an epic tradition, the first of these aspects, plot, gives rise to history or other types of empirical narrative,[8] while the second, theme, gives rise to allegory and discursive philosophical writing.[9] The present discussion is concerned with allegory rather than philosophical writing. As Ricoeur comments, allegory is generally a mode of hermeneutics, within a tradition, rather than "a spontaneous creation of signs."[10] Midrash represents a specific type of allegorical interpretation.[11] It provides a means of relating the themes and mythic patterns of the "epic" tradition to new situations and ideas.

The new elements. The new elements that are related to the older patterns of thought correspond to what Ricoeur terms the symbolic meaning of an allegory, which is related to the primary meaning, in this case, the patterns of thought found in the sacred tradition, through the process of translation.[12] In the case of allegory, or allegorical interpretation, the symbolic meaning is derived from another system of thought, which is related to the pattern of thought in the sacred text on a one-to-one basis. Philo interprets scripture by relating its patterns of thought to those of Greek philosophy. In the case of midrash, interpretive materials may be derived from a number of places, including popular tales, Hellenistic traditions, and even other passages of scripture, all of which are seen as related to the themes and motifs of the basic passage of scripture, and the resulting pattern of thought is then related to the structure of present experience or of future expectation.

Midrash and the continuity of the Jewish tradition. The distinction of deposit of tradition, method of interpretation, and interpretive elements provides a conceptual framework with which to address the problem of continuity and Hellenization. If the problem is considered from the standpoint of method of interpretation, it is apparent that, insofar as Jewish apocalyptic utilizes a midrashic method, it represents the inner development of the Jewish tradition. This judgment is not based on any observation that midrash is uniquely Jewish, but rather that midrash represents the appropriate mode of interpretation for that particular phase of development of the Israelite-Jewish tradition. In contrast, Philo's use of the allegorical method, which he has *consciously* borrowed from Greek philosophy, represents a degree of Hellenization of the Jewish tradition, both in terms of the method of interpretation and the interpretive elements brought to the hermeneutical situation. It is interesting to observe, however, that, although Philo is using a Hellenistic hermeneutical method, it corresponds to a native method, midrash, in use in Palestine and probably elsewhere. That Philo is aware of this correspondence is suggested by his description of the hermeneutic of the Essenes as allegory.[13]

If the problem of Hellenization and continuity is considered from the standpoint of interpretive elements, the solution becomes more complex. It might be best here to distinguish between degrees of Hellenization related to the proportion of interpretive elements derived from scripture or distinctive elements of Jewish culture to that derived from the larger Hellenistic world. This solution, of course, leaves a number of ambiguities, since it is not possible in each case to definitively determine how closely any particular traditional unit is related to Hellenistic material. However, this approach also makes it possible to relate the question of Hellenization to individual elements within a tradition without making it necessary to decide whether a whole religious movement within a particular religious tradition is discontinuous with its past.

It can be determined, for example, that the myth of the fallen angels in its various forms is based on a theme that is definitely discontinuous with the Jewish past. Ascription of the origin of evil to sources external to man is definitely out of place in a tradition that has been concerned with the responsibility of man, as an individual and as a community, for evil. On the other hand, Jewish apocalyptic continues to be concerned with themes that are central to the Jewish tradition. The sovereignty of the one God over the worlds of nature and men continues to be central to

apocalyptic, and even though that sovereignty has become
problematic in the present age, the apocalypse reaffirms it in
a visionary fashion with an account of the judgment and
punishment of the evil powers, the kings and mighty of the
earth in the Parables, who are the cause of evil in the present
situation. Several scholars have also shown recently that the
apocalyptic patterns used in works like the Parables of Enoch
represent a continuous development reaching back into the
Jewish tradition,[14] although at least some of the patterns of
thought associated with apocalyptic represent related and
parallel developments to patterns of thought in other native
cultures of the time.[15]

The inner development of Judaism must also be considered in an examination of the problem of continuity and
Hellenization. Where themes and motifs are borrowed from
Hellenistic culture, the ground has probably been prepared by
developments within the Jewish social or religious situation.
Plöger uses this argument to explain the origin of dualism in
Jewish apocalyptic by relating it to a sociological split
between the theocratic establishment in Jerusalem, which believes
that it represents the apex of God's relationship with his
people, and the Ḥasidim, who believe that there is more to
come.[16] The version of the myth of the fallen angels in 1 En.
6-11, which accounts for evil by the mixture of the heavenly
and earthly realms, could be concerned at the illustrative
level with the divisions created within the Jewish community
by the impact of Hellenistic culture on Jewish society and the
acculturation of the upper classes.[17] In contrast, the use of
the Is. 24:17-23 midrash in the Parables could reflect,
through the polemic against the kings and host of heaven, the
impact of external political and military power on Jewish
society. In either case, the ground has been laid for a theme
that treats evil as, in origin, external to man.

At the same time, Hellenistic material is adopted
through its relation, by means of the allegorical method of
midrash, to themes or motifs found in scripture, and the
adoption can result in the transformation of the foreign
material as well as of the native tradition. The myth of the
complaint of the earth, which has been used in the traditions

behind 1 En. 6-11 to interpret Gen. 6:1-4, has been transformed
to a certain degree by that passage of scripture, and the
resulting combination has been interpreted by reference to
Jewish laws concerning mixed fruits and *mamzerim*.[18]

A distinction should be made between syncretism involving the adoption of Hellenistic motifs that are thematically
related to Jewish motifs and that involving the transformation
of the underlying themes. The Is. 24:17-23 midrash is related
to a theme dealing with the rebellion and punishment of divine
beings, a theme known from the ancient world. This theme has
existed on the periphery of the Israelite-Jewish tradition,
being related to Is. 14 as well as to the Levithan motif.
While the use of this theme in the Is. 24:17-23 midrash and
the Parables of Enoch may give the theme more importance than
it has enjoyed in the previous tradition, it does not result
in the introduction of a new theme. On the other hand, the
reinterpretation of Gen. 6:1-4 through a myth dealing with the
complaint of the earth has resulted in the thematic transformation of that passage of scripture from a myth dealing with
the limit of human life to one dealing with the introduction
of evil by heavenly beings.

While it might be said that Judaism in the Hellenistic
period is Hellenistic in character, either through the perva-
sive influence of the latter culture in all segments of Jewish
society, or through the definition of Hellenization as
involving the reaction of a number of native cultures to the
impact of Greek rule and culture, the examination of Judaism as
a religious tradition requires a means of defining the continuity of its elements with the past as well as a means of isolat-
ing the inevitable transformations that take place in any
tradition as it related to both its own past and its environment. The identification of midrash as a hermeneutical method
that relates the deposit of tradition, scripture, to the
present situation through the introduction of new interpretive
elements provides such a means. It thus becomes possible to
look at Jewish apocalyptic as both a Jewish and a Hellenistic
phenomenon.

*The Kings and Mighty and the
Understanding of History
in Apocalyptic*

The kings and mighty of the earth are symbolic of "history" in the Parables in that they represent the larger world of public events to which the apocalyptic circle that produced the work is reacting. The symbolism of the kings and mighty can be examined from the standpoint of both the sociology of religion and the history of religion.

The sociology of religion. Recently, some attention has been paid to the social setting of apocalyptic and proto-apocalyptic texts in the second temple Judaism.[19] In general, apocalyptic seems to arise as a result of the reaction of a particular class in Palestinian Judaism to rule of the nation and its homeland by a foreign power and to the adjustment that other competing groups have made to the rule of that power. In light of this situation, the heavenly realm in the Parables of Enoch seems to form a collective representation of the human realm.

It has already been noted that the use of the Is. 24:17-23 midrash, with its concern for the punishment of angelic beings, has been used for its thematic value rather than for its precise identity with other motifs in the Parables and that there is a certain degree of fluidity between the heavenly and earthly realms in the symbolism of the work.[20] These observations lead to the conclusion that the heavenly realm reflects the social situation of the earthly realm. The host of Asael is the heavenly parallel to the kings and mighty of the earth, the emperor and powerful men of the Roman empire in the first century A.D. There are also correspondences between the human community of the righteous and the angels and messianic figure in the Parables. Nickelsburg has pointed out that, in the use of the servant song of Is. 52-53 in 1 En. 62, the kings and mighty of the earth are asked to recognize in *the Elect one* who judges them, *the elect ones* whom they have persecuted.[21]

While the lack of concrete details in the Parables makes it difficult to translate the symbolism into history, a study of the symbolism illuminates the social situation in

which the work was produced. The kings and mighty are seen
as part of a cosmic rebellion against the power of God, while
the present sufferings of the righteous servants of an omnipotent God are sanctioned by reference to the eschatological
reversal that will take place. The symbolism of the Parables
functions as a means of integrating the present experience
of the righteous of a world that does not seem to be structured according to the laws of their God with their belief
in a God who, as the divine lawgiver, rewards in concrete ways
the community of his chosen ones when it is faithful to his
law. While a collective representation of a social order
generally functions as a means of sanctioning the structure
and authority of that order, in an apocalyptic system such a
representation must sanction the overthrow or fall of the
oppressive order and the establishment of a new society.

The history of religions. While the sociology of
religion is useful in the study of religious phenomena, when
used to the exclusion of other methods, the resulting understanding of religion is limited. An adequate method for the
study of religion must attempt to understand religious phenomena as the spiritual creations of mankind.[22] Ultimately,
religious phenomena must be understood as expressing the
understanding of a culture of man's existential situation
or "mode of being in the world."[23]

The existential situation or mode of being in the
world expressed by apocalyptic symbolism is one of alienation
from history[24]--history being understood as the actions of
powerful men, the kings and mighty of the earth, in time.
Von Rad has come close to this understanding of apocalyptic
in his characterization of that movement as ahistorical;[25]
however, his perspective is limited by his identification of
history with the salvation history of the prophetic movement.
While Gnosticism might be characterized as ahistorical,
apocalypticism represents an anterior mode of religious experience in which the *mysterium tremendum*, the awe-inspiring
aspect of the sacred, is perceived, at least in part, in
history. This perception represents a degree of dualism of
religious experience in which the more threatening aspects of
divinity have been split off and used to develop a symbolism

of evil that identifies the structure of evil with the structure of history. In the case of Dan. 7, history is symbolized by the four beasts. Therefore, it is incorrect to understand history in apocalyptic as the realm of the progressive self-revelation of God.[26] It is rather the dualistic reflection of certain negative elements of divinity that are now declared as less than ultimate by the symbolism of the judgment and imprisonment or destruction of the beasts, kings, and angels, the last of which are specifically said to act *as if they were God* in 1 En. 68:4.

Von Rad is correct in perceiving a difference between the prophetic and apocalyptic understanding of history; however, apocalypticism should not be understood as ahistorical but rather as expressing a profound alienation from history. History has two aspects to the apocalypticist: active history, or the evil deeds of great men, and passive history, or the experience of the suffering of the righteous. In both cases, the righteous are alienated from history: in the first through the perception of the expression of evil in history, and in the second through a desire for a new age. That new age is present to the seer in his vision, and that vision, whether actual or a literary fiction, acts as a means of transformation that permits the righteous to transcend the alienation characteristic of their existential situation.

This structure of religious experience is found in the Parables of Enoch. The kings and mighty of the earth, through their association with the host of Asael, represent the numinous presence of evil in the world, while, beyond history, the righteous seer is able to perceive through his vision the heavenly world that will bring the self-important powers of history under divine judgment. Thus, the seer becomes obsessed with the fate of the righteous and the wicked, themes that are related to the selection of the genre *mašal*. The numinous character of the perception of evil in history is suggested by the idea in 1 En. 68:4 that the fallen angels act as if they were God and might thus be considered the *counterfeit* of divine power. This idea could be related to the cult of the emperor in which the ruler, possibly Gaius Caligula in the case of the Parables, asked the Jews to recognize in him the supreme hierophany.

While the Parables of Enoch contains little in the way of allegorical representation of the course of history, it is concerned with a theology of history that identifies the structure of evil with that of time. In 1 En. 67:4-12, the poet is faced with the problem of integrating a myth of the origin of evil, a myth that places the origin of evil in the rebellion of the host of heaven prior to the flood, with a perception of the presence of evil in the actions of the kings and mighty of the earth, who are contemporaries of the author. The problem is resolved by ironically identifying the current pleasure of the kings and mighty in a spa, which is associated with a thermal spring, with the punishment of the fallen angels, who were imprisoned in the earth prior to the flood and whose punishment is the cause of the warmth of the waters of this spring. The poet has thus moved from a myth of the origin of evil to a theology--or demonology--of history.

Ultimately, the alienation of the righteous from history is an alienation from time itself. Eliade's characterization of the Guaranis makes the role of time in this alienation clear.

> The Guaranis desired to live as their mythical ancestors lived in the beginning of the world--in Judeo-Christian terms, to live as Adam, before the Fall, lived in Paradise. This is not an absurd and peculiar idea. At a certain time in their history, many other primitive peoples believed that it was possible to return periodically to the first days of Creation--that it was possible to live in a dawning and perfect world, such as it had been *before it had been consumed by Time* and vilified by History.[27]

The previous discussion has related the eschatological understanding of history to the creation myth by suggesting that the destruction of the old world and the creation of the new age represents the identification of the eschatological activity of God with his creative activity.[28] This interpretation, however, can be carried further. In apocalypticism, the time of the creation myth has been identified with *the course of history*. The present age represents the time of the incursion of the powers of chaos, and the eschaton represents the final *agon* between those powers and God. In the older national civilizations, time could be regenerated yearly through the ritual appropriation of the creation myth. In the Parables of Enoch, however, that yearly reappropriation is no longer possible. Regeneration of time is possible only symbolically through the visionary experience of the seer or the recounting of that experience in the book of the Parables of Enoch.

NOTES

PREFACE

[1] H. St. J. Thackeray (vols. 1-5), Ralph Marcus (vols. 5-8), Allen Wickgren (vol. 8), and Louis Feldman (vol. 9), *Josephus*, LCL, 9 vols. (Cambridge: Harvard University Press, 1926-65).

[2] F. H. Colson (vols. 1-10) and G. H. Whitaker (vols. 1-5), *Philo*, LCL, 10 vols. (Cambridge: Harvard University Press, 1929-62).

[3] Hugh G. Evelyn-White, *Hesiod, the Homeric Hymns and Homerica*, LCL (Cambridge: Harvard University Press, 1914).

[4] A. M. Harmon (vols. 1-5), K. Kilburn (vol. 6), and M. D. Macleod (vols. 7-8), *Lucian*, LCL, 8 vols. (Cambridge: Harvard University Press, 1913-67).

[5] Bruce M. Metzger, ed., *The Oxford Annotated Apocrypha: The Apocrypha of the Old Testament: Revised Standard Version* (New York: Oxford University Press, 1965).

[6] See J. T. Milik and Matthew Black, eds., *The Books of Enoch: Aramaic Fragments of Qumrân Cave 4* (Oxford: Clarendon Press, 1976).

[7] See ibid., pp. 89-98.

[8] *Grammatica elementare della lingua Etiopica*, Pubblicazioni dell'istituto per l'oriente (Rome: Istituto per l'oriente, n.d.), pp. 3-4.

CHAPTER I: INTRODUCTION

[1] J. T. Milik ("Problèmes de la littérature hénochique à la lumière des fragments araméens de Qumrân," *HTR* 64 [1971]: 348) gives ʽAšaʼel as the form of the name found at Qumran.

[2] Milik gives the form of this name at Qumran as Šemîḥazah (ibid).

[3] See Albert B. Lord, *Singer of Tales* (New York: Atheneum, 1974).

CHAPTER II: THE PROVENANCE OF THE PARABLES OF ENOCH

[1] In this dissertation, form criticism will be understood as including the examination of the history of traditions.

²See R. H. Charles, *The Book of Enoch or 1 Enoch*, rev. ed. (Oxford: The Clarendon Press, 1912), pp. lii-liii, and Milik, "Problèmes," pp. 343-60.

³*Book of Enoch*, pp. xxx-xlvi.

⁴"Toward a Date for the Similitudes of Enoch: An Historical Approach," *NTS* 14 (1967-68): 551-65.

⁵Cf. Lars Hartman, *Prophecy Interpreted: The Formation of Some Jewish Apocalyptic Texts and of the Eschatological Discourse Mark 13 Par.*, trans. Neil Tomkinson and Jean Gray, ConB: NT Series, no. 1 (Lund, Sweden: CWK Gleerup, 1966), pp. 88-91.

⁶Ibid., p. 89.

⁷The relationship between "Son of Man" in the Parables of Enoch and in Christianity will be dealt with below in connection with Milik's position. It should be noted here that the second century A.D. seems too late for a polemic against the Christian use of the title. The latter group has forgotten its eschatological significance and is interested in it as a means of talking about the human nature of Jesus in a developing Christological controversy: cf. *Ign. Eph.* 20:2 and *Barn.* 12:10.

⁸See "Problèmes," pp. 333, 375-78.

⁹Ibid., p. 375.

¹⁰Ibid., pp. 335, 338.

¹¹See Hugo Odeberg, *3 Enoch or the Hebrew Book of Enoch*, with a new Prolegomenon by Jonas C. Greenfield, reprint ed. (New York: Ktav Publishing House, 1973). Greenfield (pp. XXI-XXIII) points out that the correct title of the work is *Sefer ha-Hekhaloth* and that the title assigned to it by Odeberg, 3 Enoch, has no basis in the textual tradition and is poorly supported by the contents of the work. Greenfield's protest against the designation of these works as *1*, *2*, and *3* Enoch (see pp. XVIII and XXI) is well taken to the extent that the reader is misled into believing that they are part of a single literary tradition. However, the same protest could be registered against similar titles in the Ezra and Baruch cycles, or, for that matter, in the designations applied to parts of Isaiah or Zechariah. Since the non-specialist reader is easily confused by the proliferation of possible titles for these works, it seems best to use the ones that are most common as long as it is understood that they are only the conventions of modern scholarship.

¹²Cf. Carsten Colpe, "ὁ υἱὸς τοῦ ἀνθρώπου," *TDNT*, 8:423, and Geza Vermes, *Jesus the Jew: A Historian's Reading of the Gospels* (London: Collins, 1973), pp. 173-75. The latter's remarks are particularly instructive:
"But contrary to a large body of opinion, analysis of the relevant texts, taken severally and together, never points

to the titular use of *son of man*. Phrases such as 'the Anointed' or 'the Lord of the spirits' are sufficient in themselves, they are titles. This can never be said of *son of man*, which always needs to be explained either by referring to the original vision, or to some other determining clause: for example, 'the *son of man* born unto righteousness'. Without such qualification it is neither clear, nor distinctive enough to act as an autonomous title" (ibid., p. 175).

[13] *Rediscovering the Teaching of Jesus* (New York: Harper and Row, 1967), pp. 172-99, see especially p. 173.

[14] Cf. Colpe ("ὁ υἱὸς τοῦ ἀνθρώπου," p. 425), who observes that the Elect one is depicted with greater detail than the Son of Man and is introduced prior to the latter title (cf. 1 En. 39:6; 40:5; and 45:3-4). However, he concludes that "the very breadth of the eschatology of the Elect One establishes the broadly Messianic significance of the man-concepts embedded in it" (ibid.). For further discussion of Colpe's position, see below, p. 27.

[15] See 1 En. 46:3,7-8; 47:1-2,4; 48:2-3,5,7,10; 62:10,14, 16; 63:1-12; 71:17. For the midrashic passages see 1 En. 46:1-48:10; 62:5-16; 63:1-12; 71:10-17. 1 En. 69:26-29 is the conclusion to the three parables and seems to represent a final interweaving of both the Son of Man and the fallen-angel midrashim with messianic characteristics derived from the Elect one. 1 En. 62-63 represents an earlier stage of a similar interweaving once the Dan. 7:9-14 midrash has been initially established in 1 En. 46-48. The way in which this midrash is handled in the Parables will also be examined in chapter VII below in a discussion of structure and compositional technique in the work.

[16] *Major Trends in Jewish Mysticism*, 3d rev. ed. (New York: Schocken Books, 1961), pp. 41, 43.

[17] *Jewish Gnosticism, Merkabah Mysticism, and Talmudic Tradition* (New York: The Jewish Theological Seminary of America, 1965), p. 34.

[18] Ibid., p. 29.

[19] "The Angelic Liturgy at Qumran--4Q Serek šîrôt ʿôlat Haššabbāt," *Congress Volume: Oxford, 1959*, VTSup, vol. 7 (Leiden: E. J. Brill, 1959), pp. 343-45.

[20] Ibid., pp. 335-42.

[21] Ibid., p. 319.

[22] Ibid., pp. 339-40.

[23] Prolegomenon to *3 Enoch or the Hebrew Book of Enoch*, by Hugo Odeberg, reprint ed. (New York: Ktav Publishing House, 1973), pp. XVI-XVIII and XXXII-XXXV.

[24] Ibid., p. XVII.

[25] Ibid., p. XVIII.

[26] Ibid. It has been suggested that the Ethiopic translator made his version of the Parables from either a Hebrew, Aramaic, or Syriac text and that the work may never have existed in Greek, although the rest of 1 Enoch seems to depend on the Greek version (see Nathaniel Schmidt, "The Apocalypse of Noah and the Parables of Enoch," *Oriental Studies in Honor of Paul Haupt*, ed. C. Adler and A. Ember [Baltimore: Johns Hopkins Press, 1926], p. 120, and Edward Ullendorff, "An Aramaic 'Vorlage' of the Ethiopic Text of Enoch?" *Atti del convegno internazionale di studi Etiopici*, Problemi attuali di scienza e di cultura [Rome: Accademia Nazionale dei Lincei, 1960], pp. 259-67). Charles (*Book of Enoch*, pp. lxi-lxviii) argues for Hebrew as the original language of the Parables, although he is not always consistent in his notes to the translation (see ibid., p. 135, where he translates back into Aramaic rather than Hebrew to solve a textual problem). It is extremely difficult to determine the original language of the Parables, or its subsequent history, since most problems can be explained by retranslation into both Hebrew and Aramaic. The present study assumes Hebrew on the grounds of a nationalistic tendency to use that language in the post-Maccabean period.

[27] "Prolegomenon," pp. XV-XVI, XXII-XXIII, and XXX-XXXII.

[28] *3 Enoch*, pp. 46 and 184.

[29] *Major Trends*, p. 44. In the parallels in Ezek. 1:26-2:7 and Dan. 8:15-17 and 10:2-11:1, the sage remains firmly rooted to the earth.

[30] Cf. Matthew Black ("The Eschatology of the Similitudes of Enoch," *JTS* 3 [1952]: 1-10), who observes that both 1 En. 14-16 and 71 represent "calls" but makes the mistake of using their formal similarity to argue for literary unity.

[31] "The Angelic Liturgy," pp. 339-40.

[32] Note, for example, the final lines of two of the hymns from the Greater Hekhaloth quoted by Scholem (*Jewish Gnosticism*, pp. 59-61). The phrase is found frequently in the Greater Hekhaloth (see the edition in S. Wertheimer, בתי מדרשות, 2d ed., enl. and amended by A. J. Wertheimer, 2 vols. [Jerusalem: Ktab wa-Sepher, 5728 (1967-68)], 1:63-136).

[33] See GKC, pp. 417 and 440.

[34] Cf. George Foot Moore, *Judaism in the First Centuries of the Christian Era*, 3 vols. (Cambridge: Harvard University Press, 1927-30), 3:134.

[35] See 3 En. 1:10,12; 7; 8:1; 10:1; 14:1; 15:1; 18:17, 19,22; 24:22; 26:7,11; 28:2; 33:3; 35:3; 36:1,2; 39:1; 40:1; 41:2,4; 43:2. The one exception with the pronominal suffix is 40:4.

[36] See James Hope Moulton, Wilbert Francis Howard, and Nigel Turner, *A Grammer of New Testament Greek*, 3 vols. (Edinburgh: T. and T. Clark, 1906-63), 3:214.

[37] In the Parables, the Watchers are termed "those who never sleep," *'ela 'iyenawwemu*, and are part of the divine court. Unlike 1 En. 12-16, they are not in any way identified with fallen angelic beings, another indication that the Parables is part of an independent strand of tradition.

[38] *Book of Enoch*, p. 76.

[39] *3 Enoch*, p. 184. Cf. David Flusser, "Sanktus und Gloria," *Abraham unser Vater: Juden und Christen im Gespräch über die Bibel (Festschrift für Otto Michel)*, ed. Otto Betz, Martin Hengel, and Peter Schmidt, Arbeiten zur Geschichte des Spätjudentums und Urchristentums, no. 5 (Leiden and Cologne: E. J. Brill, 1963), pp. 138-39.

[40] S. Singer, *The Authorized Daily Prayer Book* (London: Eyre and Spottiswoode, Ltd., 1929), p. 39.

[41] *3 Enoch*, p. 184; see also Flusser, "Sanctus und Gloria," p. 139.

[42] Odeberg, *3 Enoch*, translation, p. 5.

[43] On the role of onomastica in the wisdom tradition, see Gerhard von Rad, "Hiob XXXVIII und die altägyptische Weisheit," *Wisdom in Israel and in the Ancient Near East*, ed. M. Noth and D. Winton Thomas, VTSup, vol. 3 (Leiden: E. J. Brill, 1955), pp. 293-301; and *Old Testament Theology*, trans. D. M. G. Stalker, 2 vols. (Edinburgh and London: Oliver and Boyd, 1962-65), 1:425 and 2:307.

[44] *Book of Enoch*, pp. 138-39.

[45] M. Moïse Schwab, "Vocabulaire de l'angélologie d'après les manuscrits hébreux de la Bibliothèque Nationale," *MPAIBL*, 1st series, 10 (1897): 264.

[46] "The Logos Ebraikos in the Magical Papyrus of Paris, and the Book of Enoch," *JRAS*, 3d series, 33 (1901): 109-17.

[47] 3 En. 13:1 (Odeberg, *3 Enoch*, translation, pp. 34-35).

[48] *Jewish Gnosticism*, p. 79.

[49] See Jas. 2:19, where the daemons tremble in response to their belief that God is one, and the Great Paris Papyrus (PGM IV.3016), which gives the following instructions for the use of a charm: "Hang it round the sufferer; it is of every daemon a thing to be trembled at, which he fears" (John M. Hull, *Hellenistic Magic and the Synoptic Tradition*, SBT, 2d series, no. 28 [Naperville, Ill.: Alec R. Allenson, 1974], p. 17). Obviously, a daemon trembles or quakes in response to divine power, not for his own pleasure. Cf. Pr. Man. 1-5:

"(1) O Lord Almighty,
                God of our fathers, . . .
      (2) thou who hast made heaven and earth
                with all their order;
      (3) who hast shackled the sea by thy word of command,
                who has confined the deep
                and *sealed* it with thy terrible and glorious *name;*
      (4) *at whom all things shudder,*
                and tremble before thy power,
      (5) for thy glorious splendor cannot be borne,
                and the wrath of thy threat to sinners is
                irresistible."

Not only should verse 4 be compared with the trembling of the fallen angels in the oath tradition in the Parables, but the name that seals the deep in verse 3 should be compared with the secret name of 1 En. 69:14, which, as a part of the oath, functions in the same way (cf. 1 En. 69:18). In 3 En. 14, the entire heavenly host indicates its subjugation to Metatron by trembling.

[50] See *ANET*, pp. 100-101.

[51] *Patterns in Comparative Religion*, trans. Rosemary Sheed (Cleveland, Ohio, and New York: Meridian Books, 1963), pp. 443-46.

[52] *Book of Enoch*, pp. liv, 67, and 72-73.

[53] Greenfield, "Prolegomenon," p. XVII.

[54] Hindley, "Toward a Date for the Similitudes of Enoch." See p. 12 above.

[55] Greenfield, "Prolegomenon," p. XVII. It is necessary to differ with his judgment that "no sort of sophistry can suppress" 1 En. 56:5-7 and 67:7-9 as historical allusions; however, if they were to be accepted as such, his suggestion of the "early part of the first century C.E." would be in agreement with the conclusions advanced below.

[56] In other words, the passage is satirical rather than literal in intent. It represents a piece of folklore used to epitomize the *true* situation of the nobility of the Roman empire as they pampered their bodies and relaxed their spirits in their heated baths.

[57] The direction may well be part of a mythical geography rather than part of a reference to an actual thermal spring (cf. Charles, *Book of Enoch*, p. 133, n. to 1 En. 67:4).

[58] "The Angelic Liturgy," pp. 339-40. See p. 15 above.

[59] "The Angelic Liturgy," pp. 328-29, 343, and 345.

[60] Ibid., p. 239.

[61] See H. E. Tödt, *The Son of Man in the Synoptic Tradition*, trans. Dorothea M. Barton, The New Testament Library (Philadelphia: Westminster Press, 1965), p. 92.

NOTES TO PAGES 25-28

[62] "The Use of בר נש/בר נשא in Jewish Aramaic," *An Aramaic Approach to the Gospels and Acts*, Matthew Black, 3d ed. (Oxford: The Clarendon Press, 1967), pp. 310-28; and *Jesus the Jew*, pp. 160-91. Vermes accepts the possibility that Jesus used בר נשא as a circumlocution for "I" (ibid., p. 182).

[63] *Rediscovering*, pp. 164-99.

[64] Ibid., pp. 166-71; Vermes, *Jesus the Jew*, pp. 169-77; see above, pp. 13-14.

[65] Cf. Colpe, "ὁ υἱὸς τοῦ ἀνθρώπου," pp. 429-30.

[66] Cf. ibid., p. 429.

[67] See Perrin, *Rediscovering*, pp. 185-91.

[68] "ὁ υἱὸς τοῦ ἀνθρώπου," pp. 425-26.

[69] Ibid., p. 424.

[70] Ibid., p. 423. Colpe's position rests on the alternation of three different expressions for "Son of Man" in the Parables, which he assumes go back to the original text. Nathaniel Schmidt ("The Apocalypse of Noah," pp. 117-18) argues that the three Ethiopic terms correspond to three different Aramaic terms used to translate "Son of Man" by Aramaic-speaking Christians. If this is the case, it is unnecessary to use these terms to attempt to distinguish three different Son of Man traditions in the Parables, which are not Christian in origin. The three terms should be attributed to the preservation of the text by Christians.

[71] "ὁ υἱὸς τοῦ ἀνθρώπου," p. 429. Colpe does leave open the possibility that "the development of a genuinely Jewish Chr. Son of Man Christology as an important phase in the history of Jewish Messianology has also to be taken into account" (ibid.).

[72] Cf. Tödt, *The Son of Man*, pp. 84-86.

[73] Cf. ibid., p. 94: "As compared with Mark and Luke, Matthew . . . intensifies the transcendent sovereignty and power of the Son of Man."

[74] Mk. 9:12b has been treated as a post-Markan gloss (see Norman Perrin, *A Modern Pilgrimage in New Testament Christology* [Philadelphia: Fortress Press, 1974], p. 118). If this is the case, then Matthew has actually introduced a reference to Son of Man in Mt. 17:12, and the text of Matthew should then be understood as the source of the gloss in Mark.

[75] Cf. Tödt: "In making the reference to the Son of Man's coming serve the purpose of exhortation, Matthew follows Q. Matthew will, however, transfer the Son of Man sayings and their hortatory meaning from the narrower framework of an isolated logion into the wider context of carefully composed groups. Several times he endeavours to append to the concluding

sections of long passages an eschatological emphasis. He prefers to achieve this by means of Son of Man sayings. The eschatological prospect of the Son of Man elucidates the preceding text" (*The Son of Man*, p. 92). He gives as examples Mt. 19:28; 16:27; 25:31; and 13:41.

[76] Cf. Colpe, "ὁ υἱὸς τοῦ ἀνθρώπου," p. 448.

[77] Matthew places this parable as the last in a set of four parables in Mt. 24:45-25:46, which he has added to the two parables of Mk. 13:28-37 (cf. Mt. 24:32-44). The latter passage in its original Markan context was intended to emphasize the unexpected character of the coming of the Son of Man mentioned in the synoptic apocalypse. Matthew has, in effect, expanded the conclusion of the apocalypse by the addition of the four parables, the final and climactic one being the parable of the last judgment by the Son of Man (cf. Tödt's remark quoted in n. 75 above).

[78] *The Son of Man*, p. 73.

[79] See von Rad, *Old Testament Theology*, 1:46-47 and 2:155-69. For the use of this motif in the first century A.D., see William R. Farmer, *Maccabees, Zealots, and Josephus: An Inquiry into Jewish Nationalism in the Greco-Roman Period* (New York: Columbia University Press, 1956), pp. 93-116.

[80] "The Angelic Liturgy," pp. 339-40.

[81] See Emil Schürer, *The History of the Jewish People in the Age of Jesus Christ (175 B.C.-A.D. 135)*, new Eng. ver., rev. and ed. Geza Vermes and Fergus Millar, 3 vols. (Edinburgh: T. and T. Clark, 1973-), 1:388-97. Schmidt ("The Apocalypse of Noah," p. 119) favors the time of Caligula for the composition of the Parables.

[82] *Leg.* 347.

[83] See Schürer, *History of the Jewish People*, 1:305-6.

[84] Cf. ibid., 1:456 and 463-64; and Farmer, *Maccabees*, pp. 116-23. Symbolism that is here seen to be related to the Exodus tradition includes (a) leading a mob into the wilderness, (b) the anticipation that, upon their return, the waters of the Jordan would part, (c) the anticipation that, upon their approach to Jerusalem, the walls of the city would collapse, and (d) the name of one of the messianic demagogues, the Egyptian. While much of this is also symbolic of the entry into the land, the overtones of the Exodus are there (cf. Josephus, *J.W.* 2. 259, where the "imposters" are said to reveal σημεῖα ἐλευθερίας to the mob [cf. Mt. 24:24-26]).

[85] Exodus symbolism is found in midrashic use of Exodus 14-15 in 1 En. 48:8-10 and 62:6-16.

[86] The early part of Herod's reign should probably be ruled out. 1 En. 56:5-7 does not function well as an allusion to the invasion of the Parthians in 40-38 B.C. since, at that

time, they *entered* Jerusalem unopposed at the invitation of
Antigonus, a Hasmonean (see Schürer, *History of the Jewish
People*, 1:279-80), while 1 En. 56:7 anticipates that "the city
of my righteous ones will be an obstacle for their horses."
In addition, their presence at this time was probably welcomed
by the Jews as a part of growing opposition to Roman power. If
the passage is indeed a historical allusion, it must be seen
as written either prior to the approach of the Parthians in 40
B.C., which seems unlikely since that approach would have been
welcomed, or at a time sufficiently remote for the details to
have been forgotten. It is more likely that the reference to
the Parthians, insofar as it is not purely an apocalyptic
motif, functions in much the same way as "Babylon" in Revelation as a cryptic reference to the Romans.

E. Sjöberg (*Der Menschensohn im äthiopischen Henochbuch*,
Skrifter utgivna av kungl. humanistiska Vetenskapssamfundet i
Lund, no. 41 [Lund, Sweden: CWK Gleerup, 1946], pp. 35-39)
dates the work in the early part of the first century A.D. for
the following reasons: (a) the reference to the idolatry
practiced by the kings and mighty in 1 En. 46:7 is more suggestive of the Romans than the Hasmoneans, (b) 1 En. 56:5-8
refers to the Parthians as the archenemy of Israel, a reference
that he sees as possibly suggested by the entry of the
Parthians into Palestine in 40-38 B.C., and (c) the use of the
Son of Man in the Parables by Jesus and the early Christians
prohibits a date later in the first century. However, he does
not insist on the last point since, he argues, the Christians
could have obtained the Son of Man material from apocalyptic
tradition rather than directly from the Parables of Enoch.

Sjöberg is correct in allowing for the independence
of the early Christian movement from the Parables. It is not
necessary to follow Vermes (*Jesus the Jew*, pp. 175-76) in
arguing for a post-70 date in order to establish that independence since there is no evidence that the work was in wide
circulation (cf. Colpe, "ὁ υἱὸς τοῦ ἀνθρώπου," pp. 427 and
429). Vermes bases his position on the authority of Milik's
position (see pp. 12-13 above) and on the argument that the
preexistent type of messiah represented by the Son of Man in
the Parables is a late messianic concept (see *Jesus the Jew*,
pp. 137-39 and 176). However, the preexistence of the Son of
Man (cf. 1 En. 48:1-7 and 62:7) is dependent upon exegesis of
the servant song in Is. 49, and George W. E. Nickelsburg, Jr.
(*Resurrection, Immortality, and Eternal Life in Intertestamental Judaism*, HTS, no. 26 [Cambridge: Harvard University
Press, 1972], pp. 58-79) has shown that the Son of Man material
in the Parables uses exegetical traditions based on the servant
songs, traditions that are also used in the material dealing
with the righteous man in Wsd. Sol. 2 and 4-5.

[87]"Prolegomenon," p. XVIII, see above p. 21.

[88]See Georg Beer, "Das Buch Henoch," *Die Apokryphen und
Pseudepigraphen des Alten Testaments*; vol. 2, *Die Pseudepigraphen des Alten Testaments*; ed. Emil Kautzsch (Tübingen:
J. C. B. Mohr, 1900; reprint ed., Hildesheim: Georg Olms
Verlagsbuchhandlung, 1962), p. 227; and Charles, *Book of Enoch*,
pp. xlvi-xlvii, 106-7, and 129. The latter lists the

following passages: 1 En. 6-11; 54:1-55:2; 60; 65:1-69:25; 106-7 (see p. xlvii); however, he is not consistent in his notes to the translation (see p. 106).

[89]See the ספר נוח among the small midrashim collected by Adolph Jellinek (*Bet ha-Midrasch: Sammlung kleiner Midraschim und vermischter Abhandlungen aus der ältern jüdischen Literatur*, 2d ed., 6 vols. [Jerusalem: Bamberger and Wahrmann, 1938], 3:155-60). A German translation has been made by August Wünsche (*Aus Israels Lehrhallen: Kleine Midraschim zur jüdischen Eschatologie und Apokalyptik*, 5 vols. bound as 2 [Hildesheim: Georg Olms Verlagsbuchhandlung, 1967; original ed., Leipzig, 1909], 3:201-12).

[90]*Der Menschensohn*, pp. 13-35.

[91]"Man muss sich in der apokalyptischen Literatur manchmal mit einem assoziativen statt mit einem logischen Zusammenhang zufrieden geben" (ibid., p. 13).

[92]Ibid., p. 33.

[93]"Solche [sekundäre Abschnitte] sind vor allem die 'noachidischen' Abschnitte (39,1-2a; 54,7-55,2; 60; 65-69,25), *über deren besondere Herkunft schon längst Einigkeit herrscht*" (ibid., emphasis added).

PART II: INTRODUCTION

[1]Cf. Geza Vermes, *Scripture and Tradition in Judaism: Haggadic Studies*, SPB, no. 4; 2d rev. ed. (Leiden: E. J. Brill, 1973), pp. 6, 8, and 228-29.

CHAPTER III: THE IS. 24:17-23 MIDRASH

[1]"An Investigation of the Literary Form, Haggadic Midrash, in the Old Testament and Intertestamental Literature," Studies in Sacred Theology, 2d ser., no. 164 (Dissertation, Catholic University of America, 1965), p. 145.

[2]Ibid., p. 262.

[3]Ibid., pp. 91-103.

[4]*Scripture and Tradition*, pp. 228-29. Vermes treats exegetical and narrative midrash as two variations of one form.

[5]The use of formulaic language in the Parables will be examined further in chapter VII below.

[6]*Scripture and Tradition*, p. 229.

[7]Cf. Hartman (*Prophecy Interpreted*, p. 109): "We get a certain idea of how the creative mind of the author worked with the material it had learned when we are able to determine certain 'stations' for the processes of association, determine

which OT passages are echoed in the text and then consider how it came about that the author recalled these particular passages and why his 'intuition' or his exploring mind sought out just this or that passage in the OT."

[8] Cf. ibid., pp. 109-12. Hartman compares the apocalyptic material with which he is working to midrashic exegesis without, however, terming it midrash.

[9] This position represents a slight departure from Hartman's position (ibid., p. 109; see above, n. 7). Hartman assumes that it is the "author" who is carrying out the exegesis. The assumption here is that the exegetical units in the Parables are traditional in nature and that the creativity of the poet is to be found in the selection of these units and their use within the framework of the pattern that he employs (see chapter VII below).

[10] Cf. Vermes, *Scripture and Tradition*, p. 229.

[11] Otto Kaiser, *Isaiah 13-39: A Commentary*, trans. R. A. Wilson, The Old Testament Library (Philadelphia: Westminster Press, 1974), pp. 176-77.

[12] Ibid., p. 176.

[13] Ibid., pp. 178-79.

[14] Ibid., p. 178.

[15] *Resurrection*, pp. 17-18.

[16] Ibid., p. 19.

[17] Kaiser, *Isaiah 13-39*, p. 178.

[18] *Theocracy and Eschatology*, trans. S. Rudman (Oxford: Basil Blackwell, 1968), p. 77.

[19] *The Dawn of Apocalyptic* (Philadelphia: Fortress Press, 1975), pp. 313-15.

[20] Cf. Otto Eissfeldt, *The Old Testament: An Introduction*, trans. Peter R. Ackroyd (New York: Harper and Row, 1965), p. 346.

[21] Cf. Roland de Vaux, *Archaeology and the Dead Sea Scrolls* (London: Oxford University Press for the British Academy, 1973), p. 97; and Frank Moore Cross, Jr., *The Ancient Library of Qumran and Modern Biblical Studies*, rev. ed. (Garden City, N.Y.: Anchor Books, 1961), pp. 164-65.

[22] Eissfeldt, *The Old Testament*, pp. 565-66.

[23] From the Prologue to Sirach.

[24] אספה is a hapax legomenon, and KB suggests reading אסף האסיר, taking the ה as the definite article of the next

word. The change makes little difference since the word in question is to be taken as an internal object after אספו. אספה is represented in middle Hebrew by אסיפה, "assembly," and thus might be a late linguistic feature of the passage. Both the LXX and the Targum present too free a translation to be of much use in textual criticism of this section. In verse 23, for example, the Targum indicates that it is those who *worship* the sun and moon who will be ashamed.

[25] Various attempts to deal with the composition of the Isaiah Apocalypse split Is. 24:17-23 between two (or more) strata (See Kaiser, *Isaiah 13-39*, pp. 174-79 and 192-93).

[26] The translation is that of the *RSV*, which interprets רזי־לי as from the root רזה, "diminish." Kaiser (*Isaiah 13-39*, p. 189) follows the LXX and the Targum by relating the phrase to רז, "secret," although both may well represent an interpretation of the text. KB indicates that רזי is unexplained.

[27] The "reward of the righteous" is probably a reference to Is. 24:23b, where the Targum has transferred the central interest from Yahweh Ṣebaʾoth, who reigns, to the *kingdom* of the Lord of Hosts: ארי תתגלי מלכותא דיוי צבאות בטורא דציון ובירושלם וקדם סבי עמיה ביקר. The kingdom is the reward of the righteous. The perception of Is. 24:17-23 as relating to the reward of the righteous and the punishment of the wicked will be of importance in chapters VI and VII below in relating the Is. 24:17-23 midrash to the thematic structure of the Parables of Enoch.

[28] In the Ethiopic, *maʿābelt*, "instruments," has been altered to *mabāleʿt*, "foods," through metathesis.

[29] The Ethiopic reads *ʾesrat[a] mabāleʿt*, "packages [of] food," the second word of which has been dropped here as a gloss, following Charles (*The Ethiopic Version of the Book of Enoch*, Anecdota Oxoniensia [Oxford: The Clarendon Press, 1906], pp. 97-98). The gloss was obviously the result of the metathesis in verse 3 above, and *ʾesrat* should here be translated "bonds."

[30] Charles is probably correct in rejecting *wa-diba ʾanqeʿt ʾela matḥeta samāyāt*, "and in addition to the fountains that are beneath the heavens," as an obvious corruption of the original cosmology (see ibid., p. 98, n. 34).

[31] Charles is probably correct in rejecting the relative pronoun *za-* in *za-mesla māyāt*, "that [are] with the waters" (see ibid., p. 99, n. 2).

[32] The temporal reference relates to the motif of 1 En. 54:1-6, which is seen as taking place before the flood. 1 En. 55:3-56:4 returns to the motif of 54:1-6, and, according to the eschatology of the Is. 24:17-23 midrash, which will be discussed below, the imprisonment of the angels and kings takes place before or at the time of the flood.

³³Charles's translation, "seduced" (see *Book of Enoch*, p. 129), is too specific; *'asḥata* means "cause to err."

³⁴An examination of the narrative structure of the passage indicates that verse 3 belongs after verse 5; see p. 134 below.

³⁵Verses 6-8 do not seem to fit into the dialogue between Enoch and Noah, see p. 134 below.

³⁶Charles reads *yetbaddar*, "is pre-eminent," with one manuscript, rather than *yebadder*, "is swift" (*Book of Enoch*, p. 130).

³⁷The Ethiopic reads *yetḫʷēllaqʷ*, "it will be numbered," which, according to Charles (*Book of Enoch*, p. 131), is equivalent to יחשב, *nif.*, "it will be accounted," which is corrupt for יחשך, *nif.*, "it will be withheld."

³⁸Charles (ibid.) suggests that the Ethiopic represents חדשים, "months," which is corrupt for חרשים, "sorceries," an insight that he attributes to M. Joseph Hallévy ("Recherches sur la langue de la rédaction primitive du livre d'Énoch," *JA*, 6th series, 9 [1867]: 352-95).

³⁹The Ethiopic reads *malā'ekt*, "angels"; however, the context suggests that מלכים, "kings," has been corrupted to מלאכים, "angels" (see Charles, *Book of Enoch*, p. 135).

⁴⁰As it stands, *mesālyāta*, "parables," must be read as the direct object of *wahaba*, "he gave."

⁴¹Charles (*Book of Enoch*, p. 105) recognizes that Is. 24:21-23 is responsible for the idea of the common judgment of the kings and the angels, but he does nothing more with the passage in relation to the Parables of Enoch.

⁴²See Pierre Grelot, "Isaïe XIV 12-15 et son arrière-plan mythologique," *RHR* 149 (1956): 18-48.

⁴³See Nicholas J. Tromp, *Primitive Conceptions of Death and the Nether World in the Old Testament*, BibOr, no. 21 (Rome: Pontifical Biblical Institute, 1969), pp. 66-69. The double meaning, "prison" and "Sheol," is appropriate in this context.

⁴⁴*Book of Enoch*, p. 108.

⁴⁵August Dillmann, *Lexicon Linguae Aethiopicae: Cum Indice Latino*, reprint ed. (New York: Frederick Ungar Publishing Co., 1955), s.v. Dillmann's citations are not comprehensive, and the LXX stands between the Hebrew and the Ethiopic version; however, the examples provided by this method at least point toward patterns of usage.

⁴⁶KB, s.v.

⁴⁷Cf. Reginald H. Fuller, (*The Foundations of New Testament Christology* [New York: Charles Scribner's Sons, 1965], pp. 169-70), who bases his argument on Is. 42:1 rather than on 44:2.

[48] See above, n. 24.

[49] Rabbinic sources mention several thermal springs, which were said to have remained when the other fountains of the deep were closed, although not all are in the Jordan rift. They include the gulf of Gaddor, the hot springs of Tyberias, the great well of Biram, and the cavern springs of Paneas (see *Sanh.* 108a and *Gen. Rab.* 33:4). Several explanations are given for the springs, including the suggestion that they pass by the gates of Gehenna (see *Šabb.* 39a). For other references, see Dov Noy, "Motif-Index of Talmudic-Midrashic Literature" (Dissertation, Indiana University, 1954), p. 124 (A 942.1,2). See also Origen (*Contra Celsum* 5. 52), who explains the thermal springs as the *tears* of the angels imprisoned in chains in the earth. It is difficult to determine whether this reference indicates that Origin is familiar with the Parables or with a tradition initiated by the work.

[50] Cf. Martin P. Nilsson, *Geschichte der Griechischen Religion*; vol. 2, *Die Hellenistische und Römische Zeit*; Handbuch der Altertumswissenschaft, no. 5, pt. 2; 2d rev. and enl. ed. (Munich: C. H. Beck'sche Verlagsbuchhandlung, 1961), pp. 556-58; and Franz Cumont, *After Life in Roman Paganism*, Silliman Memorial Lectures (New Haven: Yale University Press, 1922), pp. 170-76. The latter argues that the Hellenistic interest in the torment of the damned has eastern origins while the former responds that "die Hölle eine griechische Erfundung ist" (*Griechischen Religion*, p. 558).

[51] *Hellenistic Influence on the Book of Wisdom and Its Consequences*, AnBib, no. 41 (Rome: Biblical Institute Press, 1970), p. 101 (emphasis added).

[52] Philo's account of the psychological torment of Flaccus (*Flacc.* 170-75) and Cain (*Praem.* 67-73) presents some interesting parallels. Flaccus is tormented in his soul for his persecution of the Jews in Alexandria, and both are condemned to a living death rather than to a swift execution. For Cain, divine justice created a transformation in the soul of the sinner:

"Death thus remains with him perpetually; observe how that is effected. There are four passions in the soul, two concerned with the good, either at the time or in the future, that is pleasure and desire, and two concerned with evil present or expected, that is grief and fear. The pair on the good side God tore out of him [Cain] by the roots so that never by any chance he should have any pleasant sensations or desire anything pleasant, and engrafted in him only the pair on the bad side, producing grief unmixed with cheerfulness and fear unrelieved" (*Praem.* 71).

[53] Charles (*Book of Enoch*, p. 133) is overly concerned with the inconsistencies related to the mountains and valleys between 1 En. 52-54 and 67. The geography involved seems to be as much mythical as actual. Charles himself quotes one Rabbinic source, *Mid. Ps.* 8, that claimed that Jehoshaphat (cf. Joel 3 and 1 En. 53:1) does not exist (ibid., p. 104).

[54] Dillmann (*Lexicon*, s.v.) gives *vergere, inclinari,* and *labascere* for *'agnana*. The last term, meaning "totter" or "threaten to fall," has been taken here.

[55] See *Prophecy Interpreted*, pp. 71-77.

[56] See Charles, *Book of Enoch*, p. 107; for Rabbinic and Kabbalistic parallels, see Ḥag. 15a; Harry Sperling and Maurice Simon, trans., *Zohar*, 5 vols. (London: Soncino Press, 1933), 1:75, 144, and 200-201; and Scholem, *Major Trends*, p. 231.

[57] Cf. 1 En. 10:7 and 67:2. In the latter case, the subjunctive *yebo'* requires an imperative rather than an indicative: "But *let* a change *occur* lest the earth remain destitute" (contrast Charles, *Book of Enoch*, p. 133). The transformation that is to take place does not refer to the fruitfulness of the seed of Noah alone but to the state of the earth, which has been polluted and made destitute by violence and bloodshed (cf. 1 En. 65:6). Philo's description of the results of the first murder in *Praem*. 68, is a relevant parallel:
"He [Cain] it was who first fell under a curse, who first brought *the monstrous pollution of human blood upon the still pure earth*, who first, when it was giving birth and growth to every kind of animals and plants and was bright with all the products of its fruitfulness, *set a bar to that fruitfulness*, who first armed dissolution against generation, death against life, sorrow against joy and evil against good."
While the motif is connected to a different legend, it is clear that bloodshed pollutes the earth, causing its destitution, and that a creative act, the meeting of the waters in 1 En. 54:7-9, is required to return the earth to its original purity. For a study of the pollution of the earth or land by the three "deadly" sins, idolatry, sexual immortality, and bloodshed, see Adolf Büchler, *Studies in Sin and Atonement in the Rabbinic Literature of the First Century*, Jews' College Publications, no. 11 (London: Oxford University Press, 1928), pp. 212-26, 278-83, 292-97.

[58] 1 En. 2-5 contrasts the order in the cosmic realm to the chaos in human society, a theme derived from the wisdom tradition, which was concerned with discerning "a hidden order in things and events" that is "kindly and righteous" and that can be discovered through observation of "analogies between processes in 'nature' and in the life of man" (von Rad, *Old Testament Theology*, 1:421 and 425). Von Rad is one of several proponents of the wisdom tradition as the source of apocalyptic, and his revised discussion of this topic can be found in *Theologie des Alten Testaments*; vol. 1, *Die Theologie der geschichtlichen Ueberlieferungen Israels*; 6th ed. (1969); vol. 2, *Die Theologie der prophetischen Ueberlieferungen Israels*, 5th rev. and improved ed. (1968); 2 vols. (Munich: Chr. Kaiser Verlag, 1968-69), 2:316-31. See also James Muilenburg, "The Son of Man in Daniel and the Ethiopic Apocalypse of Enoch," *JBL* 79 (1960): 197-209; Frank Moore Cross, Jr., "New Directions in the Study of Apocalyptic," *JTC* 6 (1969): 157-65; and Jonathan Z. Smith, "Wisdom and

Apocalyptic," *Religious Syncretism in Antiquity: Essays in Conversation with Geo Widengren*, ed. Birger A. Pearson, Series on Formative Contemporary Thinkers, no. 1 (Missoula, Mont.: Scholars Press for the American Academy of Religion, 1975), pp. 131-56.

[59] *The Old Testament*, p. 111.

[60] See also the Prayer of Manasseh, which, in verses 9-10, claims:
"I am unworthy to look up and see the height of heaven
    because of the multitude of my iniquities.
I am weighted down with many an iron fetter,
    so that I am rejected because of my sins. . . ."
It then continues in verse 13:
"Do not be angry with me for ever or lay up evil for me;
    do not condemn me to the depths of the earth."
For the inability to look up to heaven, see 1 En. 13:5.

[61] Cf. Tromp, *Primitive Conceptions of Death*, p. 67.

[62] See Stith Thompson, *Motif-Index of Folk-Literature*, Rev. and Enl. ed., 6 vols. (Bloomington, Ind.: Indiana University Press, 1955-58), 2:451-54 (E 431.10.1, 437.4, 441.2); Ödön Beke, "Texte zur Religion der Osttscheremissen," *Anthropos* 29 (1934): 49-50; and Jacqueline Simpson, *Icelandic Folktales and Legends* (Berkeley and Los Angeles, Calif.: University of California Press, 1972), p. 135. The practice of covering with stones may also have the implication of separating the sinner from God, as the parallel idea of covering Asael with darkness in 1 En. 10:5 suggests.

[63] See T. Francis Glasson, *Greek Influence in Jewish Eschatology: With Special Reference to the Apocalypses and Pseudepigraphs* (London: S.P.C.K., 1961); Victor Tcherikover, *Hellenistic Civilization and the Jews*, trans. S. Applebaum (New York: Atheneum, 1970); and Martin Hengel, *Judaism and Hellenism: Studies in their Encounter in Palestine during the Early Hellenistic Period*, trans. John Bowden (London: SCM Press Ltd., 1974).

[64] See Hans Dieter Betz ("On the Problem of the Religio-Historical Understanding of Apocalypticism," *JTC* 6 [1969]: 134-56), who argues for the discontinuity of Jewish apocalyptic with the older Israelite and Jewish tradition.

[65] See Smith, "Wisdom and Apocalyptic."

[66] Philo's exegesis of Gen. 6:1-4 in *Gig.* 6-8 is an obvious example. Palestinian Jewish syncretism of this nature is generally more subtle in the introduction of Hellenistic material, but the possibilities will become apparent in the examination of the Is. 24:17-23 midrash and the angel lists.

[67] See Theodor H. Gaster, *Myth, Legend, and Custom in the Old Testament* (New York: Harper and Row, 1969), pp. 571-72 and 574-75.

⁶⁸Cf. Glasson, *Greek Influence*, pp. 62-67.

⁶⁹Cf. ibid., pp. 65-67.

⁷⁰*Theogony* 713-20.

⁷¹*Myth, Legend, and Custom*, p. 574.

⁷²Ibid., p. 575.

⁷³Ibid., pp. 574-75. At what point the rebellious powers come to be identified with stars or planets is unclear. Gaster implies that this identification is late and gives examples from 1 En. 18 and 21 as his earliest examples. In the *Enuma elish*, the vanquished gods are fettered and trampled underfoot before the creation of the heavens (see *ANET*, p. 67). On the other hand, Grelot, "Isaïe XIV 12-15," interprets *Helel ben Shaḥar* in Is. 14:12 in terms of an astral myth related to the planet Venus, a myth that he reconstructs by relating Ugaritic material to the Greek myth of Phaëthon (see also Jack Lindsay, *Origins of Astrology* [London: Frederick Muller, 1971], pp. 24-25). Perhaps the theme of the fall of the mighty should be regarded as one having variable functions and associations with various motifs in the ancient world. It is applied in Obad. 1-4 to Edom, a nation dwelling on mountain peaks, and the reference to the eagle in verse 4 suggests the motif of the fall of the bastard eaglet to be examined below (see Erwin R. Goodenough, "The Political Philosophy of Hellenistic Kingship," *Yale Classical Studies*, Vol. 1, ed. Austin M. Harmon [New Haven: Yale University Press, 1928], pp. 82-83 and 97).

⁷⁴There is similar ambivalence concerning the ultimate fate of Prometheus in Greek mythology (see H. J. Rose, *A Handbook of Greek Mythology Including Its Extension to Rome* [New York: E. P. Dutton and Co., 1959], pp. 55-56).

⁷⁵Carsten Colpe, in a class lecture, spring, 1974.

⁷⁶Cf. Glasson, *Greek Influence*, pp. 65-67.

⁷⁷See Rose, *Greek Mythology*, pp. 54-56.

⁷⁸Julian Morgenstern ("The Mythological Background of Psalm 82," *HUCA* 14 [1939]: 29-126) argues that Ps. 82 is composed of parts of two sources, one dealing with the judgment of heavenly beings (verses 1 and 6-7) and one concerning the failure of earthly judges, or kings, to exercise justice on the earth (verses 2-5). He identifies the sin of the heavenly beings by reference to Gen. 6:1-4. A comparison, however, of verses 6-7 with Ps. 2:7 and Ezek. 28:9, indicates that the entire psalm refers to *kings*, who, in the royal ideology of the ancient world, could be termed gods or the sons of gods and who could, in the terms of Ps. 82, Is. 14, and Ezek. 28, fall from power for the abuse of power or knowledge or for excessive hubris.

⁷⁹See Goodenough, "Hellenistic Kingship," pp. 55-102.

[80]Ibid., p. 78.

[81]*Icaromenippus* 14.

[82]Goodenough, "Hellenistic Kingship," p. 83.

[83]*Die Henochgestalt: Eine vergleichende religionsgeschichtliche Untersuchung*, Skrifter utgitt av det Norske Videnskaps-Akademi i Oslo, no. II, Historisk-Filosofisk Klasse, 1939, no. i (Oslo, Norway: I Kommisjon Hos Jacob Dybwad, 1939), pp. 77-78. Possible Iranian parallels are to be found in Geo Widengren, "Iran and Israel in Parthian Times with Special Regard to the Ethiopic Book of Enoch," *Religious Syncretism in Antiquity: Essays in Conversation with Geo Widengren*, ed. Birger A. Pearson, Series on Formative Contemporary Thinkers, no. 1 (Missoula, Mont.: Scholars Press for the American Academy of Religion, 1975), pp. 120-23. The imprisonment of the kings and angels in the period between the flood and the eschaton is a idea distinct from the thousand year messianic reign in Rev. 20. The latter is probably of Iranian origin, although the eschatology of the Is. 24:17-23 midrash preserved in 1 Enoch may have had some small influence on Rev. 20. The details of the chaining and imprisonment of the serpent in Rev. 20:1-3 could reflect 1 En. 10:4-6 or 54:3-6; however, the release of Satan at the end of a thousand years in Rev. 20:11 is not derived from 1 Enoch.

[84]*Prometheus: Archetypal Image of Human Existence*, trans. Ralph Manheim, Bollingen Series 65, Archetypal Images in Greek Religion, vol. 1 (New York: Pantheon Books, 1963), pp. 27-28.

[85]Wright ("Haggadic Midrash," p. 91) assigns halakah to Rabbinic discussion and haggadah to the synagogue. Vermes comments only on haggadah, which he assigns to the synagogue (*Scripture and Tradition*, p. 228-29). See also Hartman (*Prophecy Interpreted*, p. 111), who does not distinguish between haggadah and halakah but mentions both contexts. It is possible that some discussion is needed of the relationship between haggadic and halakic midrash. The Merkabah tradition represents a form of haggadic midrash and yet seems to have been a matter of private discussion rather than public preaching. It is possible that haggadah in the sectarian context extended beyond the sermon, particularly when it involved eschatological or messianic secrets. In chapter II above, the Parables of Enoch was found to have points of contact with the Merkabah tradition, and this connection may have some implications for the precise *Sitz im Leben* of the material in the work.

[86]The term "sectarian" may have limited application in first century Judaism since it is not clear what "normative" Judaism is in that period so that one could define a sect in relation to it. The term, however, has been widely used and is here used to designate a private religious association, a form of religious community common in the Hellenistic age (cf. the "Rules of a Private Religious Association in Philadelphia," in Frederick C. Grant, *Hellenistic Religions: The Age of*

Syncretism, The Library of Liberal Arts [Indianapolis, Ind.: The Bobbs-Merrill Co., 1953], pp. 28-30). The Pharisees, Essenes, and Therapeutae are probably best described as private religious associations.

CHAPTER IV: THE LISTS OF FALLEN ANGELS

[1] For some remarks on the names in the Aramaic version from Qumran, see Matthew Black, "The Fragments of the Aramaic Enoch from Qumran," *La Littérature juive entre Tenach et Mischna*, ed. W. C. van Unnik, RechBib, no. 9 (Leiden: E. J. Brill, 1974), p. 26.

[2] For a discussion of the text-critical problem raised by the order of these names in the different versions see Adolphe Lods, *Le Livre d'Hénoch: Fragments grecs découverts à Akhmîm (Haute-Égypte) publiés avec les variantes du texte éthiopien* (Paris: Ernest Leroux, 1892), pp. 106-7; Charles, *Ethiopic Version of Enoch*, pp. 227-28; and *Book of Enoch*, pp. 16-17.

[3] For an attempt to interpret some of these names, see Léon Gry, "Mystique gnostique (juive et chrétienne), en finale des Paraboles d'Hénoch," *Le Muséon* 52 (1939): 337-78. He suggests that *'arwē*, "serpent," in 1 En. 69:12 is a mistaken reading of *naḥaš*, "divination," as *nāḥāš*, "serpent"; however, his attempt to rewrite 1 En. 69:12-15 is probably too extensive to be convincing (see pp. 342-71). He argues that Jeqon in 1 En. 69:4 is corrupt for יקרון from קרן, "horn," a name found, along with גדריאל (cf. 1 En. 69:6) in Aramaic incantation texts. He also attempts to derive *'Asbe'ēl* in 1 En. 69:5 and *Kāsbe'ēl*, the chief of the oath in 1 En. 69:13-25, from the Akkadian titles *āšipu* and *kaššapu* (cf. Heb. אשף, "conjurer," and כשף, "sorcerer"); however, this explanation depends upon the treatment of the oath tradition in 1 En. 69:13-15 as a continuation of the second angel list in 1 En. 69:4-12, a position that was rejected above in chapter II, where a different explanation for *Kāsbe'ēl* was offered.

[4] See 1 En. 9-10; 20; 40; 54:6; 71:8-9; 1QM 9:15-16.

[5] The *Sefer ha-Hekhaloth*, 3 Enoch, is constructed largely of lists of heavenly beings with their functions in the heavenly liturgy, and the angelic liturgy from Qumran seems to be similar (see Strugnell, "The Angelic Liturgy"). In the New Testament, Revelation is partially constructed of angel lists, although no names are given. In chapters 2-3, the seven letters are addressed to the *angels* of the individual churches.

[6] 1QM 9:15-16. In addition, the inscriptions on the trumpets, banners, and spears in columns 3, 4, and 7 seem to be little more than angel names, the clauses spelling out more specifically the meaning that would be packed into a theophoric name.

[7] Cf. Lord, *Singer of Tales*, pp. 86, 106.

⁸*J.W.* 2. 142.

⁹See above, n. 6. A number of these phrases use feminine or abstract words as formative elements where an angel name would have a masculine word.

¹⁰Association of the angels with natural phenomena is a common idea in the Enochic literature (see 1 En. 33:2-4; 69:13-25; and 72-82) as well as in other works from Judaism of the period (see 1QH 1:8-13; 13:1-10; and 1QM 10:11-15). Cf. Betz, "Religio-historical Understanding," p. 141; Hull, *Hellenistic Magic*, p. 38; and Hengel, *Judaism and Hellenism*, 1:231-39. See also the discussion of the oath tradition on pp. 19-23 above.

¹¹"Hiob XXXVIII," pp. 293-301, and *Old Testament Theology*, 1:425 and 2:307.

¹²Cf. von Rad, *Theologie des Alten Testaments*, 2:318. For the role of the scribes in the third century B.C., see Elias Bickerman, *From Ezra to the Last of the Maccabees: Foundations of Post-Biblical Judaism*, trans. Moses Hadas (New York: Schocken Books, 1962), pp. 68-71; and Tcherikover, *Hellenistic Civilization and the Jews*, pp. 125-26 and 196-98.

¹³The phrase *daqiqa malā'ekt [qedusān]*, "sons of the [holy] angels," is a metonym for בני האלחים of Gen. 6:2. Cf. Ps. 8:6, where the MT states that man has been created a little lower מאלחים, which the LXX renders παρ' ἀγγέλους and the Targum, ממלאכיא.

¹⁴See, for example, Gerhard von Rad, *Genesis: A Commentary*, trans. John H. Marks, The Old Testament Library (Philadelphia: Westminster Press, 1961), pp. 109-12; and Morgenstern, "Mythological Background," p. 79. The early Rabbinic tradition attempted to dispose of the suggestion that the Sons of God of Gen. 6:1-4 were angels who sinned by identifying them as sons of nobles (see Philip S. Alexander, "The Targumim and Early Exegesis of 'Sons of God' in Genesis 6," *JJS* 23 [1972]: 60-71). This interpretation has been attempted in modern scholarship by Leo Jung (*Fallen Angels in Jewish, Christian and Mohammedan Literature* [Philadelphia: Dropsie College for Hebrew and Cognate Learning, 1926], pp. 97-103) and Gustav E. Closen (*Die Sünde der "Söhne Gottes": Gen. 6,1-4: Ein Beitrag zur Theologie der Genesis*, Scripta Pontificii Institute Biblici [Rome: Päpstliches Bibelinstitut, 1937], pp. 75-155). Both attempts reflect theological presuppositions, for Jung, from the Rabbinic tradition, and for Closen, from Augustine. While Jung is correct in arguing that the text of Genesis does not attribute sin to the Sons of God, he takes the position that "in the whole range of not only '*orthodox*' literature, but of *undiluted* Jewish Folklore angels appear as impeccable, divine beings" (*Fallen Angels*, p. 97, emphasis added). Bernard J. Bamberger (*Fallen Angels* [Philadelphia: The Jewish Publication Society of America, 1952], pp. 8-9) correctly interprets the passage on the basis of the mythology and folklore of the ancient world.

[15] Cf. Bamberger, *Fallen Angels*, p. 8.

[16] Reading *mē'ôlām* with the versions rather than *mē'ărēlîm*, "of the uncircumcised," with the MT, see BH.

[17] See Theodor H. Gaster, *Thespis: Ritual, Myth, and Drama in the Ancient Near East* (New York: Harper and Row, 1966), pp. 418-35, for translation and notes. Bamberger (*Fallen Angels*, pp. 8-9) points out the parallel to the intercourse between divine beings and women but does not seem to have noticed the relationship between the depiction of the two demigods and of the giants in 1 En. 6-11.

[18] Cf. CD 5:6-7 and Ps. Sol. 8:13.

[19] J.W. 2. 150.

[20] Ezra 2:62; 9:2; Neh. 7:64; 13:29-30; and Mal. 2:10-12 all suggest that mixed marriages render unclean.

[21] See Lev. 19:19; Deut. 22:9-10; and *Kil'ayim*.

[22] See Deut. 23:2(MT, 23:3); Wsd. Sol. 3:16-19.

[23] Carsten Colpe, in a class lecture, spring, 1974, related the Greek philosophical concept of *mixture* to Dan. 2:42-43, where the feet of the statue, which are made of iron mixed with clay, are taken to symbolize a kingdom that perishes on account of mixed marriages. Empedocles uses the concept of mixture in describing the combination and separation of the four elements according to the action of Love and Strife (see A. A. Long, "Empedocles' Cosmic Cycle in the 'Sixties," *The Pre-Socratics: A Collection of Critical Essays*, ed. Alexander P. D. Mourelatos, Modern Studies in Philosophy [Garden City, N.Y.: Anchor Books, 1974], pp. 397-425). Long (pp. 416-17) sees increasing mixture as the higher value, particularly in relation to Empedocles' conception of the evolution of animal forms. If this is correct, the value of mixture is exactly opposite from that in 1 En. 6-16 and Dan. 2:42-43. It is possible, however, that the idea, having had some confusion in the world of popular philosophy, has had an impact on the Jewish passages. It will be argued below that a tradition concerning the complaint of the earth has found its way into both 1 En. 6-11 and a Hermetic text, the *Kore Kosmu* (Stobaei Hermetica, Excerpt XXIII; see Betz, "Religio-Historical Understanding of Apocalyptic," pp. 146-48). In the latter text, mixture represents the act of creation and is ultimately related to the imprisonment of souls in bodies when the souls are allowed to create something for themselves. They become overly proud of their abilities and begin to equate themselves with the gods in heaven. After their imprisonment they turn on each other in violence, like the giants in 1 En. 6-11, making the introduction of religion necessary. While 1 En. 6-11 and the *Kore Kosmu* have some motifs in common, including that of mixture, the use they make of them is different. In the latter, mixture is the condition of existence, while in the former it represents the destruction of the previously created and good order of the cosmos. The most likely explanation for

the difference in 1 En. 6-11 is the interpretation of mixture in light of specifically Jewish concepts and in the context of a different myth, the divine/human marriages of Genesis 6:1-4.

[24] See W. B. Henning, "The Book of the Giants," *BSOAS* 11 (1943): 52-74; and J. T. Milik, "Turfan et Qumran: Livre des Géants juif et manichéen," *Tradition und Glaube: Das frühe Christentum in Seiner Umwelt*, ed. G. Jeremias, H. -W. Kuhn, and H. Stegemann (Göttingen: Vandenhoeck and Ruprecht, 1971), pp. 117-27.

[25] *Myth, Legend, and Custom*, p. 79.

[26] Evelyn-White, *Hesiod*, pp. 199-201. For the connection with Gen. 6:1-4 and 1 En. 6-11, see Glasson (*Greek Influence*, pp. 57-61), although it seems more likely that in this case the relationship between the Greek and Jewish tradition has its basis in the common culture of the Ancient Near East.

[27] Wsd. Sol. 7:17-22.

[28] *Judaism and Hellenism*, 1:243.

[29] "Zur Dämonologie der späteren Antike," *ARW* 18 (1915): 134-72, see especially 165-68.

[30] "Religio-Historical Understanding of Apocalypticism," pp. 146-48.

[31] Stobaei Hermetica, Excerpt XXIII; see Walter Scott and A. S. Ferguson, *Hermetica: The Ancient Greek and Latin Writings Which Contain Religious or Philosophic Teachings Ascribed to Hermes Trismegistus*, 4 vols. (Oxford: The Clarendon Press, 1924-36; reprint ed., London: Dawsons of Pall Mall, 1968), 1:465-95.

[32] Ibid., 1:467.

[33] *Gig.* 6-8.

[34] See above, pp. 79-80 and n. 23.

[35] The work is to be dated sometime in the first few centuries of the Christian era (see Thomas J. Hopkins, *The Hindu Religious Tradition*, The Religious Life of Man [Encino, Calif.: Dickenson Publishing Co., 1971] pp. 95-97 and 99; and Louis Renou, *The Nature of Hinudism*, trans. Patrick Evans [New York: Walker and Co., 1962], p. 25).

[36] H. H. Wilson, *The Vishṇu Purāṇa: A System of Hindu Mythology and Tradition*, Introduction by R. C. Hazra, 3d ed. (Calcutta: Punthi Pustak, 1961; 1st ed., London, 1840), p. 396.

[37] Ibid., pp. 396-97.

[38] Curt Nimuendajú Unkel, "Die Sagen von der Erschaffung und Vernichtung der Welt als Grundlagen der Religion der

Apapocúva-Guaraní," *Zeitschrift für Ethnologie* 46 (1914): 335. See also Mircea Eliade, *The Quest: History and Meaning in Religion* (Chicago: University of Chicago Press, 1969), pp. 105-6.

[39]"Religio-Historical Understanding of Apocalypticism," pp. 136-39.

[40]*Ant.* 12. 160-236.

[41]See Tcherikover's analysis of Sirach in *Hellenistic Civilization*, pp. 142-51. He relates the class struggle to 1 En. 91-105 (ibid., pp. 105-6).

CHAPTER V: THE ESSENTIAL ELEMENTS OF THE IS. 24:17-23 MIDRASH AND THE LISTS OF FALLEN ANGELS

[1]See Charles (*Book of Enoch*, p. 13), who attributes the insight to August Dillmann ("Pseudepigraphen des Alten Testaments," *RE* [2d ed.], 12:352). Charles assigns 1 En. 6:3-8; 8:1-3; 9:7; and 10:11 to the Semjaza cycle because, with the addition of 1 En. 69:2, these passages treat that angel as the leader while "elsewhere in Enoch Azazel is chief and Semjaza is not mentioned" (*Book of Enoch*, p. 13). Beer ("Das Buch Henoch," p. 225) sees two Noachic cycles: one dealing with the revelation of mysteries and the punishment through the flood (1 En. 6:2b-8; 7:3-6; 8:4; 9:1-5,9-11; 10:4-11:2) and another dealing with the fall and punishment of the angels and the deeds of the giants (1 En. 7:1b; 8:1-3; 9:6-8; 10:1-3). He sees the common element in the two cycles as the marriages of angels and women. Subsequent attempts to distinguish two sources according to the names of the chief angels are undertaken by C. Kaplan, ("Angels in the Book of Enoch," *ATR* 12 [1929-30]: 423-37) and Bamberger (*Fallen Angels*, pp. 18-19). Kaplan argues that the sin of the angels in 1 En. 6-11 is adultery (?) and bloodshed and that their sin in the Parables is rebellion against God. He thus manages to perceive the major themes of the two sections but fails to recognize the role of the Is. 24:17-23 midrash in 1 En. 6-11 or that of the angel lists in the Parables. In attempting to distinguish between the two leaders' responsibilities for the introduction of various types of sin, he charges Asael with responsibility for moral corruption--ignoring 1 En. 6:1-8; 9:7-8; and 10:11-12--and Shemiḥazah with the revelation of secrets. Bamberger does a better job of distinguishing between the responsibilities of the chief angels, and he correctly recognizes that the Noachic fragments are not part of a single composition and that the fallen-angel material in the Parables of Enoch is early, prior to 200 B.C., although in the latter case he does not attempt to explain its presence in the Parables of Enoch or establish its relation to 1 En. 6-11. The problem presented by the above approaches is that they attempt to separate the two cycles on the basis of a literary-critical analysis of 1 En. 6-11 rather than through form-critical examination of the traditions in the Parables. 1 En. 6-11 is a skillfully told tale, making it difficult to

separate the interweaving of two traditional units. The
material in the Parables is more susceptible to analysis, since
the traditional units have retained more of their distinct
characters.

[2] An analysis of the narrative of 1 En. 6-11 would be
an interesting exercise but is beyond the scope of this dissertation. The scenes are constructed so that conversation
takes place between two individuals, or groups treated as
individuals. The action leads to a climax in chapter 9, which
is a verbal confrontation between the archangels and God in
which the charge of theodicy is placed against the deity in
no uncertain terms. The climax is resolved in chapter 10 with
the ascription of all sin to the fallen angels. The rhetorical
climax thus coincides with the central problem raised by the
mythological structure of the passage, which attempts to
explain the origin of evil in a good creation by reference to
the idea of the mixture of the levels.

[3] See above, n. 1.

[4] *Astrology and Religion among the Greeks and Romans*
(New York: Dover Publications, 1960), pp. 77-82.

[5] Bamberger (*Fallen Angels*, p. 6) distinguishes two
different versions of the myth, one dealing with the angels
who go astray after women and one with Satan the rebel. He
apparently sees these as related to two different exegetical
traditions, one on Gen. 6:1-4 and one on Is. 14 (see ibid.,
pp. 7-13). His sensitivity to the exegetical background of
the material is important; however, his interest in the
theological problem of theodicy and its impact on the Jewish,
Christian, and Islamic traditions seems to have prevented him
from pursuing his insight further.

CHAPTER VI: THE IS. 24:17-23 MIDRASH IN THE THOUGHT AND
STRUCTURE OF THE PARABLES OF ENOCH

[1] Hartman (*Prophecy Interpreted*, pp. 121-26) gives a
more extensive analysis of the following passage. In addition, Nickelsburg (*Resurrection*, p. 74) has related 1 En.
46:4-8 to Is. 14 in his discussion of 1 En. 62-63. Debt should
also be acknowledged to Charles, since his notes to the translation in *Book of Enoch* are the source of some of the scripture
references used in the analysis of the following passages.

[2] *Book of Enoch*, pp. 88-89.

[3] See Hartman, *Prophecy Interpreted*, pp. 122-24.

[4] Cf. Barnabas Lindars, *New Testament Apologetic: The
Doctrinal Significance of the Old Testament Quotations* (Philadelphia: Westminster Press, 1961), pp. 24-28; and Norman
Perrin, *The New Testament: An Introduction* (New York: Harcourt
Brace Jovanovich, Inc., 1974), pp. 73-74.

[5] *Book of Enoch*, p. 89.

⁶There are some ambiguities in the description of Diodorus, and Jack Lindsay (*Origins of Astrology*, p. 58) distinguishes the thirty counseling gods, which he relates to the dekans of Egyptian origin, from the thirty-six stars made up of the signs of the Zodiac and the twenty-four judges of the universe, which are of Babylonian origin.

⁷*De Legatione ad Gaium.*

⁸*J.W.* 2. 181-203; *Ant.* 18. 224-19. 211.

⁹See J. P. V. D. Balsdon, *The Emperor Gaius (Caligula)* (Oxford: The Clarendon Press, 1934), pp. 157-73.

¹⁰*Origins of Astrology*, pp. 265-66.

¹¹Cf. Charles, *Book of Enoch*, p. 89.

¹²See Philo's indictment of Gaius quoted in chapter II above, pp. 30-31. It also alludes to Is. 14:13-14.

¹³See Charles, *Book of Enoch*, p. 89; and Nickelsburg, *Resurrection*, pp. 79-80.

¹⁴See Charles, *Book of Enoch*, p. 89.

¹⁵19. 347. Nickelsburg (*Resurrection*, p. 79) considers the confession motif an important part of the tradition behind 1 En. 62-63 and Wsd. Sol. 2 and 4-5. The motif is probably Hellenistic in origin, being related to the idea of the psychological torment of the damned (see above, p. 56). Cf. the prayer of Flaccus in Philo, *Flacc.* 170-75, the Prayer of Manasseh, and the confessions of the damned in Hades in the Apocalypse of Peter (see Edgar Hennecke, *New Testament Apocrypha*, ed. Wilhelm Schneemelcher, trans. R. McL. Wilson, 2 vols. [Philadelphia: Westminster Press, 1963-65], 2:673 and 679).

¹⁶Hennecke, *Apocrypha*, 2:675.

¹⁷*Prophecy Interpreted*, pp. 67-68; see also Charles, *Book of Enoch*, p. 95.

¹⁸Hartman (*Prophecy Interpreted*, pp. 62-64) isolates a "1 En. Sim form," although this particular passage, which is included in his citation, departs from it.

¹⁹Verse 2b, *wa-kʷelo za-yeṣāmmewu la-gēgāy ḫaṭ'ān yeballeʿu*, does not seem correct. *Ḫaṭ'ān*, "sinners," must be the subject of both verbs, since there does not seem to be any other antecedent for *yeṣāmmewu*, "they produce," if *ḫaṭ'ān* is taken to be the subject of *yeballeʿu*, "they devour." Charles suggests reading *yeṣṣāmmawu*, which he translates "oppress," rather than *yeṣāmmewu* (*Book of Enoch*, p. 104); however, Dillmann (*Lexicon*, s.v.) does not list a reflexive-passive for *ṣāmawa*.

[20] The Ethiopic adds *'i-*, "not," but this reading seems to be incorrect.

[21] Here and in 1 En. 54:3, *ma'ābelt*, "instruments," has been altered to *mabāle't*, "foods," through metathesis.

[22] *Book of Enoch*, p. 104.

[23] The unavailing repentence of the kings and mighty is an important motif in the Parables, see 1 En. 48:10, where their proskynesis receives no response, and chapter 63.

[24] *Book of Enoch*, p. 105.

[25] Ibid., p. 70.

[26] The only other reference to the judgment of the host of heaven is 1 En. 61:8-9. Charles (*Book of Enoch*, p. 74) is probably correct in treating 39:1-2a as an interpolation.

[27] Nickelsburg has made this point in discussion at the Catholic Biblical Association, August, 1975.

[28] This point will be established in chapter VII below, in a structural examination of the third parable.

[29] *Resurrection*, p. 74.

[30] Ibid., p. 75.

[31] See ibid., p. 74.

[32] Ibid., pp. 70-74.

[33] See Charles, *Book of Enoch*, pp. 123-24, and Nickelsburg, *Resurrection*, pp. 72-73.

[34] ימס וכל־לבב אנוש, "and each man's heart will melt."

[35] *Jewish Symbols in the Greco-Roman Period*; vol. 4, *The Problem of Method; Symbols from Jewish Cult*; Bollingen Series XXXVII (New York: Pantheon Books for The Bollingen Foundation, 1954), p. 36.

[36] *Der Menschensohn*, p. 33.

CHAPTER VII: THE PARABLES OF ENOCH AS AN ORAL COMPOSITION AND AS A PSEUDEPIGRAPHON

[1] Robert Scholes and Robert Kellogg (*The Nature of Narrative* [New York: Oxford University Press, 1966], p. 51) suggest that, where it is impossible to identify oral composition as such on the basis of formulaic language because, as in the case of the Parables, the sample is too small, it may be distinguished provisionally on the basis of "consistency in the thematic significance of motifs and plots." See also Lord, *Singer of Tales*, p. 131.

²*Quod Omn. Prob.* 80-82.

³*Vit. Cont.* 25-31.

⁴Ibid., 75-78.

⁵Ibid., 64.

⁶*Nature of Narrative*, p. 29.

⁷Ibid., p. 28.

⁸"Haggadic Midrash," p. 59.

⁹*The Symbolism of Evil* (Boston: Beacon Press, 1969), p. 16.

¹⁰*Vit. Cont.* 29.

¹¹See his note in *Philo*, 9:129. His translation is quoted on p. 127 above.

¹²See 1QH 11:4, ותחן בפי הודות ובלשוני [תחיל]ה, "And you have placed [a hymn of] thanksgiving in my mouth and a song of praise on my tongue."

¹³The account of the excommunication of Eliezer ben Hyrcanus in *B. Mes.* 59b implies that the majority opinion of the Rabbis carries authority in the halakic interpretation of scripture, although one would not expect rabbinic interpretation to show the same freedom toward the consonantal text.

¹⁴*Book of Enoch*, p. 113.

¹⁵The ironic distance between author and narrator that is characteristic of written literature as opposed to oral narrative (see Scholes and Kellogg, *Nature of Narrative*, pp. 54-55) is poorly developed, if it exists at all. This is particularly the case if one assumes that visionary experience in apocalyptic literature is not solely a matter of literary fiction (see Hartman, *Prophecy Interpreted*, pp. 104-8, and Scholem, *Jewish Gnosticism*, pp. 18-19). The Parables are closely related to the early levels of Merkabah mysticism, and it seems unlikely that an entire mystical movement would develop from what was a literary fiction in a body of literature from an earlier age.

¹⁶For a translation of 1 En. 65:1-68:1, see pp. 49-51 above.

¹⁷For an earlier discussion of the disturbance upon the earth, see pp. 57-58 above. The present discussion assumes that the poet and the editor are closely associated and that the latter would have been familiar with the exegetical background of the three parables.

[18] Cf. Samuel's response to hearing the voice in 1 Sam. 3, and the *Enuma elish* 2. 5-10 (*ANET*, p. 63), where Ea, when he hears of the preparations of Tiamat for battle, goes to Anshar, his (fore)father, to make inquiries. The journey motif is related to the quests of Gilgamesh and Odysseus to the ends of the earth to obtain answers to important questions.

[19] See above, pp. 16-17.

[20] See Lord, *Singer of Tales*, pp. 30-98.

[21] See Charles (*Book of Enoch*, p. 69), who counts 104 occurrences of the title in the Parables.

[22] See p. 40 above.

[23] *Der Menschensohn*, pp. 13-35.

[24] For the possibility of oral composition in prose, see Scholes and Kellogg (*Nature of Narrative*, pp. 50-51). The meaning of the alternation between poetry and prose in the Parables is not clear. Homiletic midrashic fragments are in poetry while narrative midrashic fragments and astronomical material seem to be in prose, although some or all of the latter two types may represent summaries of poetic material (see below).

[25] Cf. Stanley Gevirtz, *Patterns in the Early Poetry of Israel*, Studies in Ancient Oriental Civilization, no. 32 (Chicago: University of Chicago Press, 1963), pp. 6-14. However, see also the reservations of Robert C. Culley (*Oral Formulaic Language in the Biblical Psalms*, Near and Middle East Series [(Toronto): University of Toronto Press, 1967], pp. 117-19), who believes that it *is* possible to establish an oral formulaic analysis of Hebrew poetry on metrical units rather than on parallelism of thought and line. It is possible that parallelism belongs to the level of the motif rather than formula and formulaic language, although the pairs may not always be tied to one motif. It is also possible that Philo's description of the "repetitions" in the style of the president of the Therapeutae in *Vit. Cont.* 76 is an attempt to depict the use of the parallelism of line: "His instruction proceeds in a leisurely manner: he lingers over it and *spins it out with repetitions*, thus permanently imprinting the thoughts in the souls of the hearers."

[26] *Ethiopic Version of Enoch*, p. iii; *Book of Enoch*, p. lvi.

[27] See above, n. 24.

[28] See Lord, *Singer of Tales*, pp. 99-123.

[29] See pp. 26-27 above, where it is suggested that the Elect one is initially associated with the theme of judgment, on the basis of Is. 42:1-4.

[30] It is difficult to define with any degree of precision the nature of this particular theme; however, the resurrection motif, which is associated with it in 1 En. 61:5, is also found in the second parable in 51:1. In addition, the return from the dispersion found in 57:1-3 might be seen as related to this theme since both it and the resurrection motif involve a "return" (cf. 61:5). The sources of the theme, Ezek. 40-48; Is. 34:15-17; and Zech. 1:14-17 and 2:1-5(MT, 2:5-9), are all concerned with the return from the exile, and Is. 34:16 claims that none will be missing. It seems likely that the theme should be called "the return," and that the resurrection motif is a secondary association with it.

[31] See Hartman, *Prophecy Interpreted*, pp. 62-63: "Firstly, it may not be inappropriate to warn the reader once more against the misconception that the above stages are necessarily in chronological order. They should rather be regarded as parts of a complex of ideas, or as different motifs in a stage picture (this particular comparison with a stage picture is a useful one--these pericopes are designed as visions)." However, if the elements can be reproduced in the same order in 1 En. 41:1-2 and in chapters 60-63, there must be some significance to that order.

[32] Nickelsburg, in discussion at the Catholic Biblical Association in August, 1975, has argued for linear development related to the Son of Man in the Parables.

[33] The association of the Elect one, the dwellings of the righteous, and the heavenly songs of praise in both 1 En. 39:4-14 and 61:6-13 point toward a traditional association of motifs.

[34] Cf. Perrin, *A Modern Pilgrimage*, pp. 10-12.

[35] *Anatomy of Criticism: Four Essays* (Princeton, N.J.: Princeton University Press, 1957), p. 248.

[36] Ibid., p. 251.

[37] *Singer of Tales*, pp. 86 and 106.

[38] See above, pp. 74-77.

[39] See Lord, *Singer of Tales*, pp. 94-98 and 119-23.

[40] See ibid., pp. 68-98.

[41] Cf. von Rad, *Theologie des Alten Testaments*, 2:331: "Entgegen immer wieder auftauchenden Behauptungen muss betont werden, dass die Apokalyptik in literarischer Hinsicht keine besondere 'Gattung' repräsentiert. Sie ist im Gegenteil in formgeschichtlicher Hinsicht ein mixtum compositum, das überlieferungsgeschichtlich auf eine sehr komplizierte Vorgeschichte schliessen lässt. Für die Gesamtform ihrer Bücher lässt sich eine gewisse Bevorzugung der Gattung der 'Vermächtnisrede', des 'Testaments' beobachten. Die aber ist ihrerseits wiederum nicht spezifisch apokalyptisch."

[42] KB, s.v.

[43] Cf. Lord, *Singer of Tales*, p. 21.

[44] *Der Menschensohn*, p. 33.

[45] "משׁל," *Wisdom in Israel and in the Ancient Near East*, ed. M. Noth and D. Winton Thomas, VTSup., vol. 3 (Leiden: E. J. Brill, 1955), pp. 162-69, see especially p. 166.

[46] Ibid., p. 167, emphasis added.

[47] See above, pp. 47-48.

[48] *The Parables of Jesus*, rev. ed. (New York: Charles Scribner's Sons, 1963), p. 206, n. 77, see also p. 16, n. 22.

[49] Lord, *Singer of Tales*, pp. 124-38.

[50] *Nature of Narrative*, p. 31.

[51] *Singer of Tales*, p. 129.

[52] Oral literature makes no distinction between the poet and the narrator, while a pseudepigraphon has such a distinction as an important element (cf. Scholes and Kellogg, *Nature of Narrative*, pp. 54-55). However, in the case of the Parables of Enoch, it is the editorial material that attempts to place the distance between the poet and the narrator (Enoch), and the various contradictions that arise as a result--Noah as the speaker of 1 En. 65-66, for example--indicate that the distance is artificial and poorly carried through at that.

[53] Cf. Lord, *Singer of Tales*, p. 129.

[54] See ibid., p. 94: "In a traditional poem, therefore, there is a pull toward the previous uses of the same theme. The result is that characteristic of oral poetry which *literary scholars* have found hardest to understand and to accept, namely, *an occasional inconsistency, the famous nod of a Homer*" (emphasis added). Charles (*Book of Enoch*, p. 85) is concerned with the inappropriate use of "Head of Days" in two passages that he considers interpolations from a book of Noah, 1 En. 55:1 and 60:2. The latter case is clearly an example of an element from another theme being introduced into a similar context. The vision of the heavenly court in 1 En. 60:1-6 has led to the introduction of "Head of Days" from the Dan. 7:9-14 midrash (cf. 1 En. 60:2 with Dan. 7:9 and 1 En. 60:1 with Dan. 7:10). It is possible that the "Head of Days" is associated with a "forbearance" motif (cf. Dan. 7:12 and 1 En. 60:5-6 with 1 En. 55:1-2). Such a motif, or perhaps merely the association of the Head of Days in the Dan. 7 midrash with the act of judgment, might explain the use of the title in 1 En. 55:1.

[55] It is perhaps easier to distinguish levels of organization rather than to assign specific responsibilities to poet and scribe in the composition of 1 Enoch:

(1) the traditional midrashic material
(2) traditional organizational patterns
   (a) the apocalyptic pattern (cf. 1 En. 41:1-2)
   (b) the *mašal* and its visionary concern with the fate of the righteous and wicked
   (c) the messianic motifs and their relationship
(3) the three parables produced according to the techniques of oral composition by a poet or poet-scribe
(4) the editorial work necessary to transform the three parables into a pseudepigraphon, by a scribe or poet-scribe

[56] *Quod Omn. Prob.* 82.

[57] *Vit. Cont.* 31.

[58] Ibid., 75.

[59] *Quod Omn. Prob.* 81, "In these they are instructed *at all other times*, but particularly on the seventh days."

[60] Scholem (*Jewish Gnosticism*, p. 38) quotes Origin, *Prologus in Canticum*, concerning the Song of Songs: "It is said that the custom of the Jews is that no one who has not reached full maturity is permitted to hold this book in his hands. And not only this, but although their rabbis and teachers are wont to teach all the scriptures and their oral traditions [*Mishnayoth*; Origen uses the Greek term *deuteroses*] to the young boys, they defer to the last [in the original: *ad ultimum reservari*] the following four texts: The beginnings of Genesis, where the creation of the world is described; the beginning of the prophecy of Ezekiel, where the doctrine of the angels is expounded [in the original: *de cherubim refertur*]; the end [of the same book] which contains the description of the future temple; and this book of the Song of Songs" (brackets are Scholem's).

    The expounding of the astrological wisdom is obviously related to Gen. 1, and the connection between the creation narrative can be demonstrated from 1 En. 60:7-10,24, where the account of the creation of Leviathan and Behemoth is found (see Charles, *Book of Enoch*, p. 115). That this tradition is part of the midrashic interpretation of the creation narrative is obvious from the parallels in 4 Ezra 6:49-52 and 2 Bar. 29:4, which also make it obvious that wisdom based on the creation narrative was not limited to the Enochic tradition. In 1 En. 60:9-10, Enoch asks to be shown the power of the two monsters and is told that he is inquiring about what is hidden. The angel then shows Enoch the astrological secrets and returns to Leviathan and Behemoth in verse 24, at which point the text breaks off. As 4 Ezra 6:45-52 makes clear, the astrological secrets are associated with the fourth day of creation and the two beasts with the fifth day. In 1 En. 60:11-24, when the "angel" expounds these secrets to Enoch, he follows the same order: (1) astrological secrets, 60:11-23, and (2) the two beasts, 60:24. Had the text not broken off at that point, it would have repeated the tradition concerning the eschatological function of the two beasts as food for the righteous.

According to the Mishnah, it was forbidden to expound the secret of creation to more than one hearer; however, according to Moore (*Judaism*, 1:383), "The restriction. . .does not apply to the exposition of what took place on the six days of creation, nor to what is within the expanse of heaven. But what was before the first creative day, or what is above, beneath, before, behind, it is forbidden to teach in public."

[61] *Vit. Cont.* 29.

[62] See above, pp. 129-30.

[63] See Lord, *Singer of Tales*, p. 106.

[64] While this fluidity between the human and angelic realms appears elsewhere in Judaism of the period--Dan. 7, for example--it is definitely less at home in 1 En. 6-16, where the illegitimate mixing of the two realms is used to explain the origin of evil.

CHAPTER VIII: THE PARABLES OF ENOCH AND THE STUDY OF APOCALYPTIC

[1] "Religio-Historical Understanding of Apocalypticism," pp. 136-39; see above, pp. 88-89.

[2] *Theologie des Alten Testaments*, 2:316-31.

[3] See above, pp. 41-42 and 89.

[4] *Nature of Narrative*, p. 28.

[5] Cf. ibid., p. 40.

[6] See above, pp. 112-13 and 118-19.

[7] *Nature of Narrative*, p. 28.

[8] Here the narrative arts of second temple Judaism should be located, for example, 1 and 2 Maccabees, Judith, Daniel, and Tobit. These narratives frequently utilize the narrative patterns of the "epic" tradition, scripture, to give meaning to their accounts. 2 Macc. 9, for example, tells of the death of Antiochus in terms of Is. 14.

[9] Scholes and Kellogg, *Nature of Narrative*, p. 28.

[10] *Symbolism of Evil*, p. 16.

[11] See above, pp. 128-29.

[12] *Symbolism of Evil*, p. 16.

[13] *Quod Omn. Prob.* 82.

[14] See Plöger, *Theocracy and Eschatology*; Hartman, *Prophecy Interpreted*; and Hanson, *The Dawn of Apocalyptic*.

[15] See Smith, "Wisdom and Apocalyptic."

[16] *Theocracy and Eschatology*, pp. 46-52.

[17] See above, pp. 84, 90, and 99-100.

[18] See above, pp. 80-81.

[19] See Plöger, *Theocracy and Eschatology*, and Hanson, *The Dawn of Apocalyptic*.

[20] See above, pp. 120-23 and 154-55.

[21] *Resurrection*, p. 72.

[22] See Eliade, *The Quest*, pp. 4-7. As he puts it, one must attempt to understand religious phenomena "*on their own plane of reference*" (ibid., p. 4). Elsewhere, he warns against "the fallacy of demystification" (ibid., pp. 68-71).

[23] Ibid., p. 10.

[24] Cf. ibid., pp. 110-11.

[25] *Theologie des Alten Testaments*, 2:316-31.

[26] See Wolfhart Pannenberg et al. (*Revelation as History*, trans. David Granskou [London: The Macmillan Co., 1969]) for this viewpoint.

[27] *The Quest*, p. 111. See above, p. 88.

[28] Eliade identifies the time of creation in the creation myth with the eschaton in "Messianic visions" (see *Cosmos and History: The Myth of the Eternal Return*, trans. Willard R. Trask [New York: Harper and Row, 1959], p. 106). While he alternates in considering history as profane time and as a series of negative or positive hierophanies (ibid., pp. 95 and 107), he is unable to distinguish between the prophetic movement, which discerned the action of Yahweh in history, and the apocalyptic movement, in which evil forces intervene in history. When that distinction is made, it is then possible to discern the parallel between the incursion of evil in the time of creation in the ritual vision of the world and its appearance in history in apocalypticism.

SELECTED BIBLIOGRAPHY

Alexander, Philip S. "The Targumim and Early Exegesis of 'Sons of God' in Genesis 6." *JJS* 23 (1972): 60-71.

Balsdon, J. P. V. D. *The Emperor Gaius (Caligula)*. Oxford: The Clarendon Press, 1934.

Bamberger, Bernard J. *Fallen Angels*. Philadelphia: The Jewish Publication Society of America, 1934.

Beer, Georg. "Das Buch Henoch." In *Die Apokryphen und Pseudepigraphen des Alten Testaments*. Vol. 2: *Die Pseudepigraphen des Alten Testaments*, pp. 217-310. Edited by E[mil] Kautzsch. Tübingen: J. B. C. Mohr, 1900; reprint ed., Hildesheim: Georg Olms Verlagsbuchhandlung, 1962.

Beke, Ödön. "Texte zur Religion der Osttscheremissen." *Anthropos* 29 (1934): 39-69, 371-98, and 703-37.

Betz, Hans Dieter. "On the Problem of the Religio-Historical Understanding of Apocalypticism." *JTC* 6 (1969): 134-56.

Bickerman, Elias. *From Ezra to the Last of the Maccabees: Foundations of Post-Biblical Judaism*. Translated by Moses Hadas. New York: Schocken Books, 1962.

Black, Matthew. "The Eschatology of the Similitudes of Enoch." *JTS* 3 (1952): 1-10.

──────. "The Fragments of the Aramaic Enoch from Qumran." In *La Littérature juive entre Tenach et Mischna*, pp. 15-28. Edited by W. C. van Unnik. Rech Bib, no. 9. Leiden: E. J. Brill, 1974.

──────, ed. *Apocalypsis Henochi Graece*. PVTG, no. 3. Leiden: E. J. Brill, 1970.

Bonner, Campbell. *The Last Chapters of Enoch in Greek*. SD, no. 8. London: Christophers, 1937.

Bousset, Wilhelm. "Zur Dämonologie der späteren Antike." *ARW* 18 (1915): 134-72.

Büchler, Adolf. *Studies in Sin and Atonement in the Rabbinic Literature of the First Century*. Jews' College Publications, no. 11. London: Oxford University Press, 1928.

Charles, Robert Henry. *The Book of Enoch or 1 Enoch*. Revised ed. Oxford: The Clarendon Press, 1912.

──────, ed. *The Ethiopic Version of the Book of Enoch*. Anecdota Oxoniensia. Oxford: The Clarendon Press, 1906.

Closen, Gustav E. *Die Sünde der "Söhne Gottes": Gen. 6,1-4: Ein Beitrag zur Theologie der Genesis.* Scripta Pontificii Institute Biblici. Rome: Päpstliches Bibelinstitut, 1937.

Colpe, Carsten. "ὁ υἱὸς τοῦ ἀνθρώπου." In *TDNT*, 8:400-477.

Colson, F. H. (vols. 1-10), and Whitaker, G. H. (Vols. 1-5). *Philo.* LCL. 10 vols. Cambridge: Harvard University Press, 1929-62.

Cross, Frank Moore, Jr. *The Ancient Library of Qumran and Modern Biblical Studies.* Revised ed. Garden City, N.Y.: Anchor Books, 1961.

─────. "New Directions in the Study of Apocalyptic." *JTC* 6 (1969): 157-65.

Culley, Robert C. *Oral Formulaic Language in the Biblical Psalms.* Near and Middle East Series. [Toronto]: University of Toronto Press, 1967.

Cumont, Franz. *After Life in Roman Paganism.* Silliman Memorial Lectures. New Haven: Yale University Press, 1922.

─────. *Astrology and Religion among the Greeks and Romans.* New York: Dover Publications, 1960.

Denis, Albert-Marie. *Introduction aux pseudépigraphes grecs d'Ancien Testament.* SVTP, no. 1. Leiden: E. J. Brill, 1970.

Dillmann, August. "Pseudepigraphen des Alten Testaments." In *RE* (2d ed.), 12:341-67.

─────. *Lexicon Linguae Aethiopicae cum Indice Latino.* Reprint ed. New York: Frederick Ungar Publishing Co., 1955.

Eissfeldt, Otto. *The Old Testament: An Introduction.* Translated by Peter R. Ackroyd. New York: Harper and Row, 1965.

Eliade, Mircea. *Cosmos and History: The Myth of the Eternal Return.* Translated by Willard R. Trask. New York: Harper and Row, 1959.

─────. *Patterns in Comparative Religion.* Translated by Rosemary Sheed. Cleveland, Ohio: Meridian Books, 1963.

─────. *The Quest: History and Meaning in Religion.* Chicago: University of Chicago Press, 1969.

Evelyn-White, Hugh G. *Hesiod, the Homeric Hymns and Homerica.* LCL. Cambridge: Harvard University Press, 1914.

Farmer, William R. *Maccabees, Zealots, and Josephus: An Inquiry into Jewish Nationalism in the Greco-Roman Period.* New York: Columbia University Press, 1956.

BIBLIOGRAPHY

Flusser, David. "Sanktus und Gloria." In *Abraham unser Vater: Juden und Christen im Gespräch über die Bibel (Festschrift für Otto Michel)*, pp. 129-52. Edited by Otto Betz, Martin Hengel, and Peter Schmidt. Arbeiten zur Geschichte des Spätjudentums und Urchristentums, no. 5. Leiden: E. J. Brill, 1963.

Frye, Northrop. *Anatomy of Criticism: Four Essays*. Princeton, N.J.: Princeton University Press, 1957.

Fuller, Reginald H. *The Foundations of New Testament Christology*. New York: Charles Scribner's Sons, 1965.

Gaster, Moses. "The Logos Ebraikos in the Magical Papyrus of Paris, and the Book of Enoch." *JRAS*, 3d series, 33 (1901): 109-17.

Gaster, Theodor H. *Myth, Legend, and Custom in the Old Testament*. New York: Harper and Row, 1969.

_____. *Thespis: Ritual, Myth, and Drama in the Ancient Near East*. New York: Harper and Row, 1966.

Gevirtz, Stanley. *Patterns in the Early Poetry of Israel*. Studies in Ancient Oriental Civilization, no. 32. Chicago: University of Chicago Press, 1963.

Glasson, T. Francis. *Greek Influence in Jewish Eschatology: With Special Reference to the Apocalypse and Pseudepigraphs*. London: S.P.C.K., 1961.

Goodenough, Erwin R. *Jewish Symbols in the Greco-Roman Period*. Vol. 4: *The Problem of Method; Symbols from Jewish Cult*. Bollingen Series XXXVII. New York: Pantheon Books for The Bollingen Foundation, 1954.

_____. "The Political Philosophy of Hellenistic Kingship." In *Yale Classical Studies*, 1:55-102. Edited by Austin M. Harmon. New Haven: Yale University Press, 1928.

Grant, Frederick C. *Hellenistic Religions: The Age of Syncretism*. The Library of Liberal Arts. Indianapolis, Ind.: The Bobbs-Merrill Co., 1953.

Greenfield, Jonas C. Prolegomenon to *3 Enoch or the Hebrew Book of Enoch*, by Hugo Odeberg. New York: Ktav Publishing House, 1973.

Grelot, Pierre. "L'Eschatologie des Esséniens et le livre d'Hénoch." *RevQ* 1 (1958-59): 113-31.

_____. "La Géographie mythique d'Hénoch et ses sources orientales." *RB* 65 (1958): 33-69.

_____. "Isaïe XIV 12-15 et son arrière-plan mythologique." *RHR* 149 (1956): 18-48.

————. "La Légende d'Hénoch dans les apocryphes et dans la Bible: Origine et signification." *RSR* 46 (1958): 5-26 and 181-210.

Gry, Léon. "Mystique gnostique (juive et chrétienne), en finale des Paraboles d'Hénoch." *Le Muséon* 52 (1939): 337-78.

Hallévi, M. Joseph. "Recherches sur la langue de la rédaction primitive du livre d'Hénoch." *JA*, 6th series, 9 (1867): 352-95.

Hanson, Paul. *The Dawn of Apocalyptic*. Philadelphia: Fortress Press, 1975.

Harmon, A. M. (vols. 1-5), Kilburn, K. (vol. 6), and Macleod, M. D. (vols. 7-8). *Lucian*. LCL. 8 vols. Cambridge: Harvard University Press, 1913-67.

Hartman, Lars. *Prophecy Interpreted: The Formation of Some Jewish Apocalyptic Texts and of the Eschatological Discourse Mark 13 Par*. Translated by Neil Tomkinson and Jean Gray. ConB: NT Series, no. 1. Lund, Sweden: CWK Gleerup, 1966.

Hengel, Martin. *Judaism and Hellenism: Studies in Their Encounter in Palestine during the Early Hellenistic Period*. Translated by John Bowden. London: SCM Press Ltd., 1974.

Hennecke, Edgar. *New Testament Apocrypha*. Edited by Wilhelm Schneemelcher. Translated by R. McL. Wilson. 2 vols. Philadelphia: Westminster Press, 1963-65.

Henning, W. B. "The Book of the Giants." *BSOAS* 11 (1943): 52-74.

Hindley, J. C. "Toward a Date for the Similitudes of Enoch: An Historical Approach." *NTS* 14 (1967-68): 551-65.

Hopkins, Thomas J. *The Hindu Religious Tradition*. The Religious Life of Man. Encino, Calif.: Dickenson Publishing Co., 1971.

Hull, John. *Hellenistic Magic and the Synoptic Tradition*. SBT, 2d series, no. 28. Naperville, Ill.: Alec R. Allenson, 1974.

Jansen, Herman Ludin. *Die Henochgestalt: Eine vergleichende religionsgeschichtliche Untersuchung*. Skrifter utgitt av det Norske Videnskaps-Akademi i Oslo, no. II, Historisk-Filosofisk Klasse, 1939, no. 1. Oslo, Norway: I Kommisjon Hos Jacob Dybwad, 1939.

Jellinek, Adolph. *Bet ha-Midrasch: Sammlung kleiner Midraschim und vermischter Abhandlungen aus der ältern jüdischen Literatur*. 2d ed. 6 vols. Jerusalem: Bamberger and Wahrmann, 1938.

Johnson, A. R. "משל." In *Wisdom in Israel and in the Ancient Near East*, pp. 162-69. Edited by M. Noth and D. Winton Thomas. VTSup, vol. 3. Leiden: E. J. Brill, 1955.

Jung, Leo. *Fallen Angels in Jewish, Christian and Mohammedan Literature*. Philadelphia: Dropsie College for Hebrew and Cognate Learning, 1926.

Kaiser, Otto. *Isaiah 13-39: A Commentary*. Translated by R. A. Wilson. The Old Testament Library. Philadelphia: Westminster Press, 1974.

Kaplan, C. "Angels in the Book of Enoch." *ATR* 12 (1929-30): 423-37.

Kerényi, C. *Prometheus: Archetypal Image of Human Existence*. Translated by Ralph Manheim. Bollingen Series 65, Archetypal Images in Greek Religion, vol. 1. New York: Pantheon Books for The Bollingen Foundation, 1963.

Lindars, Barnabas. *New Testament Apologetic: The Doctrinal Significance of the Old Testament Quotations*. Philadelphia: Westminster Press, 1961.

Lindsay, Jack. *Origins of Astrology*. London: Frederick Muller, 1971.

Lods, Adolphe. "La Chute des anges." *RHPR* 7 (1927): 295-315.

_____. *Le Livre d'Hénoch: Fragments grecs découverts à Akhmîm (Haute-Égypte) publiés avec les variantes du texte éthiopien*. Paris: Ernest Leroux, 1892.

Long, A. A. "Empedocles' Cosmic Cycle in the 'Sixties.'" In *The Pre-Socratics: A Collection of Critical Essays*, pp. 397-425. Edited by Alexander P. D. Mourelatos. Modern Studies in Philosophy. Garden City: N.Y.: Anchor Books, 1974.

Lord, Albert B. *Singer of Tales*. New York: Atheneum, 1974.

Metzger, Bruce M., ed. *The Oxford Annotated Apocrypha: The Apocrypha of the Old Testament: Revised Standard Version*. New York: Oxford University Press, 1965.

Milik, J. T. "The Dead Sea Scrolls Fragment of the Book of Enoch." *Bib* 32 (1951): 393-400.

_____. "Hénoch au pays des aromates." *RB* 65 (1968): 70-77.

_____. "Turfan et Qumran: Livre des Géants juif et manichéen." In *Tradition und Glaube: Das frühe Christentum in seiner Umwelt*, pp. 17-27. Edited by G. Jeremias, H.-W. Kuhn, and H. Stegemann. Göttingen: Vandenhoeck and Ruprecht, 1971.

_____. "Problèmes de la littérature hénochique à la lumière des fragments araméens de Qumrân." *HTR* 64 (1971): 333-78.

Moore, George Foot. *Judaism in the First Centuries of the Christian Era.* 3 vols. Cambridge: Harvard University Press, 1927-30.

Morgenstern, Julian. "The Mythological Background of Psalm 82." *HUCA* 14 (1939): 29-126.

Moulton, James Hope; Howard, Wilbert Francis; and Turner, Nigel. *A Grammer of New Testament Greek.* 3 vols. Edinburgh: T. and T. Clark, 1906-63.

Muilenburg, James. "The Son of Man in Daniel and the Ethiopic Apocalypse of Enoch." *JBL* 79 (1960): 197-209.

Nickelsburg, George W. E., Jr. *Resurrection, Immortality, and Eternal Life in Intertestamental Judaism.* HTS, no. 26. Cambridge: Harvard University Press, 1972.

Nilsson, Martin P. *Geschichte der Griechischen Religion.* Vol. 2: *Die Hellenistische und Römische Zeit.* Handbuch der Altertumswissenschaft, no. 5, pt. 2. 2d revised and enlarged ed. Munich: C. H. Beck'sche Verlagsbuchhandlung, 1961.

Noy, Dov. "Motif-Index of Talmudic-Midrashic Literature." Dissertation, Indiana University, 1954.

Odeberg, Hugo. *3 Enoch or the Hebrew Book of Enoch.* Prolegomenon by Jonas C. Greenfield. Reprint ed. New York: Ktav Publishing House, 1973.

Pannenberg, Wolfhart; Rendtorff, Rolf; Rendtorff, Trutz; and Wilkens, Ulrich. *Revelation as History.* Translated by David Granskou. London: The Macmillan Co., 1969.

Perrin, Norman. *A Modern Pilgrimage in New Testament Christology.* Philadelphia: Fortress Press, 1974.

_____. *The New Testament: An Introduction.* New York: Harcourt Brace Jovanovich, Inc., 1974.

_____. *Rediscovering the Teaching of Jesus.* New York: Harper and Row, 1967.

Plöger, Otto. *Theocracy and Eschatology.* Translated by S. Rudman. Oxford: Basil Blackwell, 1968.

Rad, Gerhard von. *Genesis: A Commentary.* Translated by John H. Marks. The Old Testament Library. Philadelphia: Westminster Press, 1961.

_____. "Hiob XXXVIII und die altägyptische Weisheit." In *Wisdom in Israel and in the Ancient Near East*, pp. 293-301. Edited by M. Noth and D. Winton Thomas. VTSup, vol. 3. Leiden: E. J. Brill, 1955.

_____. *Old Testament Theology.* Translated by D. M. G. Stalker. 2 vols. Edinburgh and London: Oliver and Boyd, 1962-65.

_____. *Theologie des Alten Testaments.* Vol. 1: *Die Theologie der geschichtlichen Ueberlieferungen Israels.* 6th ed. (1969). Vol. 2: *Die Theologie der prophetischen Ueberlieferungen Israels.* 5th revised and improved ed. (1968). 2 vols. Munich: Chr. Kaiser Verlag, 1968-69.

Reese, James M. *Hellenistic Influence on the Book of Wisdom and Its Consequences.* AnBib, no. 41. Rome: Biblical Institute Press, 1970.

Renou, Louis. *The Nature of Hinduism.* Translated by Patrick Evans. New York: Walker and Co., 1962.

Rose, H. J. *A Handbook of Greek Mythology Including Its Extension to Rome.* New York: E. P. Dutton and Co., 1959.

Schmidt, Nathaniel. "The Apocalypse of Noah and the Parables of Enoch." In *Oriental Studies in Honor of Paul Haupt,* pp. 111-23. Edited by C[yrus] Adler and A[aron] Ember. Baltimore: The Johns Hopkins Press, 1926.

Scholem, Gershom G. *Jewish Gnosticism, Merkabah Mysticism, and Talmudic Tradition.* New York: The Jewish Theological Seminary of America, 1965.

_____. *Major Trends in Jewish Mysticism.* 3d revised ed. New York: Schocken Books, 1961.

Scholes, Robert, and Kellogg, Robert. *The Nature of Narrative.* New York: Oxford University Press, 1966.

Schürer, Emil. *The History of the Jewish People in the Age of Jesus Christ (175 B.C.-A.D. 135).* New English version, revised and edited by Geza Vermes and Fergus Millar. 3 vols. Edinburgh: T. and T. Clark, 1973-.

Schwab, M. Moïse. "Vocabulaire de l'angélologie, d'après les manuscrits hébreux de la Bibliothèque Nationale." *MPAIBL,* 1st series, 10 (1897): 113-430.

Scott, Walter, and Ferguson, A. S. *Hermetica: The Ancient Greek and Latin Writings Which Contain Religious or Philosophic Teachings Ascribed to Hermes Trismegistus.* 4 vols. Oxford: The Clarendon Press, 1924-36; reprint ed., London: Dawsons of Pall Mall, 1968.

Simpson, Jacqueline. *Icelandic Folktales and Legends.* Berkeley and Los Angeles, Calif.: University of California Press, 1972.

Singer, S. *The Authorized Daily Prayer Book.* London: Eyre and Spottiswoode, Ltd., 1929.

Sjöberg, Erik. *Der Menschensohn im äthiopischen Henochbuch.* Skrifter utgivna av kungl. humanistiska Vetenskapssamfundet i Lund, no. 41. Lund, Sweden: CWK Gleerup, 1946.

Smith, Jonathan Z. "Wisdom and Apocalyptic." In *Religious Syncretism in Antiquity: Essays in Conversation with Geo Widengren*, pp. 131-56. Edited by Birger A. Pearson. Series on Formative Contemporary Thinkers, no. 1. Missoula, Mont.: Scholars Press for the American Academy of Religion, 1975.

Sperling, Harry, and Simon, Maurice, trans. *Zohar*. 5 vols. London: Soncino Press, 1933.

Stier, Fridolin. "Zur Komposition und Literarkritik der Bilderreden des äthiopischen Henoch (Kap. 37-69)." In *Orientalistische Studien: Enno Littmann, zu seinem 60. Geburtstag am 16. September 1935*, pp. 70-88. Edited by R. Paret. Leiden: E. J. Brill, 1935.

Strugnell, John. "The Angelic Liturgy at Qumran--4Q Serek Šîrôt 'Ôlat Haššabbāt." In *Congress Volume: Oxford 1959*, pp. 318-45. VTSup, Vol. 7. Leiden: E. J. Brill, 1959.

Tcherikover, Victor. *Hellenistic Civilization and the Jews*. Translated by S. Applebaum. New York: Atheneum, 1970.

Thackeray, H. St. J. (vols. 1-5), Marcus, Ralph (vols. 5-8), Wickgren, Allan (vol. 8), and Feldman, Louis (vol. 9). *Josephus*. LCL. 9 vols. Cambridge: Harvard University Press, 1926-65.

Thompson, Stith. *Motif-Index of Folk-Literature*. Revised and enlarged ed. 6 vols. Bloomington, Ind.: Indiana University Press, 1955-58.

Tödt, H. E. *The Son of Man in the Synoptic Tradition*. Translated by Dorothea M. Barton. The New Testament Library. Philadelphia: Westminster Press, 1965.

Tromp, Nicholas J. *Primitive Conceptions of Death and the Nether World in the Old Testament*. BibOr, no. 21. Rome: Pontifical Biblical Institute, 1969.

Ullendorff, Edward. "An Aramaic 'Vorlage' of the Ethiopic Text of Enoch?" In *Atti del convegno internazionale di studi Etiopici*, pp. 259-67. Problemi attuali di scienza e di cultura. Rome: Accademia Nazionale dei Lincei, 1960.

Unkel, Curt Nimeundajú. "Die Sagen von der Erschaffung und Vernichtung der Welt als Grundlagen der Religion der Apapocúva-Guaraní." *Zeitschrift für Ethnologie* 46 (1914): 284-403.

Vaux, Roland de. *Archaeology and the Dead Sea Scrolls*. London: Oxford University Press for the British Academy, 1973.

Vermes, Geza. *Jesus the Jew: A Historian's Reading of the Gospels*. London: Collins, 1973.

_____. *Scripture and Tradition in Judaism: Haggadic Studies*. SPB, no. 4. 2d revised ed. Leiden: E. J. Brill, 1973.

_____. "The Use of בר נש/בר נשא in Jewish Aramaic." In *An Aramaic Approach to the Gospels and Acts*, pp. 310-28, by Matthew Black. 3d ed. Oxford: The Clarendon Press, 1967.

Wertheimer, S. בתי מדרשות. 2d ed., enlarged and amended by A. J. Wertheimer. 2 vols. Jerusalem: Ktab wa-Sepher, 5728 (1967-68).

Widengren, Geo. "Iran and Israel in Parthian Times with Special Regard to the Ethiopic Book of Enoch." In *Religious Syncretism in Antiquity: Essays in Conversation with Geo Widengren*, pp. 85-129. Edited by Birger A. Pearson. Series on Formative Contemporary Thinkers, no. 1. Missoula, Mont.: Scholars Press for the American Academy of Religion, 1975.

Wilson, H. H. *The Vishnu Purāna: A System of Hindu Mythology and Tradition*, with an Introduction by R. C. Hazra. 3d ed. Calcutta: Punthi Pustak, 1961; original ed., London: n.p., 1840.

Wright, Addison G. "An Investigation of the Literary Form, Haggadic Midrash, in the Old Testament and Intertestamental Literature." Studies in Sacred Theology, 2d series, no. 164. Dissertation, Catholic University of America, 1965.

Wünsche, August. *Aus Israels Lehrhallen: Kleine Midraschim zur jüdischen Eschatologie und Apokalyptik*. 5 vols. bound as 2. Hildesheim: Georg Olms Verlagsbuchhandlung, 1967; original ed., Leipzig: E. Pfeiffer, 1907-10.

SUPPLEMENTARY BIBLIOGRAPHY

Adler, W. "Enoch in Early Christian Literature." In *SBL 1978 Seminar Papers*, 1:271-75. Missoula, Mont.: Scholars Press, 1978.

Barr, J. "Aramaic-Greek Notes on the Book of Enoch (I)." *JSS* 23 (1978): 184-98.

Black, M. "The Apocalypse of Weeks in the Light of 4QEn^g." *VT* 28 (1978): 464-69.

_____. "The 'Parables' of Enoch (1 En. 37-71) and the 'Son of Man.'" *Exp Tim* 88 (1976): 5-8.

_____. "The New Creation in I Enoch." In *Creation, Christ and Culture*, pp. 13-21. Edited by R. W. A. McKinney. Edinburgh: Clark, 1976.

_____. "The Throne-Theophany Prophetic Commission and the 'Son of Man': A Study in Tradition-History." In *Jews, Greeks and Christians: Religious Cultures in Late Antiquity* (W. D. Davies Festschrift), pp. 57-73. Edited by R. Hamerton-Kelly and R. Scroggs. Leiden: E. J. Brill, 1976.

Black, M. "The 'Two Witnesses' of Rev. 11:3f. in Jewish and
Christian Apocalyptic Tradition." In *Donum Gentilicium:
New Testament Studies in Honour of David Daube*, pp. 227-37.
Edited by E. Bammel, C. K. Barrett, and W. D. Davies.
Oxford: Clarendon Press, 1978.

Cantinat, J. *Les Épitres de Saint Jacques et de Saint Jude*.
Paris: Lecoffre, 1973. (See especially pp. 270-76).

Caquot, A. "Léviathan et Behémoth dans la troisième 'Parable'
d'Hénoch." *Sem* 25 (1975): 111-22.

―――――. "Remarques sur les chap. 70 et 71 du livre éthiopien
d'Hénoch." *Lectio Divina* 95 (1977): 111-22.

Casey, M. "The Use of Term 'Son of Man' in the Similitudes of
Enoch." *JSJ* 7 (1976): 11-29.

Charlesworth, James H. *The Pseudepigrapha and Modern Research*.
SBLSCS, 7. Missoula, Mont.: Scholars Press, 1976. (See
especially pp. 98-107.)

―――――. "The SNTS Pseudepigrapha Seminars at Tübingen and
Paris on the Books of Enoch." *NTS* 25 (1979)·: 315-23.

Collins, Adela Yarbro. *The Combat Myth in the Book of
Revelation*. Missoula, Mont.: Scholars Press, 1976. (This
book and the following one by John Collins deal with
recurrence or recapitulation in other apocalyptic
writings.)

Collins, John J. *The Apocalyptic Vision of the Book of Daniel*.
Missoula, Mont.: Scholars Press, 1977.

―――――. "Methodological Issues in the Study of I Enoch:
Reflections on the Articles of P. D. Hanson and G. W.
Nickelsburg." In *SBL 1978 Seminar Papers*, 1:315-22.

Coppens, J. "Miscellanea biblica 33: Le Fils d'homme
daniélique, vizir céleste." *ETL* 40 (1964): 72-80.

―――――. "La vision du très-haut en Dan. VII et Hén. Éthiop.
XIV." *ETL* 53 (1977): 187-89.

Coughenour, R. A. "The Woe-Oracles in Ethiopic Enoch." *JSJ* 9
(1978): 192-97.

Dalton, W. J. "Light from the Book of Enoch." In *Christ's
Proclamation to the Spirits*, pp. 163-76. AnBib. Rome:
Pontifical Biblical Institute, 1965.

Dautzenberg, G. "Das Offenbarungsverständnis im aethiopischen
Henoch." In *Urchristliche Prophetie: Ihre Erforschung,
ihre Voraussetzungen im Judentum und ihre Struktur im
ersten Korintherbrief*, pp. 76-89. BWANT, Folge 6, Heft 4.
Stuttgart: Kohlhammer, 1975.

Dexinger, F. *Henochs Zehnwochenapokalypse und offene Probleme
der Apokalyptikforschung*. Leiden: E. J. Brill, 1977.

Dimant, D. "I Enoch 6-11: A Methodological Perspective." In *SBL 1978 Seminar Papers*, 1:323-39. Missoula, Mont.: Scholars Press, 1978.

Doeve, J. W. "Lamech's achterdocht in 1Q Genesis Apocryphon." *Nederlands Theologisch Tijdschrift* 15 (1961): 401-15.

――――――. "De tien-weken-Apokalyps (I Henoch 93:1-10; 91:12-17): een Qumrandocument." In *Vruchten van de Uithof* (H. A. Brongers Festschrift), pp. 7-27. Utrecht: Theologisch Instituut, 1974.

Fitzmyer, J. A. "Implications of the New Enoch Literature from Qumran." *TS* 38 (1977): 332-45.

Glasson, T. F. "The Son of Man Imagery: Enoch 14 and Daniel 7." *NTS* 23 (1976): 82-90.

Greenfield, J. C., and Stone, M. E. "The Enochic Pentateuch and the Date of the Similitudes." *HTR* 70 (1977): 51-65.

Grelot, P. "Hénoch et ses écritures." *RB* 82 (1975): 481-500.

Hammershaimb, E. "Om lignelser og billedtaler i de gammeltestamentlige pseudepigrafer." *SEA* 40 (1975): 36-65.

Hanson, Paul D. "Rebellion in Heaven, Azazel, and Euhemeristic Heroes in 1 Enoch 6-11." *JBL* 96 (1977): 195-233.

――――――. "A Response to John Collins' 'Methodological Issues in the Study of 1 Enoch.'" In *SBL 1978 Seminar Papers*, 1:307-9. Missoula, Mont.: Scholars Press, 1978.

Hartman, Lars. "'Comfort of the Scriptures'--An Early Jewish Interpretation of Noah's Salvation, I En. 10:16-11:2." *SEA* 41-42 (1976-77): 87-96.

Himmelfarb, M. "A Report on Enoch in Rabbinic Literature." In *SBL 1978 Seminar Papers*, 1:259-69. Missoula, Mont.: Scholars Press, 1978.

Klijn, A. F. J. "From Creation to Noah in the Second Dream-Vision of the Ethiopic Henoch." In *Miscellanea Neotestamentica*, pp. 147-59. NovTSup, 47. Leiden: E. J. Brill, 1978.

Knibb, M. A. "The Date of the Parables of Enoch: A Critical Review." *NTS* 25 (1979): 345-59.

Knibb, M. A., and Ullendorff, E. *The Ethiopic Book of Enoch: A New Edition in the Light of the Aramaic Dead Sea Fragments*. 2 vols. Oxford: Clarendon Press, 1978.

Kraft, Robert A. "Philo (Josephus, Sirach and Wisdom of Solomon) on Enoch." In *SBL 1978 Seminar Papers*, 1:253-57. Missoula, Mont.: Scholars Press, 1978.

Lindars, B. "A Bull, a Lamb and a Word: I Enoch XC.38." *NTS* 22 (1976): 483-86.

Luck, U. "Das Weltverständnis in der jüdischen Apokalyptik
dargestellt am äthiopischen Henoch und am 4 Ezra."
ZTK 73 (1976): 283-305.

Marcheselli, C. C. "Come risorgeranno i morti? Osservazioni
su alcuni letterari di 1 Henoch." *Asprenas* 23 (1976):
182-208.

Mearns, C. L. "Dating the Similitudes of Enoch." *NTS* 25
(1979): 360-69.

_____. "The Parables of Enoch." *Exp Tim* 89 (1978): 118-19.

Milik, J. T., and Black, Matthew. *The Books of Enoch:
Aramaic Fragments of Qumrân Cave 4.* Oxford: Clarendon
Press, 1976.

Milik, J. T. "Écrits prééséniens de Qumrân: d'Hénoch
à Amran." *BETL* 46 (1978): 91-106.

_____. "Fragments grecs du livre d'Hénoch (P. Oxy. VII
2069)." *Chronique d'Egypte* 46 (1971): 321-43.

Neugebauer, O. "Notes on Ethiopic Astronomy." *Orientalia*,
n.s., 33 (1964): 49-71.

Nibley, H. "A Strange Thing in the Land: The Return of the
Book of Enoch." *Ensign* (December, 1975): 72-76; (February,
1976): 64-68; (March, 1976): 62-66; (April, 1976): 60-64;
(July, 1976): 64-68; (October, 1976): 76-81; (December,
1976): 73-78.

Nickelsburg, George W. E. "The Apocalyptic Message of *1 Enoch*
92-105." *CBQ* 39 (1977): 309-28.

_____. "Apocalyptic and Myth in 1 Enoch 6-11." *JBL* 96
(1977): 383-405.

_____. "Enoch, Book of." In *IDBSup*, pp. 265-68.

_____. "Enoch 97-104: A Study of the Greek and Ethiopic
Texts." In *Armenian and Biblical Studies*, pp. 90-156.
Edited by M. E. Stone. *Sion*, Sup. 1. Jerusalem: St.
James, 1976.

_____. "Reflections upon Reflections: A Response to John
Collins' 'Methodological Issues in the Study of I Enoch.'"
In *SBL 1978 Seminar Papers*, 1:311-14. Missoula, Mont.:
Scholars Press, 1978.

_____. "Riches, the Rich, and God's Judgment in 1 Enoch
92-105 and the Gospel According to Luke." *NTS* 25
(1979): 324-44.

Nola, A. M. di. "Enoch, Libri apocrifi di." In *Enciclopedia
delle Religioni*, 9:1156-60. Florence: Vallecchi, 1970-76.

Osburn, C. D. "The Christological Use of 1 Enoch i.9 in Jude
14,15." *NTS* 23 (1977): 334-41.

Pearson, B. A. "The Pierpont Morgan Fragments of a Coptic Enoch Apocryphon." In *Studies on the Testament of Abraham*, pp. 227-83. Edited by G. W. E. Nickelsburg. SBLSCS. Missoula, Mont.: Scholars Press, 1976.

Philonenko, Marc. "Une allusion de l'Asclepius au Livre d'Hénoch." In *Christianity, Judaism, and Other Greco-Roman Cults: Studies for Morton Smith at Sixty; pt. 2, Early Christianity*, pp. 161-63. Edited by Jacob Neusner. Leiden: E. J. Brill, 1975.

_____. "La plainte des âmes dans la Koré Kosmou." In *Proceedings of the International Colloquium on Gnosticism* (Kungl. Vitterhets Histoirie och Antikvitets Akademiens Handlingar, Filol.-filos. ser. 17), pp. 153-56. Stockholm: Vitterhets, 1977.

Rau, E. "Kosmologie, Eschatologie und die Lehrautorität Henochs: Traditions- und formgeschichtliche Untersuchungen zum äth. Henochbuch und zu verwandten Schriften." Dissertation, Hamburg University, 1974.

Sneen, D. "The First Book of Enoch." In *Visions of Hope: Apocalyptic Themes from Biblical Times*, pp. 55-70. Minneapolis, Minn.: Augsburg, 1978.

Stone, M. E. "The Book of Enoch and Judaism in the Third Century B.C.E." *CBQ* 40 (1978): 479-92.

_____. "Lists of Revealed Things in the Apocalyptic Literature." In *Magnalia Dei: The Mighty Acts of God*, pp. 414-52. Edited by Frank Moore Cross, Werner E. Lemke, and Patrick D. Miller, Jr. Garden City, N.Y.: Doubleday and Company, 1976.

Suter, David W. "Apocalyptic Patterns in the Similitudes of Enoch." In *SBL 1978 Seminar Papers*, 1:1-13. Missoula, Mont.: Scholars Press, 1978.

_____. "Fallen Angel, Fallen Priest: The Problem of Family Purity in 1 Enoch 6-16." *HUCA* 50 (1979): in press.

INDEXES

INDEX OF MODERN AUTHORS

Alexander, Philip S., 188
Balsdon, J. P. V. D., 193
Bamberger, Bernard J., 188-89, 191-92
Beer, Georg, 177, 191
Beke, Ödön, 184
Betz, Hans Dieter, 85, 157, 184, 188-89
Bickerman, Elias, 188
Black, Matthew, 169, 172, 187
Bousset, Wilhelm, 85
Büchler, Adolf, 183
Charles, Robert Henry, 11, 18, 23, 108, 111, 114-15, 139, 154, 170, 172, 174, 177, 180-83, 187, 191-94, 196, 198-99
Closen, Gustav E., 188
Colpe, Carsten, 27, 170-71, 175-77, 185, 189
Colson, F. H., 129, 169
Cross, Frank Moore, Jr., 179, 183
Culley, Robert C., 196
Cumont, Franz, 100, 182
Dillmann, August, 138, 181, 183, 191, 193
Eissfeldt, Otto, 63, 179-80
Eliade, Mircea, 23, 166, 201
Evelyn-White, Hugh G., 169, 190
Farmer, William R., 176
Feldman, Louis, 169
Ferguson, A. S., 190
Flusser, David, 15, 173
Frye, Northrop, 144
Fuller, Reginald H., 181
Gaster, Moses, 22

Gaster, Theodor H., 67, 82, 184, 189
Gevirtz, Stanley, 196
Glasson, T. Francis, 184-85, 190
Goodenough, Erwin R., 121-22, 185-86
Grant, Frederick C., 186
Greenfield, Jonas C., 15, 32, 170, 174
Grelot, Pierre, 181, 185
Gry, Léon, 187
Hallévi, M. Joseph, 181
Hanson, Paul, 44
Harmon, A. M., 169
Hartman, Lars, 170, 178-79, 186, 192-93, 195, 197
Hengel, Martin, 184, 188
Hennecke, Edgar, 193
Henning, W. B., 190
Hindley, J. C., 12, 174
Hopkins, Thomas J., 190
Howard, Wilbert Francis, 173
Hull, John, 173
Jansen, Herman Ludin, 71
Jellinek, Adolph, 178
Jeremias, Joachim, 148
Johnson, A. R., 147-48
Jung, Leo, 188
Kaiser, Otto, 42-43, 179-80
Kaplan, C., 191
Kellogg, Robert, 128, 149, 158, 194-96, 198, 200
Kerényi, C., 72
Kilburn, K., 169
Lindars, Barnabas, 192

Lindsay, Jack, 109, 185, 193
Lods, Adolphe, 187
Long, A. A., 189
Lord, Albert B., 5, 145, 149, 169, 187, 194-98, 200
MacLeod, M. D., 169
Marcus, Ralph, 169
Metzger, Bruce M., 169
Milik, J. T., ix, 12-13, 169, 170, 190
Moore, George Foot, 172, 200
Morgenstern, Julian, 185, 188
Moulton, James Hope, 173
Muilenburg, James, 183
Nickelsburg, George W. E., Jr., 43, 117, 177, 192-94, 197
Nilsson, Martin P., 182
Noy, Dov, 182
Odeberg, Hugo, 18-19, 170, 173
Pannenberg, Wolfhart, 201
Parry, Milman, 5
Perrin, Norman, 13, 25, 175, 192, 197
Plöger, Otto, 43, 200-201
Rad, Gerhard von, 75, 157, 164-65, 173, 176, 183, 188, 197
Reese, James M., 56
Renou, Louis, 190
Ricoeur, Paul, 128, 159
Rose, H. J., 185
Schmidt, Nathaniel, 172, 175-76
Scholem, Gershom G., 14, 22, 172, 195, 199
Scholes, Robert, 128, 149, 158, 194-96, 198, 200
Schürer, Emil, 176-77
Schwab, M. Moïse, 173
Scott, Walter, 190
Simpson, Jacqueline, 184

Singer, S., 173
Sjöberg, Erik, 33, 122, 147, 177
Smith, Jonathan Z., 183-84, 201
Sperling, Harry, and Simon, Maurice, 183
Strugnell, John, 15, 24-25, 187
Tcherikover, Victor, 184, 188, 191
Thackeray, H. St. J., 169
Thompson, Stith, 184
Tödt, H. E., 28, 174-75
Tromp, Nicholas J., 181, 184
Turner, Nigel, 173
Ullendorff, Edward, 172
Unkel, Curt Nimeundajú, 190
Vaux, Roland de, 179
Vermes, Geza, 25, 40-41, 175, 177-79, 186
Wertheimer, S., 172
Wickgren, Allen, 169
Widengren, Geo, 186
Wilson, H. H., 190
Whitaker, G. H., 169
Wright, Addison G., 39-40, 128, 186
Wünsche, August, 178

INDEX OF SUBJECTS

Absalom: burial related to punishment of Asael, 64

Adam literature, 90

Agrippa, 111

Alexander Jannaeus, 23

Alienation in apocalyptic understanding of history, 164-65. See also Apocalyptic; History

Allegory and midrash, 128-30, 152, 159

Angelic liturgy, 15, 75

Angels: as culture heroes, 84-85; associated with natural phenomena, 99-100, 188. See also Archangels; Asael; Shemiḥazah

Antiochus IV Epiphanes, 110-11

Anti-royal polemic, 12, 29-32, 70-71, 105, 111-12, 115-16, 120. See also Divinity of Roman emperor; Royal power, limits of

Apocalypse of Peter, 56

Apocalypse of the Animals (1 En. 85-90), 28, 59

Apocalyptic: alienation from history in, 164-65; history in, 201; overthrow of social order sanctioned in, 164; structure of time in, 166; study of, 6

Apocalyptic writings: relation to times of crisis, 31

Aquarius, 110

Archangels: commissioned in 1 En. 10, 98; number of, 76; prayer in 1 En. 9, 97

Asael: form of name at Qumran, 169; host of, 52-53, 58, 66; as leader of fallen angels, 2, 91; and Prometheus, 69; punishment of, 63-64; responsibility for sins of angels, 3, 96-98

Astrology, 73, 109, 199; as a religion, 100

Astronomical book (1 En. 72-82), 76

Authority of midrashic exegesis and of pseudepigrapha, 130, 150-51, 153

Authorship in oral and written literature, 149-51. See also Oral Composition

2 Baruch: concerned with fall of Jerusalem, 29

Baths (thermal), 55

Berossus, 71

Bloodshed: pollutes the earth, 183

Book of Noah, 2, 32, 37, 102, 105, 122, 154

Cain: in Philo, 182

Callirhoe: location of thermal springs at, 24

Canon: formation of, 44

Cherubim, 17

Collective representation, 164

Complaint of the earth, 85-89, 97, 100

Continuity of a religious tradition, 6. See also Judaism and Hellenism

Creation myth: and cosmological oath, 23; and time of history in apocalyptic, 6, 166-67

Culture heroes, 68-69, 83-85, 89-90, 97

Defilement, 80; of angels, 89. See also Purity

Demigods, 78. See also Giants

Demons, 173-74

Diodorus Siculus, 109-10

Divine-human marriages, 78-79, 82-83. See also Marriage

Divinity of Roman emperor, 4, 29-32. *See also* Anti-Royal polemic; Gaius Caligula; Royal power, limits of

Earth polluted by bloodshed, 183

Editorial framework of Parables, 5, 130-35, 150

El, 79

The Elect one: enthronement of, 116-17; as formula in Parables, 135; as judge of kings and mighty, 107; predominant messianic designation in Parables, 13; and Son of Man, 26, 171

Emperor, 6. *See also* Anti-royal polemic; Royal power, limits of; Gaius Caligula

Enoch: as heavenly scribe, 76, 84; name associated with editorial framework of Parables, 130-31, 156; role in Enochic tradition, 16

1 Enoch 6-11: date of composition of, 11

2 Enoch (Slavonic Enoch), 13

3 Enoch (*Sefer ha-Hekhaloth*), 13, 16, 17, 19, 22, 170, 187

Enuma elish, 61, 67, 185, 196

Epic stage of culture, 7, 158

Eschatology: of Parables, 6; of Is. 24:17-23 midrash, 3, 54-55, 58-61

Essenes (and Therapeutae): assemblies as *Sitz im Leben* for midrash, 5, 126; and lists of angels, 74; interpreter of scripture in, 151; as sect, 187

Exodus tradition: used in popular movements, 176

4 Ezra: and fall of Jerusalem, 29; Son of Man in, 25

Fallen angels, 1; myth discontinuous with Jewish tradition, 160; and mythology of ancient world, 81-90; related to kings and mighty in Parables, 163-66

Fall of heavenly beings: not central concern of Parables: 115-16, 120-21

Fetter motif, 62-64

Flaccus, 182

Flood, 46-47, 57-58, 61, 98-99, 133-35, 180

Folklore: European, 64; angels in, 188

Folktales, 55, 96

Form criticism, 1, 11, 33, 169

Formulas and formulaic language, 135-39, 196. *See also* Oral Composition

Gaius Caligula, 30, 109-11, 115, 166. *See also* Divinity of Roman emperor

Genre: lists of angels as, 73, 93; midrash as, 39-40, 91; of Parables, 105, 146-49

Geography, mythical, 174, 182

Ghost. *See* Laying a ghost

Giants, 52-54, 79, 191; avoided in Parables, 81, 90, 102; as *mamzerim*, 80, 98

Gilgamesh Epic, 133

Gnosticism, 69

Guarani Indians, 88, 166

Harrowing of hell, 67

Ḥasidim, 90, 161

Heavenly ascent, 16

Hekhaloth tradition, 14

Helel ben Shaḥar, 52

Hell, origin of notion of, 182

Hellenism. *See* Judaism and Hellenism; Syncretism

Hermetic literature. *See* *Kore Kosmu*

Hermon, Mt., 96

Herod the Great, 176-77; his final illness and 1 En. 67:7-9, 24; as object of polemic in Parables, 30-31

Hesiod, 66, 82

History: alienation from, 6, 165; apocalyptic and prophetic understanding of, 164-65; of religions, 164-67

Idolatry, 183

Impurity. *See* Defilement

Imprisonment: of angels, 55, 59, 97; of kings and angels, 66, 115, 120, 180, 186; of seven stars, 67

Isaiah Apocalypse (Is. 24-27), 2, 42-45, 58

Jamnia: destruction of emperor's statue by Jews in, 30

Jerusalem, fall of: and date of Parables, 29

Josephus: on Gaius Caligula, 109; on lists of angels, 74

Judaism and Hellenism, 65, 69, 84, 88-90, 100-102, 121-23, 157-62

Judgment: function of the Elect one in Parables, 26; of kings and angels paralleled, 52-56; of kings and mighty, 107

Kabbalism, 61

Kil'ayim. *See* Mixed fruits

Kings and mighty of the earth, 107; as formula in Parables, 135; identity of, 23, 30; imprisonment or punishment paralleled to that of fallen angels, 52-54, 60, 163-66

Kore Kosmu, 85-89, 94, 100, 157, 189

Laying a ghost related to punishment of Asael, 64

Lists: of fallen angels, 1, 4, 21, 37, 73-91; of angels, 74-77, 84-85, 93, 187; of archangels, 21. *See also* Onomasticon

Literary criticism, 1, 11, 33; two source theory in 1 En. 6-11, 3, 91-92, 95-96

Logos Ebraikos, 22-23

Lord of Spirits, 26; as formula in Parables, 135; predominant divine name in Parables, 14; reflects language of Qumran, 15

Maccabeans, 23

Mamzerim, 80, 86, 95, 98, 162

Marriages: of angels with women, 96-98, 191; of gods and humans, 82-83

Mašal, 33; as genre of Parables, 4, 105, 146-49; as oral genre, 125; *Sitz im Leben* of, 152

Matthew: compositional methods in, 25-29, 175-76; relation to Parables, 25-29

Merkabah mysticism, 14

Metatron, 16

Michael, 21, 59

Midrash: and allegory, 128-30; as characteristic of cultural stage, 7, 157-58; on Dan. 7:9-14, 14, 26, 107, 117; on Ex. 14-15, 113, 118-19; as form of oral tradition, 41; on Gen. 6:1-4, 37, 79; on Is. 24:17-23, 1, 3, 4, 37, 39-72, 91; problem of definition of, 39-42; *Sitz im Leben* of, 72, 186. *See also* Authority; Scripture

Mixed fruits (*Kil'ayim*), 80, 86, 95

Mixed marriages, 189. *See also* Marriages

Mixture, 80, 86, 189

Mystical ascent. *See* Heavenly ascent; Throne-chariot; Throne of his Glory

Mythological patterns, 37, 65-72, 92

Myths of the origin of evil, 37, 79, 90, 160-62, 166

Names: of leaders of fallen angels as key to tradition history, 2, 91, 93; of sages in pseudepigrapha sociological in character, 156. *See also* Lists

Nephilim, 78, 83, 85

Noah, 59, 133. *See also* Book of Noah

Oath: in 1 En. 6:4-5, 96; in 1 En. 69:13-25, 19-23, 174

Odyssey, 133

Onomasticon, 20, 75-77, 173. *See also* Lists

Ophannin, 15, 17, 23

Oral composition, 125; formulas and formulaic language in, 135; identification of, 194; inconsistencies characteristic of, 150, 154-55, 198; and *mašal*, 148-49; in Parables, 106, 135-51; relation to written composition, 149-51, 153-54, 155-56; role of lists in, 4; and structure, 139; theory of, 5

Ornamental function: of fallen-angel material in Parables, 123, 145-46; of lists in popular literature, 4, 74, 77, 90, 102, 145

Ouranology of Parables, 15, 24

Parable of the last judgment (Mt. 24:31-46), 28

Parables of Enoch: absent from Qumran, 1; date of composition of, 11, 23-32, 176-77; levels of composition in, 199; Milik's treatment as a third century, Christian composition, 12; original language of, 172; proto-merkabah in origin, 23; provenance of, 11; as pseudepigraphon distinct from three parable structure, 132; relation to rest of 1 Enoch, 1, 15, 32-33, 98, 102; structure of, 4, 139-45

Parthians, 12, 24, 176-77

Pharisees, 23, 187

Philo: on Essenes and Therapeutae, 5, 126-30, 152; on Gaius Caligula, 30, 109

Poem of the Gracious Gods, 79

Poetry in the Parables, 139

Pogroms in Alexandria, 115

Prometheus, 68-69

Provenance of Parables a problem, 1

Pseudepigraphon, 5, 125; distance between author and narrator in, 195, 198; *Sitz im Leben* of, 152-53; transmission motif in, 131-35. *See also* Authority

Pseudo-scientific material, 61-62

Psychological tortures of the guilty, 56, 182

Punishment: of angels central to Is. 24:17-23 midrash, 3, 92; of angels and kings paralleled, 52, 120; of angels derived from Is. 24:17-23 midrash in 1 En. 6-11, 94; of Asael, 59, 63-64, 97

Purity: central concern in angel-list tradition and 1 En. 6-11, 2, 4, 90, 95 102. *See also* Defilement

Qeduššah, 16, 18-19, 116

Qumran: and the Parables, 1, 11-13, 32; pesharim at, 61; pseudepigrapha at, 152-53

Recurrence of themes, 4, 116, 125, 140-45

Redaction criticism, 4, 11, 33, 105

Righteous man, exaltation of, 117-18

Royal ideology, 110, 123

Royal power, limits of, 2, 3, 70-71, 92, 102. *See also* Anti-royal polemic

Sadducees, 23

Scenic duality, law of in 1 En. 6-11, 95

Scribes and lists of angels, 76-77

Scripture: exposition of by Essenes and Therapeutae, 128-30, 152; interpretation related to foreign mythologies, 65; use in 1 En. 62-63, 118; use in Is. 24:17-23 midrash, 61-64; use as key to traditional unit, 91; use as key to continuity of Jewish tradition, 101. See also Midrash

Sect, 186

Sectarian Judaism. See Essenes (and Therapeutae)

Sefer ha-Hekhaloth. See 3 Enoch

Sefer Noaḥ, 154

Seth, sons as culture heroes, 84

Shemiḥazah, 59, 77; form of name at Qumran, 169; as leader of fallen angels, 2, 93; responsibility for sins of angels, 3, 96-98

Sibylline Oracles, 12

Sins: of angels, 73, 77, 79-80, 191; in angel-list tradition, 2, 93; in Is. 24:17-23 midrash, 2, 92; three that pollute the earth, 183. See also Purity

Sirach, 44

Sociology of religion, 163-64

Son of Man: Aramaic and Ethiopic equivalents for, 175; and Christology, 170; as eschatological judge, 27; as formula, 135; in Parables, 12-13, 107; as title, 25, 171

Sons of Elohim, 2, 78, 96-99

Sources in 1 En. 6-11. See Literary criticism

Structure of Parables. See Parables of Enoch

Synagogues, 115

Syncretism, 89, 101, 122, 162. See also Judaism and Hellenism

Targum Jonathan, treatment of Is. 24:17-23 in, 47-48, 180

Teaching of secrets by angels, 69, 83-84

Testament of Levi, 25

Theodicy, 4, 192

Theology of history, 166

Therapeutae. See Essenes (and Therapeutae)

Thermal springs: at Callirhoe, 24; in which the kings and mighty are punished, 55-56, 166; in Rabbinic sources, 182

Throne-chariot: in angelic liturgy, 15; in Parables, 24

Throne of his glory: formula in Matthew, Parables, and Hekhaloth tradition, 25, 28; object of mystical ascent, 17

Titans, 66, 68, 72, 121-22

Tobiads, 90

Tradition: importance in Judaism, 101; and midrash, 41; role in composition of the Parables, 1. See also Oral composition

Tradition history, 2, 32, 95-100, 169

Transmission motif in pseudepigraphon, 131

Uriel, 59

Value of a theme or motif, 121-22

Vishnu Purāna: complaint of the earth in, 57, 85-89, 100

Vulcanic activity, 55

War in heaven, 66

War Scroll, 74-75
Watchers, 19, 173

Wisdom tradition, 183
Zodiac, 109-10, 193

INDEX OF REFERENCES TO ANCIENT LITERATURE

Hebrew Scriptures

Genesis

1:1-25	20
6-9	62
6:1-4	2,37, 60,68,77-83,85-86, 89-96,98-100,102,157, 162,184,188,190,192
6:2	188
6:3	78
7:11	61
22:2	53
25:28	53
37:3-4	53
44:20	53
49:4	138

Exodus

14-15	113, 118,176
14:13	112, 119
14:17-18	56
14:26-27	112-13
14:28	112
14:30	112-13
14:30-31	119
15:1-18	119
15:7	112
15:10	112
15:14-16	112, 118
15:17	119

Leviticus

19:19	189

Deuteronomy

22:9-10	189
23:2	189
33:12	53
34:5	119

Joshua

1:13	119
7:26	64
8:29	64
8:31,33	119
11:12	119
12:6	119
13:8	119
14:7	119
18:7	119
22:2,5	119

1 Samuel

3	196

2 Samuel

7:10	119
7:11	112, 114
18:17-18	64

2 Kings

18:12	119

Isaiah

1-39	44
2:4	114
5:1	53

6:3	18,136	26:14	43, 112
13:7-8	112, 118	26:19	42-43
14	30,70, 105,108,118,147,162,185, 192,200	34:15-17	197
		34:17	140
		40:12	111
14:4	148	40:21-26	20
14:4-7	114	41:13	113
14:4-21	107, 111-12,122	42:1	13, 53,181
14:7	112-13	42:1-4	26, 118,196
14:9	108	42:6	113
14:10	112	44:2	53,181
14:11	111-12	45:1	113
14:12	185	46:2	112
14:12-21	43,52	47:14	112
14:13-14	72, 109-10,193	49	118, 177
18:7	114	49:1	154
22:23	17	49:1-2	119
24-27	2,39, 42	49:7	107, 112
24:14-16	47	49:8	119
24:16	47-48, 122,148	49:23	112
		52-53	118-19, 163
24:17-18	46	66:20	114
24:17-23	2-4, 37,39,43,45-48,51-52,54, 59-60,62,67-68,70-71,89, 91-92,98,102,122,154,180	66:24	112
		Jeremiah	
24:18	45, 47,57-58,61	5:22	20
24:18-20	46, 57-58,60	10:13	62
		14:21	17
24:19-20	57-58	31:35	111
24:21	47-48, 52	48:43-44	46
		51:16	62
24:21-22	58	*Ezekiel*	
24:21-23	42, 46,181		
24:22	52, 56-59,62,67-68	1-3	15,17
		1:15-21	15
24:23	54, 58,99,180	1:26	13
25:6-8	42		

Ezekiel (continued)

1:26-2:7	172
1:28-2:7	133
2:1-7	134
3:12	18
10	17
17:2	147
28	185
28:1-19	43
28:2	72
28:4-9	108
28:5-6	72
28:9	72, 185
32:27	78
40-48	140, 197

Joel

3	114-15, 182

Obadiah

1-4	185

Micah

1:4	114
2:4	147-48

Nahum

1:5	114

Habakkuk

2:6	147-48

Zechariah

1:14-17	140, 197
2:1-5	140, 197
12	44
13:9	114
14	44

Malachi

2:10-12	189
3:2-3	114
4:1	112

Psalms

2:2	113
2:2-3	72
2:3	63
2:7	53,185
3:7	107
8:6	188
19:1-5	20
24:2	20
36:12	112
44:2	119
48:5-6	118
49	146-47
58:6	107
60:7	53
68	114
68:2	114-15
68:28-31	114
68:29	115
74:8	108, 115
76	114
76:11-12	114-15
78	146
78:2	147
78:49	119
78:69	114
82	43, 70,185
84:2	53
97:5	114
104	19,77
107:10-11	62
107:10	107
108:7	53

127:2	53
132:3	138
132:7-8	138
132:14	138
135	22,77
135:6-7	19
135:7	62
136	22,77
136:4-9	19
140:10	112
148	19,77
149:8-9	63

Job

15:15	69
17:13	107-8, 138
17:14	107
21:26	107
25:5	58,69
26:5-14	20
30:11	107
31:24-28	69
31:26-28	58
36:7-12	63
38-41	20, 76,77
38:8-11	111
38:22	62

Proverbs

1:6	147
8:22-31	20

Koheleth

1:4	114

Lamentations

3:6	107
3:6-9	63
3:47	46
3:53	63

Daniel

2:42-43	189
7	25-27, 165,200
7:9	13
7:9-14	14, 25-27,107,118,136,171, 198
7:11-12	26
7:13	13
7:13-14	27
7:26	26
8:10	108
8:15-17	172
8:18	133
8:18-26	134
10:2-11:1	172
10:9-10	133
10:10-14	134
12:2	43

Ezra

2:62	189
9:2	189

Nehemiah

7:64	189
13:29-30	189

Apocrypha

4 Ezra

6:45-52	199

Wisdom of Solomon

2	118, 177,193
3:16-19	189
4-5	112, 118,177,193
6:1	109
7:17-22	20, 83-84,190
9:10	17
17:1-21	121-22
17:2-21	56
18:21	119

Sirach

39:1	44
43	77
43:14	62
45-49	44
47:17	147
48:22-25	44
48:22-49:12	44

Baruch (1 Bar.)

3:29-37	20

Song of the Three Young Men

35-60	77
35-68	20

Prayer of Manasseh

1-5	173-74
9-10	184

2 Maccabees

9	200
9:1-29	111-12
9:4,7-8	72
9:8	110
9:18	112

Pseudepigrapha

1 Enoch

1-36	45,76, 155-56
2-5	183
6-11	1,3-4,6, 11,32,37-38,45,52,54,57, 59-60,67,74,77,79,81-82, 85-102,145,154-57,161-62, 178,189-92
6-16	52,91,95, 189,200
6:1-3	96
6:1-8	191
6:3	77
6:7	73-77, 84-85,93,96
7:1	79,96,191
7:3-5	80
7:3-6	191
7:6	85,98
8:1-2	96
8:1-3	4,73-75, 83-84,93,154,191
8:4	98,191
9-10	187
9:1-5	191
9:2	85
9:2-3	98
9:4	17
9:6-8	97,191

9:7-8	77,191	18:12-19:2	67
9:8	79	20	155,187
9:9-11	191	20-36	76
10	59,66,74, 97-98,192	21	76,185
		21:1-6	68
10:1-3	191	21:1-10	67
10:4-5	63-64	33-36	76
10:4-6	3,59, 94,97,186	33:2-4	188
		33:4	20,76
10:4-11:2	191	37	131,142
10:5	184	37:1	131,148
10:7	80,183	37:1-5	131-32,150
10:8	69,97	37:2-3	131
10:9	79-80	37:2-5	148
10:9-10	83	37:3-4	151
10:11	79-80	37:5	146,151
10:11-12	77,191	38	148
10:11-13	3,59, 94,97	38-44	26
		38:1	115,136
10:12	52-53, 79,83	38:1-6	131
		38:1-39:2	142
10:12-13	67	38:2	26
10:18-22	80	38:2	136
12-13	76	38:2	138-39
12-16	173	38:5	26,107
12:1	156	39	143
12:5-6	67	39:1-2	178,194
13:5	184	39:2	131
14-16	16,76,172	39:3-8	117
14:1	76	39:3-14	116,142
14:6	53,83	39:3-40:10	141
14:10-17	24	39:4-5	138-39
14:18	16-17	39:4-14	197
14:24-15:1	133	39:6	171
14:25-16:4	134	39:6-7	141,143
15:3-10	80	39:9	137
15:11	80	39:9-10	136
16:3	81,84,99	39:9-14	16,139,143
16:4	67	39:10-13	18
18	185	39:10-14	19
18:12-16	68		

1 Enoch (continued)

39:12	136
40	74,131,187
40:1-10	142
40:2	137
40:5	171
40:8	137
40:9-10	21
41	15
41:1	122,155
41:1-2	140-42, 146,154,197,199
41:2	136
41:3-7	21
41:3-9	142
41:4-5	62
41:7-8	139
42	142-43
43-44	142
43:1-44:1	21
43:3	137
45	142,148
45-46	117
45-57	26,107
45:2	26,136
45:2-3	26
45:3	18,116-18
45:3-4	171
45:6	136
46	142-44
46-47	26
46-48	171
46-53	141,144
46:1	13,136
46:1-3	107,118
46:1-48:10	171
46:2	137,139
46:3	171
46:4-8	26,30,107-8, 112,118,176,192
46:5-6	111
46:5-7	63,117
46:7	26,30,54, 72,108-10,117,136,177
46:7-8	171
46:8	30,115,117
47	142
47:1-2	171
47:2	16,136-37
47:4	171
48	142-44
48:1-7	177
48:2	154
48:2-3	171
48:2-7	118
48:5	136,171
48:7	171
48:8-10	112-13, 118-19,158,176
48:9	155
48:10	30,136, 171,194
49	142-43
49:4	116
50-51	142
51	144
51:1-5	143
52	142
52-54	56,182
52:1-5	139
52:3	137
52:5	137
52:6	114
52:8-9	114
53	120,143
53:1	120,139,182
53:1-7	113-15
53:2	136
53:2	139,193
53:3	48
53:3-5	54

53:4	137	57:1-3	197
53:5	26	58	131,143,148
53:6-7	115	58-69	26,116
54:1	115,120,146	58:1	149
54:1-5	63	58:3	137-38
54:1-6	48,52,54,180	58:6	138
54:1-55:2	178	59	143
54:1-56:4	1-2,32-39,45,48-49,54,59-61,66,102,113,115,119-20,143	60	32,154,178
		60-63	140-41,143,146,154,197
54:2	26,48,54,63	60:1	110,131,198
		60:1-6	117
54:3	115,180,194	60:1-6	141,143,198
54:3-6	186	60:1-63:12	141
54:4	137	60:2	198
54:4-5	55	60:3	139
54:4-6	3,97	60:4-6	134
54:5	57,63-64,115	60:7-10	199
54:5-6	59	60:7-24	140,143
54:6	52,58,187	60:8	131
54:7	59	60:11-23	22
54:7-9	183	60:11-24	199
54:7-55:2	48,52,133-34,152,178	60:12,19-21	62
		60:24	137,199
54:8	61	60:25	117,141,143
55	144	61	144
55:1-2	198	61:1-2	139
55:3-56:4	48,180	61:1-5	140,143
55:4	18,27,52,54,116-18,143	61:3	137
		61:5	197
56:1	54,115	61:6	139
56:1-4	52-54	61:6-11	122,140,143
56:2	137	61:6-13	116-17,197
56:3	57	61:7	136
56:3-4	91	61:8	18,27,155
56:4	30,137,139	61:8-9	52,109,194
56:5-7	24,174,176	61:9	136-37
56:5-8	12,31,143,177	61:9-12	16
56:7	29,177	61:10	15
57	143		

1 Enoch (continued)

61:10-11	139
61:12	136
61:12-13	140,143
62	144,163
62-63	26,112,117-20,171,192-93
62:1	26,139
62:1-3	117
62:1-63:12	141,143
62:2-3	18
62:4-5	118
62:5	14,18,26,117-18,144
62:5-16	171
62:5-63:12	117
62:6	26,136,139
62:6-16	176
62:7	119,177
62:7-13	158
62:8	115,119
62:9	26
62:10	117,171
62:11	117,119
62:12-13	119
62:13-16	140
62:14,16	171
63	55,194
63:1	26,139
63:1-12	171
63:1-64:2	54
63:2	136
63:4-7	30
63:7	26,72,117,136-37
63:10	57,117,139
63:10-11	55
63:12	26,139
64	54-55,120,146
64:1-68:1	2,37,39,45,49-51,54-55,59-61,100,106,115,134,143
64:1-69:12	33,35
64:1-69:25	32,102
65-66	57,133-34,198
65:1	57-58
65:1-66:3	133
65:1-67:3	52,57
65:1-68:1	131-32,195
65:1-69:25	178
65:3	57-58,134,181
65:4	133
65:5	134,181
65:6	183
65:6-7	54
65:6-8	68,100,134,181
65:9	57,133-34
65:10-11	134
65:11	60,68
65:12	139
67	182
67:1-3	133-34
67:2	183
67:4	24,55-56,174
67:4-7	55,60
67:4-12	166
67:4-13	54-55
67:6	56
67:6-7	63
67:7-9	24,174
67:8	24,26,136
67:8-13	55-56
67:10	26,136
67:12-13	133
67:12-69:1	132
67:13	132
68:1	129,131-33,146

INDEXES

68:2-5	132
68:2-69:1	143
68:4	54,68, 72,100,110,165
69:2	77,191
69:2-3	2,73-75, 84-85
69:2-12	1,21,37, 73,81,89-90,143,145
69:4	21
69:4-12	2,4,21, 73-74,77,83,154,187
69:5	79,187
69:8-11	84
69:9-11	151
69:12-15	187
69:13-14	21
69:13-25	19-23, 139,143,187-88
69:14	174
69:18	174
69:24	136-37
69:26	136
69:26-27	154
69:26-29	14,131, 143,171
69:27	144
70	143
70-71	131
70:1-4	131-32
71	16,134, 143,172
71:5-7	24
71:7	15,17
71:8-9	187
71:10-17	171
71:11	136
71:12	139
71:14	16
71:17	171
72-82	76,188
72:1	76
76:12-13	114
81:5-6	76
82:10-20	76
83	57-58,76
83:3-11	133
83:8-10	57
83:10	76
84	76
85-90	67,76,155
86:1-89:9	59
87:2	76,155
88:3	67
90:20-27	28,59
91-105	102,191
98:4	102
99:5	53
106-7	32,133,178

2 Enoch

22:5-23:6	134

3 Enoch

1:10	172
1:10-12	19
1:12	172
6:3	16
7	172
8:1	172
10:1	172
13:1	22
14	174
14:1	172
14:3-4	84
15:1	172
18:17,19,22	172
24:22	172
26:7,11	172
28:2	172
33:3	172
35:3	172

3 Enoch (continued)

36:1,2	172
39:1	172
40:1,4	172
41:1-4	22
41:2,4	172
43:2	172

Jubilees

2:1-16	20
4:17	84
10:13-14	32
12:16-18	100
21:10	32

Testament of Levi

2:7-3:9	25
5:1	17

2 Baruch

29:4	199

Psalms of Solomon

8:13	189

Qumran Literature

Damascus Document (CD)

5:6-7	189

Hôdāyôt (1QH)

1:8-13	188
1:8-15	20,77
4:27-29	151
11:4	195
13:1-10	188
13:7-9	20

Milḥāmāh (1QM)

3-4	187
7	187
9:15-16	187
10:11-15	188

$4QpIs^a$

D,3	17

4QS1

40:24 24,29	15,17,

Philo

De Abrahamo

68-80	100

In Flaccum

170-75	182,193

De Gigantibus

6-8	85,184,190

De Legatione ad Gaium

	193
347	30-31,112

De Praemiis et Poenis

67-73	182
68	183
71	182

INDEXES

Quod Omnis Probus Liber		29	129,152
80-82	126,130	31	151
81	199	64	128
82	151,200	75	151
		75-78	127-28
De Vita Contemplativa		76	196
25-31	126-27, 129-30		

Josephus

Antiquities		*Jewish War*	
1. 69-71	84	2. 142	74
12. 160-236	191	2. 150	80
18. 224-19. 211	193	2. 181-203	193
19. 343-52	111-12	2. 259	176

New Testament

Matthew		9:12-13	28
9:6	13	13:28-37	176
10:23	13	*Luke*	
13:24-30	28	12:8-9	25
13:41	176	22:30	28
13:41-43	28	23:35	13
16:13-17:13	27	*Acts*	
16:27	27-28,176	12:20-23	111-12
16:28	28	*James*	
17:9-13	27-28	2:19	173
17:12	27,175	*1 Peter*	
19:28	17,28,176	3:19-20	67
24:45-25:46	176	1:17	53
25:31	17,28,176	*Revelation*	
25:31-46	28,148	2-3	187
Mark		20	186
1:11	53	20:1-3	186
8:38	25,27	20:11	186
9:1	28		
9:7	53		

Early Christian Literature

Barnabus		*Origen, Contra Celsum*	
12:10	170	5. 52	182
Ignatius to the Ephesians			
20:2	170		

Greek Literature

Hesiod, Theogony		*Lucian, Icaromenippus*	
713-20	66	14	70
Diodorus Siculus			
2. 30. 6	109		
2. 31. 4	109		

Talmud, Midrashim

Baba Meṣiʿa		*Midrash on Psalms*	
59b	195	8	182
Genesis Rabbah		*Sanhedrin*	
33:4	182	108a	182
Ḥagiga		*Šabbat*	
15a	183	39a	182
Kilʾayim			
	189		

www.ingramcontent.com/pod-product-compliance
Lightning Source LLC
Chambersburg PA
CBHW021807220426
43662CB00006B/212